**PELLISSIPPI STATE
LIBRARY SERVICES
P.O. BOX 22990
KNOXVILLE, TN 37933-0990**

WEST ACADEMIC PUBLISHING'S LAW SCHOOL ADVISORY BOARD

JESSE H. CHOPER
Professor of Law and Dean Emeritus
University of California, Berkeley

JOSHUA DRESSLER
Distinguished University Professor Emeritus,
Frank R. Strong Chair in Law
Michael E. Moritz College of Law, The Ohio State University

RENÉE McDONALD HUTCHINS
Dean and Joseph L. Rauh, Jr. Chair of Public Interest Law
University of the District of Columbia David A. Clarke School of Law

YALE KAMISAR
Professor of Law Emeritus, University of San Diego
Professor of Law Emeritus, University of Michigan

MARY KAY KANE
Professor of Law, Chancellor and Dean Emeritus
University of California, Hastings College of the Law

LARRY D. KRAMER
President, William and Flora Hewlett Foundation

JONATHAN R. MACEY
Professor of Law, Yale Law School

DEBORAH JONES MERRITT
Distinguished University Professor, John Deaver Drinko/Baker &
Hostetler Chair in Law
Michael E. Moritz College of Law, The Ohio State University

ARTHUR R. MILLER
University Professor, New York University
Formerly Bruce Bromley Professor of Law, Harvard University

GRANT S. NELSON
Professor of Law Emeritus, Pepperdine University
Professor of Law Emeritus, University of California, Los Angeles

A. BENJAMIN SPENCER
Justice Thurgood Marshall Distinguished Professor of Law
University of Virginia School of Law

JAMES J. WHITE
Robert A. Sullivan Professor of Law Emeritus
University of Michigan

ISLAMIC LAW
IN A NUTSHELL®

HAIDER ALA HAMOUDI
Professor of Law and Vice Dean
University of Pittsburgh School of Law

The publisher is not engaged in rendering legal or other professional advice, and this publication is not a substitute for the advice of an attorney. If you require legal or other expert advice, you should seek the services of a competent attorney or other professional.

Nutshell Series, In a Nutshell and the Nutshell Logo are trademarks registered in the U.S. Patent and Trademark Office.

© 2020 LEG, Inc. d/b/a West Academic
      444 Cedar Street, Suite 700
      St. Paul, MN 55101
      1-877-888-1330

West, West Academic Publishing, and West Academic are trademarks of West Publishing Corporation, used under license.

Printed in the United States of America

ISBN: 978-1-62810-042-6

PREFACE

Addressing the subject of Islamic law in "nutshell" form presents a series of unusual challenges. The most obvious of them is that the scope of what is normally understood as "Islamic law" is quite different from that of modern legal systems generally. When most devout Muslims think of Islamic law, the most pressing questions that come to their minds relate to questions of worship and ritual, such as fasting, prayer, and the pilgrimage to Mecca. Obviously, these are not matters with which the law of most modern states, Muslim or non-Muslim, is particularly concerned. By contrast, there are vast areas of law that are fundamental to the operation of a modern state about which Islamic law has relatively little to say. These include such disparate fields as corporate law, nationality law, and administrative law and regulation. Islamic law is therefore broader than most modern legal systems in some respects, and narrower in others.

Another key distinction, related to the first, is that Islamic law is not historically the product of a state. In fact, as Chapter One makes clear, in its most traditional and classical form, Islamic law emanates from learned scholars, known as jurists, who operate within schools of thought that are independent of the state. The state's apparatus, at best, would be used to enforce Islamic law, but not to pronounce it. This historic feature of Islamic law has eroded substantially in the modern world, where the idea that the state has a complete monopoly on law has been internalized among legal and political elites, including Islamist elites, in almost all modern Muslim societies. Nevertheless, the influence of the corpus of rules developed in the classical era remains. Thus, when Muslims states purport to apply Islamic law, they almost always begin with the classical rules of the major Islamic schools, even if they depart in important ways thereafter. The state's power to "declare" Islamic law is therefore circumscribed in a manner that is not true of more positivist based modern legal systems.

Finally, because it is not as closely tied to a state, and in light of its scope, much of the structure of Islamic law resembles an ethical system as much as a legal one, at least as modern systems envisage the term "legal". To take one of the most salient examples of this, Muslim jurists have traditionally categorized acts as falling within five primary categories. These are the obligatory, the recommended, the permissible, the disfavored or reprehensible, and the forbidden. The categories do not map particularly easily onto a modern state's legal system, whether or not the state purports to be Islamic. A Muslim woman who appears in a county clerk's office in order to file papers to dissolve her marriage to her husband is not particularly interested in the clerk's views on whether or not her actions are "recommended" or "reprehensible." She merely wishes to know whether or not she is legally empowered to end her marriage.

On the other hand, the same Muslim woman may very well wish to solicit the views of a cleric or an imam as to whether the effort to dissolve her marriage is reprehensible, even if permitted, and this might affect her decision to appear in the clerk's office in the first place. Similarly, she may seek the cleric's advice on marital concerns long before she considers filing for dissolution of her marriage. To the extent she has questions on religious ritual, these will almost be certainly directed to a cleric, and almost never to a state officer.

Accordingly, we might very well think of Islamic law applying in modern societies in different ways. One of these would be a private, ethical constraint on conduct, administered by nonstate actors guiding believers on a purely voluntary basis on how to live their lives in a manner that best accords with God's Will. There is no shortage of Arab satellite television programming on various channels hosting clerics who answer the questions of the pious on any topic imaginable, including marital discord, the proper way to perform absolution before prayer, and the permissibility of serving in the police force of a non-Muslim country. The effect of a cleric answering such matters in quick succession on a one hour television program can be dizzying, but ratings seem to suggest the forum is quite attractive to broad sections of the Muslim population. Imams in local mosques and internet personalities issuing "cyberfatwas" serve similar roles. Specifically, they offer nonbinding opinions on Islamic law (which is precisely what the term "fatwa" denotes) to the pious. In almost no case do the clerics answering these questions seem to think they are providing guidance on a matter that relates to state law. Indeed they would very likely deflect any actual legal question to an attorney, who would know better.

Another manner in which Islamic law applies in modern societies is as a form and feature of the law of the modern state, or as guiding legal doctrine in relations between states. This primarily occurs when a modern state incorporates elements of Islamic law into its legal system. There are various ways that a modern state can undertake this effort. The most common is codification, whereby the state simply enacts a particular interpretation of Islamic law and declares it applicable in the state. To the extent that Islamic criminal law remains relevant in the modern world, for example, it is almost always through the process of state codification. Another way to include Islamic law in the state would be more court centered. It would involve the state directing courts to adjudicate particular disputes by reference to a given interpretation of Islamic law. This is done at times in the context of family law, in states as varied as Egypt and India. A third method, more recent but very much in vogue, involves the constitutionalization of Islamic law, through obligating the legislature not to violate core principles of Islamic law, and empowering a constitutional court to invalidate legislation if it does violate such principles. A fourth method might be the state regulation of entire fields of Islamic law on a voluntary basis, among those who choose to be bound within those fields. Islamic finance in states such as Malaysia operates on this basis. One might imagine "sharia tribunals" to resolve family law disputes in non-Muslim states serving the same function.

PREFACE

To be clear, the two approaches described above—of either voluntary adherence or state enforcement—are not exclusive of other potential uses of Islamic law in modern societies. For example, Iraqi tribes often reference Islamic law in private disputes that arise with some frequency between them. This places Islamic law in a third space, as Iraqi tribal members do not really adhere to tribal determinations voluntarily, but neither are such determinations sanctioned, let alone enforced, by the state.

This Nutshell addresses the subject of Islamic law as it operates as part of the law of modern states. Given this constraint, it is not concerned with the vast area of Islamic law that addresses ritual, for the reasons set forth above. Moreover, it does not deal with those more conventionally "legal" areas of Islamic law that were certainly of some state concern historically, but are not now. The most obvious is the law of slavery, which played a prominent role both in juristic texts and in premodern Islamic societies. However, the practice of Islamic slavery is of quite limited relevance today. Extremist movements aside, nearly all modern Muslims, and the states they occupy, have come to shun slavery and regard it as an abomination that their sacred texts had to grudgingly accommodate in a particular historical context that is thankfully no longer with us.

Approaching Islamic law in the manner articulated above is subject to criticism. Some would point out that if the pith and pit of Islamic law is juristic in nature, and therefore divorced from state practice, and if Islamic law in its most traditional sense is as ethical as it is legal, then to focus on the manner in which a state gives Islamic law life in the modern world is to focus on the contortions, and indeed, distortions, to which Islamic law has been subjected in modernity, rather than Islamic law on its own terms. To this criticism, it might be noted that hundreds of millions of Muslims, and in some cases non-Muslims, must live their lives in compliance with state enforced laws and court rulings that purport to be traditional understandings of classical Islamic law. Seeking therefore to understand Islamic law with reference to these applications of it in our times is extremely relevant. In the end, the issue may be one of nomenclature, with some perhaps preferring my Nutshell to be entitled "State Distortions of Islamic Law in a Nutshell." In any case, it is difficult to maintain that the subject is unworthy of study, whatever it might be called.

In light of the approach outlined above, there is one final challenge to preparing a Nutshell on Islamic law that is quite important to mention at the outset; namely, that there is no single state, or even small set of states, on which a Nutshell such as this can coherently focus. There are in fact 57 states that are members of the Organization of Islamic Cooperation, the multinational organization that describes itself as the "collective voice of the Muslim world." In terms of their incorporation of Islamic law into their legal systems, these states vary greatly. In some, such as Turkey, Islamic law has almost no formal role to play at all. In others, such as Saudi Arabia, Islamic law plays a preeminent and foundational role. Most states fall somewhere between these two poles. Moreover, Islamic law plays an important role in some states that are not majority Muslim. At times, this is because it is the governing law for the Muslim population as concerns family law and potentially inheritance law. India, Singapore, and Israel are all examples of this phenomenon. At other times, Islamic law is relevant because a non-Muslim state takes steps to accommodate Islamic practices, in particular in the financial sector, or because non-Muslim courts are forced for one reason or another to consider Islamic law issues.

Islamic law is therefore relevant in many of the world's legal systems. To attempt to describe how it is relevant in each state on each question of potential applicability would therefore be a nearly impossible task, and hardly an edifying one. The result would be more of a catalog than a narrative explanation of how Islamic law tends to operate in modern legal systems as a general matter.

Accordingly, I instead seek to identify general *trends* within modern states, and then often describe examples of such a trends. Obviously, some states will not fit within a broader trend, and some readers will feel that actual state practice in one jurisdiction, or set of jurisdictions, should have been described and were not. Ultimately, once it is clear that a comprehensive account of Islamic law in all modern states is not possible, editorial decisions on what to include and what leave out become important. I have made them as best as I am able on the basis of my own experience and judgment, accepting responsibility for any errors and omissions I may have made in the process.

In light of the above considerations, the outline of the Nutshell is as follows. The first chapter lays out the origins of Islamic law, or the classical corpus from which modern states often draw in order to determine Islamic law outcomes. In so doing, the chapter lays out the sources of Islamic law, describes who has authority to decide what Islamic law is as a traditional matter, and then turns to the Sunni-Shi'i divide, which has quite significant implications for Islamic law outcomes and methods in our times.

From there, the chapters deal sequentially with areas of Islamic law that are salient in the modern state. In the second chapter, I introduce family law, the field where Islamic law in its traditional form most continues to capture the imagination of Muslims and where indeed the classical corpus proves the most determinative in modern Muslim states. That said, while many (though certainly not all) of the classical era *rules* respecting Islamic marriage and the Muslim family are retained in most Muslim states, the fundamental *conception* of marriage has changed dramatically, in a manner that creates some tensions in the jurisprudence, as the Chapter will make clear.

Chapter Three of the Nutshell turns to the area of inheritance law, which is also largely governed by Islamic law in most modern Muslim states. Here again we will see tensions as between the seeming dictate of the classical rules—still putatively the source of decisions in most Muslim courts—and actual Muslim expectations.

The next subjects are the historic Islamic endowments known as the *waqfs* in Chapter Four and Islamic finance in Chapter Five. The two subjects are interestingly almost mirror images of one another. While the *waqf* was the focus of much classical juristic attention and had a significant impact on the economic and social life of Muslims in medieval times, its relevance has declined in many, though not all, modern Muslim states. By contrast, though it purports to be built upon the foundation of classical rules, in fact Islamic finance did not exist as a practice until the latter half of the twentieth century, and its importance has grown over time. Despite this growth, as we shall see, some of the underlying, existential tensions that accompanied its founding continue to exist.

From there, the Nutshell moves to the area of public law, and specifically criminal law. Unlike family law and inheritance law, the application of Islamic criminal law remains more of an exception in Muslim states than a rule. Nevertheless, it is an important feature of no small number of Muslim states, and we will examine where it is relevant, and how it is applied within the context of an otherwise modern legal system. We will further ask what types of purposes and functions the Islamization of criminal law seems to serve.

The penultimate Chapter Six will address the subject of constitutional law, and in particular the rising phenomenon of Islamic constitutionalism. The

Chapter will describe various features of Islamic constitutionalism, with particular emphasis on the so-called "repugnancy clause," a constitutional provision that empowers a court or other tribunal to strike down legislation that is deemed to be insufficiently in keeping with broader principles of Islamic law. We will examine court practice with respect to repugnancy and seek to determine whether or not there are consistent methodologies that judiciaries employ when interpreting the clause.

The Nutshell concludes with a turn toward international law, and more particularly, the set of rules through which the Islamic state is expected to conduct itself vis a vis the non-Muslim world. The proper term in Arabic for this field of law is *sīyār*, or "movements." Most contemporary readers are probably unfamiliar with this term, though they are likely to know of jihad, which serves as a central plank of the *sīyār*. In this Chapter, we will explore the nature of international relations in the Islamic world, how they have evolved from classical times to modern, and the manner in which the term jihad has evolved with these changed understandings. What we will find as concerns the meaning of jihad, and indeed what we will discover throughout this Nutshell, is that Islamic law, like American law, is deeply contestable.

This might be stated even more forthrightly. There is no clear answer in Islamic law to a great many legal questions, and modern states grapple with Islamic source material no less intensely than state institutions within the United States grapple with the meaning of the U.S. constitution and federal legislation. That the source material is revelatory in nature in the Islamic case does not change this fundamental dynamic, which inheres in any legal system. While lay Muslims may underestimate the central role of human agency in understanding divine revelation, it is quite apparent that jurists operated under no such misapprehensions. In fact, following almost any juristic ruling, or any fatwa, on a given subject, jurists quasi-ritually demonstrate the deep humility that is expected to attach to the effort of interpretation, and reveal the awareness of the difference between God's Will and humanity's understanding of it, by repeating the same words—And God knows best. In other words, Islamic law is merely the product of human efforts to know God's Will, and as such reflects the same biases, presuppositions, imperfections, and manipulations characteristic of any other human enterprise. It is important not to lose sight of that fact when seeking to understand the substance of Islamic law, where it came from, and to where it seems to be evolving.

In producing this Nutshell, I am deeply indebted to my many Islamic law teachers and mentors over the years, including Professor Abdullahi an-Naim, the late, great Dean Peter Awn, Vice Provost Philip Khoury, Professor Lama Abu Odeh, and Professor Nathan Brown. I must also include in this number the many nonspecialists in Islamic law and Middle Eastern law and politics who helped refine my understanding of jurisprudence and the nature of law generally, without whom my own ideas respecting the operation of Islamic law, however imperfect, would never have developed. These include Professors Michael Dorf, George Fletcher, Vivian Curran, George Berman, Ron Brand and Harry Flechtner. Over the years, my work has benefited immensely from the intense scrutiny given to it by leading colleagues in the field. These include Professors Kecia Ali, Mohammad Fadel, Intisar Rabb, Clark Lombardi, Russell Powell, Asifa Quraishi, and Bernard Freamon, among many others. The book would not have been possible at all without Professor Mark Cammack, with whom I coauthored a separate casebook, and whose thoughts and contributions provided in that context indirectly permeate virtually this entire Nutshell. As Editor in Chief of West Academic Publishing, Louis Higgins deserves much credit as well, for his patience, and for his gentle and yet dogged nudging, poking, and prodding to ensure that the book continued to progress to completion—more gradually than either of us anticipated.

Finally, after I wake each morning to a run and the dawn prayer, I find myself alone with a cup of coffee and my thoughts and reflections for a brief period. My mind ordinarily settles upon all that I am grateful and indebted to God for providing me in this world. First, I think of my parents Ala Baqir Hamoudi and Ayser Abdul-Jabbar al-Chalabi—who through herculean efforts of their own ensured a stable home, a world class education, and the nurturing of an inquisitive spirit. I also think of my brothers Amar and Ali—whose deep (and quite often vociferous) intellectual engagement at the youngest ages forged an appreciation of scholarly debate, a respect for differing views, and the absolute necessity of distinguishing between that which is personal, and that which is not. Most of all, my thoughts come to my wife Sara and my children Ayad and Kani. If countless colleagues and mentors have made me a better scholar, my family has made me into a much better person than I could have possibly managed on my own. Their unfailing love, their kindness, their patience with my many faults, and their willingness to forgive my many wrongs offer a brightness to my day, and a motivation to stay firm in the tasks that lie before me, which have included, this past several years, the completion of this fourth book of mine. When my coffee is finished, my mind is settled, and I inevitably hear one of the children bouncing down the stairs calling for their Baba, I know how truly blessed I am, through no doing of my own. It is at this time more than any other that the words of the first verse of the opening chapter of the Holy Qur'an always ring truest to me—All praise is due to God, the Lord of the Worlds.

HAIDER ALA HAMOUDI

October 2019

EXPLANATORY NOTES

Translations of the Qur'anic verses set forth in this Nutshell are from the modern style Sahih International Translation, unless noted otherwise. My citation convention for the Qu'ran is to include only the chapter number and the verse number separated by a colon, with the entire reference in brackets. Hence, for example, the second verse of the 47th chapter of the Qur'an (entitled the Chapter of Muhammad) appears as [47:2].

Given the vast number of citations to classical, medieval, and modern era Islamic juristic and religious texts, as well as legislation, regulation, and court decisions across a wide variety of jurisdictions, I have not attempted to adopt a uniform system of citation. Instead, I have opted to include relevant information for the source in question in as consistent a fashion as I could manage.

Translations of Arabic material other than the Qur'an are my own, unless otherwise noted.

OUTLINE

PREFACE III
EXPLANATORY NOTES XVII
TABLE OF CASES XXV

Chapter 1. Introduction—Classical Islamic Law 1
A. The Sources of Islamic Law 2
    1. Prophet Muhammad and the Holy Qur'an 2
    2. Searching for a Second Source of Law— the Prophetic Sunna 6
    3. Other Sources of Law 11
B. Authority in the Sunni Paradigm 13
    1. The Sunni Schools of Thought 13
    2. The Closing of the Doors of *Ijtihād* 18
C. The Sunni-Shi'a Split 23
    1. Political Divisions 23
        a. Theological Divisions—Shi'ism and the Imamate 25
    2. Shi'ism and Law 27
    3. Shi'ism in the Era of Occultation 32
D. Barreling Toward Modernity 36

Chapter 2. Islamic Family Law 41
A. Introduction 41
B. Marriage 43
    1. Understanding the Marriage Contract ... 43
    2. Forming the Marriage Contract 48

	a.	Age and Guardianship.......................... 48
		i.	Classical Islamic Law 48
		ii.	Modern Legislation 51
	b.	The Dower 55
		i.	Classical Islamic Law 55
		ii.	Modern Laws and Court Practices 58
		iii.	Dower in American Courts 60
	c.	Polygamy 66
		i.	Classical Islamic Law 66
		ii.	Modern Legislation 69
	d.	Competency 75
	e.	Other Conditions of Marriage 79
3.	Marital Obligations 81
	a.	Maintenance 81
	b.	Non-Abstention 85
	c.	Obedience 86
		i.	Classical Rules 86
		ii.	Obedience in Modernity 89
4.	The Temporary Marriage 97

C. Divorce 101
　1. *Ṭalāq* 101
　　a. Basic Contours of the *Ṭalāq* 101
　　b. Effect of *Ṭalāq* 105
　　c. Modern Reforms and State Court Practices Pertaining to *Ṭalāq* 108
　　　i. Limited Scope of *Ṭalāq* Reforms 108
　　　ii. Notification and Registration of *Ṭalāq* 110
　　　iii. Post Marital Support and the Capricious *Ṭalāq* 115
　　　iv. The Triple Divorce 119

	2.	Other Marital Dissolutions 121
		a. Conditional or Delegated *Ṭalāq* 121
		b. Compensated Divorce (*Khul`*) 126
		c. Cause 130
		i. Classical Rules 130
		ii. Modern State Practice 132
		d. Irreconcilable Differences (*Shiqāq*) 139
D.	Child Custody 144
	1.	Classical Principles 145
	2.	Modern State Practice 150
	3.	Guardianship 152
	4.	Rearing (*Ḥaḍana*) 153
	5.	Exceptions 155
E.	Adoption 156

Chapter 3. Inheritance Law 161

A.	Role of Qur'anic Verse 163
B.	Sunni Inheritance 168
	1. The Agnates as Primary Residual Heirs 168
	a. Determining the Nearest Male Agnate 171
	b. Uterine Heirs 176
	2. Adjusting the Qur'anic Shares 177
	3. Wills 181
	4. Other Limitations 182
C.	Shi'i Inheritance 184
	1. The Inheritance Rights of Kin 186
	2. Categories of Kin and Cause 187
	3. Other Features of Shi'ism 193
D.	Modern State Practices and Innovations 195
	1. General Court Practice 195

	2.	Innovations 197

        a.   Inheritance of Daughters or Sisters.. 202
        b.   Inheritance Portion of the Wife 204
        c.   The Orphaned Grandchild 207
        d.   Wills.. 210

Chapter 4. The *Waqf*.. 213
A.   The Classical *Waqf*... 214
B.   The Decline of the *Waqf*................................... 223
C.   The Relevance of the *Waqf* Today 232

Chapter 5. Islamic Finance 241
A.   Introduction 241
B.   The Profit Sharing Ideal 246
C.   The Artifices and Their Risks......................... 256
D.   The Speculation Ban and the Lease Contract 268
    1.   General.. 268
    2.   Insurance 277
    3.   Islamic Capital Markets 280
        a.   The Dow Jones *Fatwa* 281
        b.   *Ṣukūk*... 284
        c.   Derivatives 286

Chapter 6. Islamic Criminal Law.................... 289
A.   Introduction 289
B.   Classical Islamic Criminal Law 291
    1.   The Scriptural Crimes............................. 291
    2.   The Discretionary Crimes 300
C.   Islamic Criminal Law in Modernity.............. 303

1. The Scriptural Crimes in Modern Courts 303
   a. Scriptural Crime as Instrument of Repression 304
   b. Uneven Implementation of the Punishments for Scriptural Crimes 317
2. Legality and the Transformation of the Islamic Criminal System 319
   a. Discretionary Crimes Reinvented 319
   b. Discretionary Sexual Crimes 323
   c. Blasphemy as Discretionary Criminal Law 328
D. The Law of Retaliation and Islamic Criminal Law 334

Chapter 7. Islamic Constitutionalism 337
A. Introduction 337
B. The Roots of Islamic Constitutionalism 339
C. Islamic Constitutional Commitments 342
   1. Islam as Religion of the State 343
   2. Islamic Law as a Source of State Law 345
   3. Repugnancy Clauses 348
   4. Implementations of Repugnancy 352

Chapter 8. Islamic International Law and Relations 369
A. The Origins of Islamic International Law 371
   1. The Era of the Prophet Muhammad 371
   2. Early Juristic Theory: Shaybānī's *Sīyār* 375

B. International Law After the Early Years 385
   1. Ibn Taymiyya and the Defensive Jihad 385
   2. The Ottomans and Permanent International Relations 387
C. Modern International Law and Relations 388
   1. Conventional Developments 388
   2. Jihad and the Modern World 391
   3. The Challenge of the Transnational Movements: Al Qaeda and the Islamic State 398

INDEX 405

TABLE OF CASES

References are to Pages

Abul Fata Mahomed Ishak And Ors. v. Rasamaya Dhur Chowdhuri And Ors., 226
Appeal 5/1989, Sharia Appeal Board (Kuala Lumpur), 123
Arab-Malaysian Finance Bhd. v. Taman Ihsan Jaya Sdn. Bhd. et. al., 264
Case 27/2010, Islamic Court of Kutacane (Indonesia), dated December 10, 2010, 325
Case 285/Personal Status Panel/2008, Court of Cassation of Iraq, decided December 31, 2008, 309
Case 318/General Panel/2000, Court of Cassation of Iraq, decided Feb. 14, 2000, 309
Case 5916/2011, Personal Status Panel, Court of Cassation of Iraq, 144
Case No. 1/1977/ Islamic High Court of Surabaya, 84
Case No. 2601/2001, Personal Status Court of Kadhimiyya, 95
Case No. 287 of Judicial Year 111, District 14, Personal Status Appeals Court of Cairo, Egypt, 314
Chaudhry v. Chaudhry, 60
Danial Latifi v. Union of India, 119
Decision 20/JY 1, Supreme Constitutional Court of Egypt, decided May 4, 1985, 348, 367
Decision 29/JY11, Supreme Constitutional Court of Egypt, decided March 26, 1994, 355
Decision 45/2012, Federal Supreme Court of Iraq, decided September 19, 2012, 358
Decision 6/JY9, Supreme Constitutional Court of Egypt, decided March 18, 1995, 361
Decision 60/2010, Federal Supreme Court of Iraq, decided December 21, 2010, 357
Decision July 29, 2006, Court of Cassation, Mudawwana al-aḥkām al-qaḍā'iyya 3:367, 320
Decision May 30, 2006, Da'er General Court, Mudawwana al-aḥkām al-qaḍā'iyya 3:364, 320

General Panel, Court of Cassation of the Autonomous
    Kurdistan Region of Iraq, decided December 25, 2004,
    310
H. Sapinah, Estate of, 177
Hazoor Bakhsh v. Federation of Pakistan, 362
Investment Dar Company KSCC v. Blom Developments
    Bank SAL, 267
Islamic Investment Company of the Gulf (Bahamas) Ltd.
    v. Symphony Gems N.V. & Others, 259
Jones v. Wolf, 62
Lina Joy v. Muslim Religious Council for the Federal
    Territory of Putrajaya et al., 312
Mohamed bin Mohd Ali v. Roslina binti Mohd Yusoff, 102
Mohammad Ahmad Khan v. Shah Bano Begum, 119
Mst. Khurshid Bibi v. Muhammad Amin, 129
Mutchilim Alias Ashrhin, Re, 180
National Group for Communications and Computers Ltd.
    v. Lucent Technologies, 272
Nazar Muhammad v. Shahzada Begum, 196
Obaidi & Qayoum, In re Marriage of, 62
Odatalla v. Odatalla, 62
Soleimani v. Soleimani, 63
Suparman v. Tien, 74
Syed Abdullah al-Shatri v. Shariffa Salmah, 52
Y.A.M. Tengku Muhammad Fakhry Ibn Sultan Ismail
    Petra v. Manohara Odelia Pinot, 93
Yaneta Binti Hakam v. Syafnil Bin Ahmad, 109
Zafran Bibi v. The State, 307

ISLAMIC LAW
IN A NUTSHELL®

CHAPTER 1
INTRODUCTION—CLASSICAL ISLAMIC LAW

Islamic law in modern states borrows heavily from the classical corpus of Islamic law. This corpus was developed by medieval jurists from roughly 750 C.E. (approximately one hundred years after the Prophet Muhammad's death) to roughly the end of the nineteenth century. This classical period also coincides with what is broadly regarded as Islam's golden era, though the Islamic world was in political and economic decline well before the end of this period.

Given the role that classical Islamic law plays in at least framing religious questions of contemporary relevance, it is therefore helpful to understand the origins, evolution and authority of classical Islamic law in the premodern Islamic state. This chapter endeavors to do this, in brief fashion. It begins by describing the sources of classical Islamic law, and then proceeds to explain the nature of authority in Islamic law and jurisprudence in the classical era. Following this is a short description of the Sunni-Shi'a split, with particular reference to its relevance in determining the substance of Islamic law. The Chapter concludes by describing the relevance of all of this premodern material on the practice of modern Muslim states.

By way of preface, it should be noted that there is a rich academic literature that surrounds the origins and development of classical Islamic law that challenges my traditional assumptions of it. However, this literature, valuable as it is in any number of contexts, is hardly relevant to this Nutshell. This is because it has a dramatically reduced effect on the manner in which Islamic law is understood among modern Muslims, and in particular those state officials and bureaucrats who are responsible for implementing and applying Islamic law in modern Muslim states. As with the founding in the United States and the early years of the republic, the blossoming of classical Islamic law within Muslim empires has attached to it a series of legends, broadly accepted and internalized among the Muslim population. Valuable as they are for other purposes, critical reappraisals of these legends do not have the effect of displacing the legends, much less changing the nature of Islamic jurisprudence as it is understood today. Hence, this Nutshell will assume Islam's core foundational legends on their own terms. We begin with the story upon which all of the others are built, respecting an illiterate merchant and former shepherd who went to a cave to meditate, and there heard the voice of the angel Gabriel commanding him to read.

A. THE SOURCES OF ISLAMIC LAW

1. PROPHET MUHAMMAD AND THE HOLY QUR'AN

The illiterate merchant referred to above was, of course, the Prophet Muhammad, born near the end of the sixth century C.E. in the trading city of Mecca, to a respectable clan within a respectable tribe.

Known for his unusually high moral character, he was orphaned at an early age, raised by his uncle, and later employed by the wealthy widow to be known among Muslims as Khadija al-Kubra, or Khadija the Great. She proposed marriage to him when he was 25 years old. A deeply thoughtful person concerned about the materialism, lack of spirituality, and social injustices around him, the Prophet Muhammad developed the habit of frequenting the cave of Hira, in the hills above Mecca, in order to meditate quietly and develop his own spiritual life. It was here at the age of forty that he received the revelation that serves as Islam's first source of law— the literal Word of God conveyed through the angel Gabriel, known to Muslims as the Qur'an.

There is some irony to describing the Qur'an as a source of law, much less the first source of law, given how little legal content it has. Of over 6000 verses, no more than a few dozen can truly be called legal, though the number expands into several hundred if one includes rules of ritual and worship. The overwhelming bulk of the Qur'an, and certainly the revelations that the Prophet Muhammad received while in Mecca, were not rules-based, but rather spiritual in nature. They conveyed the core ideas that there is a single true God, that worship of Him was a fundamental duty of each human being, and that this God out of mercy to humanity sent to the world a series of Prophets, beginning with Adam, through to Noah, Abraham, Ismail, Isaac, and the Prophets of Israel, including Jesus, and ending with Muhammad. Hence, early verses urge submission to the one and only God—"submission" being the best translation of the term "Islam"—and the performance of good deeds, which include charity to the poor, care for the vulnerable, including in particular women and slaves, and kind treatment of the orphan. In fact, the Qur'an goes so far as to promise punishment to those who pray, and yet withhold sustenance from the poor. Beyond rejecting or polytheizing God, there are few sins in the Qur'an more unequivocally condemned than hoarding wealth or obsessing over material gain.

The Prophet Muhammad spread his radical new message among the Meccans, and met with modest success. Unsurprisingly, as the faith grew, so did resistance to it. In particular, Mecca was of some importance as a pilgrimage center, where many would come to worship various idols set near the Ka`ba, a large black cube placed within a praying ground in the middle of the city. Muhammad's message of social justice and castigation of soulless materialism was troublesome enough for the tribal elites. Entirely intolerable, however, was the characterization of idol worship as fundamental sin, along with the indication that the Ka`ba itself was the house of Abraham, the Prophet who within the Qur'an is nearly burned alive for destroying idols. Muhammad was effectively challenging the very way of life of the leading Meccan tribes. As a result, once he reached a certain level of success that his message could no longer be ignored, the Meccans decided to kill him.

The Prophet soon learned of these designs, and decided to flee to the town of Yathrub, around 300 miles away, where his preaching had already led to the conversion of leaders of the two major tribes prevailing there. In Yathrub, the Prophet Muhammad took on the role of political leader alongside his spiritual role. At the same time, the verses revealed from the angel Gabriel began to change in character as well. For example, in introducing the themes of monotheism and social justice, the Meccan verses had emphasized some level of commonality as between Muslims and the other major monotheistic religions, and especially Christianity and Judaism. By contrast, the Medinan verses tended to emphasize Islam's distinctiveness. In particular, the newer verses were more explicit and strident in rejecting both the Christian notion of God having a son, and the Jewish one of the possibility of a chosen people.

Even more relevant for the purposes of this Nutshell, the Medinan verses contained actual rules, both governing areas of worship and ritual, known in Arabic as the `ibādāt, as well as societal and interpersonal relations, known as the *mu`āmalāt*. Some of these rules-based verses were quite specific. For example, as Chapter Three will show, several Qur'anic verses lay out in some detail the precise fractional shares of a decedent's estate to which certain relatives are entitled. Other verses are far more general. This includes a verse exhorting believers to fulfill their obligations, which can only serve as the very start of the development of a coherent body of contract law.

The new faith expanded dramatically throughout the region following the Prophet's flight to Yathrub, later renamed Medina, which is short for Medinat al-Nabi, or the City of the Prophet. Through conversions and a series of successful military ventures, the Prophet was able to return to Mecca late in his life, clear the Ka`ba of its idols, and energize a disparate group of tribes and peoples into a nascent community—the *'umma*—which proved ready, willing, and able to spread Muhammad's message to the entire world. Less than one hundred years after the Prophet Muhammad's death, the `Abbasid empire had conquered Persia in the east and in the west, Tariq ibn Ziyad sailed his army across the straits of Gibraltar, thereby initiating the Muslim conquest of Spain that would last for over seven centuries.

2. SEARCHING FOR A SECOND SOURCE OF LAW—THE PROPHETIC SUNNA

In many ways, the speed and manner of the dramatic Muslim expansion revealed the need for an Islamic law. As opposed to the spread of Christendom, which took place within a Roman Empire that did not lack for legal sophistication, the Islamic *'umma* displaced existing disparate legal systems of varying degrees of sophistication, and required something to replace them with. To draw from the Christ of the New Testament, the idea of rendering unto Caesar that which belongs to Caesar presupposes a Caesar—that is, a sovereign administering a coherent body of law to whom the believer could be expected to submit. This was not possible in the case of Islam. The areas it had taken over were too disparate, and the legal systems too distinct from one another, to simply incorporate as the functioning law of the *'umma*. Islam needed its own body of law that would define its own political community. Quite clearly, the Qur'an was not substantial enough as a legal document to serve that purpose on its own.

Various options were plausible. One could imagine, for example, reliance on the Muslim community itself to develop its own legal traditions and mores, and the building of institutions for these purposes. The twentieth century reformist Fazlur Rahman spoke often of a "living Sunna", which he conceived of as a dynamic and ever evolving communal effort to replicate the exemplary conduct of the Prophet Muhammad across place and time, with communal determinations ultimately being the basis of Islamic legitimacy. Another possibility, and one with strong resonance throughout Islamic history, was to permit reason to serve as a source of law alongside the Qur'an. Advocates of this view within Sunnism, plainly enamored of the works of the ancient Greek philosophers whose work they had played a fundamental role in preserving, were known as the *Mu`tazila*. Indeed, this view of reason as primary legal source continues at least in theory to be the prevalent Shi'i view, though it is less so in practice, as we shall see.

Ultimately, Sunni jurists settled upon a third approach, which was to elevate the practices, utterances, gestures, and actions of the Prophet

Muhammad—referred to collectively as the Sunna—as a coequal source of law alongside the Qur'an. The earliest major proponent of this view was the early Muslim jurist Muhammad ibn Idris al-Shafi'i, the eponym of one of the four major schools of thought within Sunnism. In advancing his claim, Shafi'i had critics during his lifetime and indeed long after. The primary criticism was not that there was some inherent problem in emulating the Prophet Muhammad given how revered he was within the *'umma,* for obvious reasons. Rather, Shafi'i's critics wanted to know precisely how Muslims were supposed to know everything the Prophet said and did. This problem arose because, unlike the Qur'an, which was meticulously collected shortly after the Prophet Muhammad's death, nobody sought to meticulously compile every life story concerning the until long after he had died.

Shafi'i's response was that the authenticity of Sunna could be determined through reliance on chains of trustworthy narrators, wherein one person of trust heard from another who heard from a third, and in some cases a fourth or a fifth, that the Prophet had made a particular statement or undertaken a particular action. An example of such a narration, involving a Sunna that is of fundamental importance to Islamic finance and the ban on money interest, is as follows:

Abu Bakr said that Waki' said that Isma'il bin al-Muslim al-Abdi said that Abu Al-Mutawakkil al-Naji reported from Abu Sa'id al-Khudri, who said he heard the Prophet of God state . . .

Whatever criticisms might be made of this approach of discovering authentic Sunna—and certainly there have been some—it suffices to note that it ultimately came to prevail over time within Sunni Islam. With this newfound consensus, the process of Sunna compilation gathered momentum decades and in some cases more than a century after the Prophet's death, as prominent figures sought to determine who of the narrators could be trusted, and who could not. Over time, there arose within Sunni Islam a broad consensus on the soundness of the Sunna contained in four compilations that have reached near canonical status. Still, disputes on the reliability of any given single Prophetic report can erupt from time to time, even in contemporary times.

The legal effects of the points made above—that the Sunna ultimately came to serve as a *coequal* source of law with the Qur'an, and that Sunna validity was tested against the reliability of its narrators and not compatibility with the Qur'an—should not be gainsaid. Most radically, the Sunna can in their coequal role serve to *displace* Qur'anic verses. An excellent example of this lies in the case of inheritance. Verse 176 of the second chapter of the Qur'an reads as follows:

> Prescribed for you, when death draws nigh to one of you, and he leaves behind some property, is the making of a testament in favor of his parents and relatives who are reputable—an obligation on the God-fearing.

Later verses of the Qur'an specify that particular portions of the estate must be left to parents and relatives. For example, verse 11 of the fourth chapter indicates ". . . to his parents to each one of the two the sixth of what he leaves, if he has children; but if he has no children, and his heirs are his parents, a third to his mother. . . ." Separately, there is a Sunna that prohibits a decedent from leaving any portion of their estate to a relative beyond the share specifically granted to that relative under Qur'anic verse.

Shafi'i reads all of this together to come to the conclusion that the first verse requiring the making of a testament to parents and relatives is *abrogated and no longer in effect,* both because of the later verse specifying portions, and because of the Sunna proscribing the making of a will to benefit one already entitled to legally inherit. The role of the Sunna in serving to abrogate the verse is thus central to Shafi'i's analysis and reveals the larger point. A Sunna with a sound narrative chain seeming to stand in contradiction to the Qur'anic verse does not have its validity questioned. Rather, the earlier verse must be abrogated in some cases, or limited in others, to be read harmoniously with Qur'anic text.

Other examples of this phenomenon exist as well. For example, the Qur'an describes the punishment for fornication as 100 lashes and a Sunna suggests that the punishment for adultery is stoning. Shafi'i's conclusion was that the Sunna limited the scope of the Qur'anic fornication punishment to unmarried fornicators, despite there being no such limitation in the Qur'anic verse itself, while the Sunna would apply to fornicating adulterers. These particular interpretations of Islamic law as concerns adultery and inheritance remain the dominant ones to this day notwithstanding what seems to be contradictory Qur'anic verse.

Thus, in summary, following some earlier ferment respecting the question, the broad view within Sunni jurisprudence is that the Sunna serve as the second source of law, alongside the Qur'an, and coequal to it. While there are other sources of Islamic law, none of them are remotely as influential as these first two. Hence, to this day, religious exhortations of virtually any sort, from Friday sermons to written guides to the devout, make repeated reference to Qur'an and Sunna together as the two major sources of Islamic law, without making much of a distinction between them. To the extent that there was ever a debate respecting the primacy of the latter of these two sources, it was long ago put to rest.

3. OTHER SOURCES OF LAW

The rise of the Sunna, and the determination of its soundness through the quasi-scientific method of examining the reliability of the narrative chain delivering it, reveal a certain discomfort among many early Muslim jurists with the use of unbridled moral reasoning to determine God's Will. Analytical reason was obviously deployed—it is needed to examine the reliability of a narrative chain, for example—but, to use Shafi`i's analogy, early jurists understood this to be no different than a sailor determining location in the open seas from the positioning of the stars. The jurist, that is, was not attempting to determine whether an action was right or wrong on the basis of reason, but merely deploying it in the service of the "discovery" (*istinbāṭ*) of legal rulings.

There have been schools of thought within Sunnism and Shi'ism that have taken these suspicions of reason to their ultimate extreme to prohibit its use as a source of law altogether. The most well-known of these was the Zahiris, a fifth school of thought within Sunni Islam that died out in the classical era. By and large, the consensus that emerged among Sunni jurists was that there was at least one form of inductive reasoning that could be used as a source of law. This was analogical reasoning. Hence, for example, the Qur'an urges the believers to shun *khamr*, which is understood to refer to wines, or alcoholic beverages arising from fermented juices. At the time, the primary wine was date wine, though grape wines existed as well. Using analogy, most classical jurists outside of the Hanafi school understood the prohibition to extend to all intoxicants, and therefore include alcoholic beverages made from barley, wheat, or rice, such as beer or whiskey.

Consensus served as a fourth source of law. Though in its earliest forms it seemed to require the agreement of all Muslims on a particular point of law, the doctrine was largely refined to involve only jurists. The idea was that, per a statement of the Prophet Muhammad, the Muslim community would never collectively agree on an error. Hence, if the jurists in a given time all agreed on a particular legal rule, this consecrated it as valid as a per se matter.

These four sources of law—Qur'an, Sunna, consensus, and analogy—are those upon which all of the Sunni schools agree. Beyond these four universally agreed upon sources, the schools differed on what might be used to derive a legal rule. Public interest (*maṣlaha*) served as a source among some jurists, particularly from the Maliki school, and a type of equity or fair dealing served as a Hanafi source. The later Hanafi jurists who wrote the major Ottoman era compilation of Islamic law known as the *Majalla* relied extensively on custom. By contrast, jurists from the Hanbali school tended to be less willing to derive Islamic law rules from any source beyond the four universally agreed upon.

Over time, the differences between the schools narrowed considerably. This is because, in practice if not in theory, later classical jurists tended not to make explicit use of sources of law beyond the first four very often. Many modern Islamic law reformists who advocate for a return to Islamic law rulemaking call for a more robust use of some of the more marginal sources of law, including public interest and fair dealing, in order to render Islamic law more progressive. The success of these efforts to date is very much debatable.

B. AUTHORITY IN THE SUNNI PARADIGM

1. THE SUNNI SCHOOLS OF THOUGHT

Perhaps even more important than the question of the valid sources from which to derive Islamic law rules is one concerning who is responsible for undertaking the effort, or, in Arabic, *'ijtihād,* to do the derivations. That is, who has the authority to determine what Islamic law is, using the sources referred to in the previous section?

A fundamental point to note in this context, and one that has deep implications on the nature of Islamic law in our times, is that the state—the quintessential lawgiver of our era—was given almost no role in determining Islamic law. There is a historical reason for this. After the death of the Prophet Muḥammad, the Sunni view was that the community was left to choose his successor, or "caliph", to use the Arabic term. The community did so by selecting one of the Prophet's closest companions, Abū Bakr al-Ṣiddīq. Upon his death, another noted companion, ʿUmar ibn al-Khaṭṭāb, served as caliph, followed by ʿUthmān ibn ʿAffān and finally, the Prophet's son in law, ʿAlī ibn 'Abī Ṭālib. Together, these four are referred to as the rightly guided caliphs, and highly revered within Sunnism. It would be anachronistic to describe the caliphal selection during this period as being somehow democratic—in fact, each caliph was selected differently, and in no case was there anything that resembled a modern election. Nevertheless, one could say with some justification that according to the classical Sunni legends, the caliphs were determined through reference to the will of the community, or at least its elites.

Following the death of the fourth caliph, there was a significant profaning of the office. Effectively, it became a hereditary position, and any role for the community in the selection was reduced to a fiction. Thus, unlike the Prophet or the first four caliphs, the leaders of the *'umma* came to be regarded as kings who represented power in this world. They were not categorically models of piety, as the rightly guided caliphs were, and they thus had no obvious claim over the power to interpret and proclaim the substance of God's Law. If anything, their capacity to undertake this task was dramatically compromised by their own political ambitions. The task of finding Islamic law was left instead to individuals known as jurists.

Jurists are different from judges, in that they generally hold no state office. The ideal vision of the jurist is one who works in isolation of the state, and has no interest in sullying a hard earned reputation in study and effort to understand God's Law with the temptations of the life of this world, whether they be wealth or power. As for their training, jurists learned their craft within institutions known as *madhāhib,* or schools of thought. The schools themselves are best not conceived as brick and mortar institutions. Rather, to borrow from the noted Islamicist George Makdisi, they served more like the trade guilds of the medieval era that governed professions such as blacksmithing or shoemaking. Among other things, like the guilds, the schools were self-regulated, relied on a form of apprenticing, and held a monopoly in the training of jurists. Anyone who wanted to be a jurist was effectively required to apprentice through a school, and spend decades perfecting the craft before they could do so.

Ultimately, Islam settled on four such schools. They were named after early juristic figures, though the extent to which each school was actually founded by its respective eponym is a matter of some debate. The schools were known as the Hanafi, after 'Abū Ḥanīfa, the Shafi'i, after Muḥammad 'ibn 'Idris al-Shāfi'ī, the Maliki, after Mālik 'ibn Anas, and the Hanbali, after the Sunna compiler Aḥmad 'ibn Ḥanbal.

The prominence of a jurist in any given school depended largely on his scholarly reputation. Partly to burnish this reputation, jurists wrote compendia in which they laid out Islamic law rules, largely on the basis of casuistic reasoning involving asking, and answering, how particular hypothetical factual situations should be resolved. These various juristic compendia, emanating from jurists within the four Sunni schools across continents and over hundreds of years, coming to different, and in some cases evolving, conclusions over an untold number of subjects, constitute the corpus of classical Islamic law. The proper Arabic term for this corpus would be *fiqh,* rather than sharia. Classically, the latter term referred to an idealized, and as such largely unknowable, conception of God's Will—the True Path, as it were. *Fiqh,* by contrast, refers to human attempts to understand the sharia. While that conceptual distinction is fundamental among Islamic philosophers and theologians, in point of fact, among lawmakers, judges, and practitioners dealing with Islamic law in modern states, the two terms are largely conflated. This is an error of category that reformists often emphasize when seeking change in understanding how an ideal Islamic state is to be constructed.

It is important to note that while at least in the purest conceptions of Islamic law, the jurist serves no role in the state and operates independently of it, this was not always true. Later Islamic empires in particular appointed jurists with official titles such as Chief Mufti, and provided considerable, enticing emoluments to accompany the position. Moreover, leading political figures were often encouraged as part of state policy to found seminaries through the Islamic charitable endowment vehicle known as the *waqf*, which served as another means through which the state could use its influence to fund jurists and juristic training.

Just as the state paid some cognizance to juristic authorities and sought to influence them, the jurists similarly did not ignore the state when developing Islamic law rules. There were juristic rules, for example, respecting the qualifications for caliph. There were also theories on when the caliph could or could not create his own binding rules—known as *sīyāsa*—that operated alongside Islamic law in the true Islamic state. The legend of the ideal jurist may have been of a person who was uninterested in the state and in the sullying temptations of wealth and power that it promised, and this legend may well continue to captivate the Muslim imagination. However, the fact is that Sunni jurists were never entirely isolated from the state, nor did they fail to consider its role in rulemaking. Indeed, juristic considerations of these subjects have proven quite important in modernity, as future chapters will show.

2. THE CLOSING OF THE DOORS OF *'IJTIHĀD*

One consequence of the settling of Sunni juristic authority into four schools was the limiting of the sources to which jurists could turn when developing their own compendia. Where at least in theory early jurists would deploy their exertions, or *'ijtihād,* to create rules directly from Islam's core source material, identified in the first section of this chapter, there seems to have been a distinct turn away from this method of creating rules around 1000 C.E., in favor of *taqlīd,* or "imitation." This involved using already developed sources within a given Sunni school to create a compendium. Thus, where earlier jurists would make reference to Sunna to defend a conclusion, later ones would instead place a particular statement in the mouth of the eponym of their school—"Mālik said,"—as justification for a rule.

The traditional Islamic studies accounts of Islamic law, from luminaries such as Noel Coulson and Joseph Schacht, maintained that the move from interpretation to imitation signified an end to the creative period of Islamic jurisprudence, and the start of its stultification. Following the closing of the doors, rules grew more arcane, less dynamic, and less capable of evolving sensibly with the times. Indeed, from early twentieth century Egyptian reformer Muḥammad 'Abduh forward there have been no shortage of Muslim progressives who find in the reopening of the doors of *'ijtihād* a potential for an Islamic rebirth and reawakening.

More recent scholarship has cast some doubt on the traditional accounts, at least as a historical matter. In the first place, it is an exaggeration to say that the doors of *'ijtihād* closed entirely. Some notable scholars—the fourteenth century 'Ibn Taymiyya, for example, or the 12th century 'Ibn Rushd—reached conclusions in contradiction to those of their schools largely on the basis of deploying *'ijtihād,* long after the supposed closing of the gates. 'Ibn Taymiyya most notably rejected the validity of the notorious "triple divorce", wherein a husband irrevocably divorces his wife by pronouncing the divorce formula orally three successive times. This view is not held by any of the Sunni schools, and his defense of it is based largely on Sunnaic exegesis that runs contrary to earlier jurists within his school.

As to the broader shift away from *'ijtihād,* valuable scholarship points out that this really was not about, nor did it lead to, a lack of creativity or dynamism in Islamic jurisprudence. Simply put, the use of "imitation" is not in and of itself stultifying. To take a simple, modern example, Islamic finance is largely based on the idea of imitative *taqlīd*. It plainly develops modern financial practices from the extant rules of classical jurists rather than using primary Sunni sources to create new rules. Whatever criticisms might be made of Islamic finance—and certainly, there have been some, as we shall see—it can hardly be described as somehow lacking in adaptability or flexibility. Indeed, its problem may be something of the reverse.

Similarly, largely through *taqlīd*, there has been juristic evolution in the doctrine of jihad from an era in which Muslim armies seemed to win every war they fought to the late Ottoman era, when they began to lose them with increasing frequency. Analogies can be made to United States jurisprudence, where courts bound by earlier Supreme Court rulings show remarkable creativity in how they interpret and apply those rulings to new cases and circumstances. Again, there is nothing blind or uncreative about this process.

Nevertheless, if imitation through *taqlīd*, like *stare decisis*, is not the caricature of blind, unthinking aping of previous rulings that it is made out to be, it is also fair to point out that it is more constraining than pure interpretation of original sources is. Again, the analogy of lower courts bound by Supreme Court precedent is a useful one, in that such courts are clearly not as free to interpret the Constitution as they would be in the absence of such precedent.

Why would later generations of classical jurists—or modern Muslim scholars developing the rules of Islamic finance, for that matter—choose to constrain themselves in this manner rather than return to the original sources of divine revelation to justify their rulings? According to the noted Islamic law scholar Sherman Jackson, such constraints carry with them the advantage of deeper legitimacy. An interpretation of Sunna by a modern jurist that seems to bless a particular modern financial vehicle may strike some as self-serving, if the modern jurist could not point to a classical rule that seems to justify the position being adopted. Certainly modern legislators find it far easier to create Islamic rules—granting women expanded rights to dissolve their marriages for example—where they can do so by adopting the rules of any of the Sunni schools rather than by claiming to find new rules directly from the Sunna. Again, this is not to suggest that *'ijtihād* is not possible in the modern world—courts in modern Islamic states quote directly from the Qur'an or Sunna to justify positions with frequency—but only that the imprimatur of authority comes more naturally from the classical sources than from earlier and necessarily more ambiguous revelatory ones.

As to whether or not this constrains Islamic jurisprudence unduly, there is no doubt that in some cases it certainly seems to. The classical Islamic conceptions of marriage, as Chapter Two shows, are deeply at odds with modern Muslim understandings and inherently patriarchal, coming uncomfortably close to treating women's sexual organs as items for purchase. There is an abundance of source material in both Qur'an and Sunna out of which a more modern, more woman friendly and more progressive marriage regime can be developed.

At the same time, it would be a mistake to ignore the dangers inherent in freeing Islamic law and jurisprudence entirely from the authority that inheres to those same classical sources. Precedents do not constrain progressives alone, and various parts of the Sunna could be read in a fashion that might justify deplorable actions that classical law places beyond the bounds of the acceptable. An obvious example lies in the case of the September 11 hijackers, who engaged in what they claimed was a form of military attack against the United States while present in the United States under visas issued by it. Under classical law, their lawful and conditional presence as Muslims in a non-Muslim state would be referred to as an *'amān,* or covenant of protection, and the person enjoying the covenant would be a *musta'min.* There are few more obvious violations of Islamic international law than engaging in violence in a territory in which one is a *musta'min,* no matter how oppressive the state. A *musta'min* could certainly leave the state in which she has been granted protection, disavow the covenant, and emigrate to an Islamic state to wage war under the authority of the caliph, but she could not attack the state where she has been given protection from within. This then begs the obvious question, and one in fact framed to Bin Laden himself, of where in the manuals of the classical doctors he could find defense for the September 11 attacks he helped to orchestrate. His response was that where others might follow the Sunna of the classical doctors, he would follow the Sunna of the Prophet Muhammad. This should at least cause careful reflection among those enamored of *'ijtihād* as some sort of necessaritarian progressivist panacea. In the end, Islam's revelatory material, like the text of the United States Constitution, is not inherently more progressive than the centuries of established jurisprudence interpreting it. It is merely more ambiguous, and this ambiguity can be used by the terrorist no less effectively than by the progressive.

C. THE SUNNI-SHI'A SPLIT

1. POLITICAL DIVISIONS

To this point, the discussion of classical Islamic law has concerned the Sunni branch of Islamic law. However, as the other major branch of Islam, Shi'ism plays a significant role in no small number of modern Muslim legal systems. Modern Shi'i political theory serves as the basis for the Iranian state, and has an outsized influence on the manner in which Iraq is governed. Shi'ism is also relevant in the legal systems of other states to a lesser extent, including Lebanon, Bahrain, and India. This section therefore introduces the core tenets of Shi'ism, with a particular focus on the manner in which these tenets have an impact on understandings of Islamic law.

The core historical legends concerning the Sunni-Shi'a divide, and the theological underpinnings associated therewith, have been described in much academic and mainstream literature and are easy to summarize. As noted above, the Sunni view is that upon the death of the Prophet Muhammad, the Muslim community was left to determine his political successor, and did, in the form of the first caliph. The Shi'i view is that God never intended to leave such a decision to the community, and in fact had designated the Prophet's successor as his son in law 'Alī, who later become the fourth Sunni caliph.

In the Shi'i legends, the Prophet made this clear late in his life. Specifically, on his way back to Medina after performing his final pilgrimage in Mecca, he stopped at the valley of *Ghadīr Khum* and declared to the community that he would leave behind him two weighty things, the Book of God, and the People of his House, and that they would not be separated from one another until they joined him in heaven. Following this, the Prophet raised the hand of 'Alī and declared that whoever followed Muhammad must now follow 'Alī. The designation, again in the Shi'i accounts, could therefore hardly have been clearer.

Under this telling of Islamic history, the events following the death of the Prophet Muhammad take on a significantly different cast. The first three caliphs, deeply revered within Sunnism, are usurpers. The first, Abu Bakr, was feeble minded and heartless, having denied to the Prophet's daughter Fāṭima a piece of real property known as the Fadak that had been given to her by her father. The second, 'Umar, was even worse—a thug and a misogynist with a proclivity of violence towards women, and in particular the women of Muhammad's household. The third, 'Uthman, was an incompetent whose shortcomings led to the political disaster of the Umayyad dynasty. Such characterizations of such deeply respected Sunni figures continues to be a source of significant tension between the sects today.

There is some convergence after this, in that 'Alī was ultimately selected as the fourth Sunni caliph. However, civil war erupted almost immediately afterwards, first in the noted Battle of the Camel waged between 'Alī and the Prophet's wife 'Ā'isha, and then between 'Alī and the founder of the Umayyad dynasty. Following 'Alī's assassination by a group hostile to both sides, the path was cleared for the Umayyads to assume the caliphate, and the position then became a hereditary one. The enmity of 'Alī's partisans against the Umayyads became forever sealed when the second caliph of the Umayyads killed Ḥusayn the son of 'Alī for failing to pledge political loyalty. The place where that occurred, located in modern Iraq, is now known as Karbala', a concocted Arabic name from the root words *karb*, or tragedy, and *bala'*, or tribulation, and the day was the tenth of Muharram, known as 'Ashūrā. The Shi'i mantra since then, in the words of the founder of Shi'i jurisprudence, is that every day is 'Ashūrā, and every land is Karbala'. The wrong done by the leader of the Sunni community to the Prophet's revered grandson is not one that the Shi'a have ever forgotten, nor do they particularly wish to forget it.

a. Theological Divisions—Shi'ism and the Imamate

Despite the deep emotional resonance of these legends among modern Shi'is, it is easy to overemphasize the political dimensions of the Sunni-Shi'a dispute. It might well be noted that Shi'ism's first leader did become the fourth caliph under Sunni accounts, that any hostilities directed against him were therefore for that reason almost *per se* illegitimate within Sunni doctrine and that there is no theological tenet within Sunnism that necessitates any sort of reverence to any of the caliphs after the rightly guided. It is, that is, entirely consistent with Sunnism to decry the death of the Prophet's grandson in Karbala' at the hands of a corrupt caliph.

The much deeper theological split is much harder to reconcile. This is because 'Alī was not, in Shi'i accounts, merely the *political* successor to the Prophet Muhammad, as the first caliph was in Sunni accounts. Rather, he held the distinct position of *Imam*, which was as much a religious office as a political one. While not exactly a Prophet who receives direct revelation from God, the Imam was divinely inspired and blessed with particular capacities that ordinary humans lacked. Most importantly, he was infallible, and he could understand hidden meanings of the Qur'an. Therefore, his authority, both religious and temporal, was as absolute as that of the Prophet. Nothing remotely similar could be said about the Sunni caliphs, even the rightly guided ones.

Hence, to fail to recognize the Imam within Shi'ism is a significant shortcoming of faith, as the Imam is the only one who can properly guide the believers. This does not consign Sunnis necessarily to eternal damnation. Indeed, for all transactional purposes, including marriage, Shi'ism regards Sunnis as fellow Muslims. Yet the denial of the Imamate is not a small matter within Shi'ism. Conversely, within the Sunni view, the concoction of a doctrine of an Imam who is infallible and seems vaguely similar to a Prophet seems itself deviant and suspicious. (It might be noted in this context, and to avoid confusion, that the word "Imam" in Arabic can also mean "leader" in a more generic sense. As a result, Sunnis and Shi'a often use it to refer to the religious or spiritual head of a mosque, for example. This uncontroversial use of the word is fundamentally different from the Shi'i use in the context of the Imamate, as described herein).

Given the centrality of the role of the Imam, Shi'i doctrine posits that one is always with humanity following the passing of the Prophet Muhammad. 'Alī was the first Imam, and then his son Ḥasan, and later Ḥusayn, killed at Karbala'. Ḥusayn's lineal male descendants subsequently serve as the successive Imams of their times up to the twelfth Imam, the Mahdī, who ultimately goes into hiding in what is known as the Greater Occultation. Importantly, he remains with us today, over one thousand years after his disappearance. To this day, Shi'a frequently invoke his name and call for him to reappear and reassert his position of Imam. Perhaps unsurprisingly, such calls become more fervent in politically turbulent times.

2. SHI'ISM AND LAW

The legal consequences of the rather deep theological divisions described above are not as great as might be imagined. The reasons for this are relatively easy to summarize. Both Shi'is and Sunnis accept as primary source the text of the Qur'an, and both accept the authority of the Prophet Muhammad and rely on narrative chains to determine the soundness of Sunna. Both also accept that a juristic consensus can serve as a source of law. While these similarities thus result in significant legal convergence, there are distinctions that require elaboration.

Most importantly, the understanding of what constitutes Sunna is different in Shi'ism relative to Sunnism in several ways. First, Shi'ism would not regard the narrative chains of all Sunni narrators to be particularly reliable. The Shi'a would dismiss as suspect some prominent Sunni narrators, in particular those close to 'Alī's enemies. The most famous of these is the narrator 'Abu Hurayra, a favorite of the Umayyads, who reports a number of statements on the Prophet's authority despite not having been particularly close to him for very long. Conversely, if the Sixth Shi'i Imam were to report a statement of the Prophet Muhammad, the Shi'i view would be that the Infallible Imam must know it to be the truth, somehow and in some way. The Sunni view would be that a report of a Prophetic statement from someone six generations removed from the Prophet would be highly suspect in the absence of a narrative chain connecting the two individuals.

What this means is that at important times, there are Sunna that the Shi'a reject as weak or inauthentic, and vice versa. This can lead to a substantive distinction in Islamic law. For example, the Shi'a do not believe that the Prophet prohibited bequests to those already entitled to inherit by law, because they question the narrative chain that

Sunnis have accepted. This means that a person can increase, for example, a daughter's inheritance above her required legal share by making a bequest in her favor.

Another important distinction as concerns the Sunna is the fact that the Shi'a would regard as authoritative, and a form of Sunna, any statement coming not only from the Prophet, but from an Imam. This adds a considerable body of source material to Sunna within the Shi'i paradigm that is not present in the Sunni one. Ironically, at times, this actually results in rule convergence. For example, the Prophet Muhammad prohibited trades of gold, silver, and other commodities for gain and with delay, meaning that one cannot purchase 10 pounds of gold today in exchange for a promise to pay back 15 pounds in the future. The Sunni Hanafi position is that the same prohibition applies by analogy to any item whose value is ascertained through its weight or its volume. Hence, for example, one could not purchase 10 barrels of oil today in exchange for a promise to pay back 15 barrels in the future. (This prohibition, incidentally, serves as the basis for the modern ban on money interest for a loan.)

For their part, the Shi'a accept the Prophetic Sunna, but reject the idea that it can be extended by analogy because to the Shi'a, analogy is not a valid source of Islamic law, as described more fully below. However, the Shi'a then hold that items measurable by weight or volume cannot be traded for gain or with delay, on the authority of a statement from the Third Imam. The methods used to reach the legal rule are therefore quite different in the Hanafi school and among the Shi'a, but the legal rule turns out to be identical.

Finally, the Shi'a cast significant suspicion over the so called *khabar wāḥid,* or solitary Sunna. This is a Sunna that seems to have a sound narrative chain but an isolated one, meaning that the statement of the Prophet or Imam is reported by only one narrator. The possibility of an error on the part of a narrator is too great in the Shi'i view to render the solitary Sunna a reliable source in the absence of other supporting material. At most, a rule derived from a solitary report of the Prophet should be followed out of precaution rather than certainty respecting its soundness.

Apart from differences over the substance of the Sunna, the other major point of distinction as between the Sunnis and the Shi'a over Islamic law source material concerns the use of analogy on the one hand, and reason on the other. Even as Shi'ism unambiguously rejects the idea that legal rules can be expanded through the use of analogy, it claims that moral reason can be used as a means through which an Islamic law rule is deduced. In fact, some of the most polemical debates in the premodern era concerned this very subject, with the Shi'a (and a Sunni group known as the Mu'tazila) insisting that reason was a source of Islamic law, and that the moral character of an act could be known through the deployment of reason alone, without the aid of revelation. The main arguments advanced in favor of this position were two. First, human societies everywhere, whether Islamic or not, had largely converging ideas on right and wrong. The awareness of this suggests an ability to discern the quality of moral actions from reason given that many of these communities do not rely on Islamic revelation to guide their moral actions. Second, one could not know that revelation itself was being truthful in its description of right and wrong, save for the use of reason to know that lying is wrong. God's indication that lying is wrong in revelation would hardly be enough, as God could be lying about that very point. The conception of a God lying about his plans in the Hereafter and therefore rewarding the wicked and punishing the righteous can be refuted as absurd by one source alone, and this is reason.

The traditional Sunni counterargument is that if God is subject to reason, and the moral character of His actions known by reference to it, this renders the Omnipotent into an automaton who ends up serving as a slave to the reason He created. This then raises the question of whether reason is an attribute of God, or a creation of God, which in turn raises the question of whether Revelation, and in particular the Qu'ran, is attribute or creation, a subject which obsessed medieval Islamic philosophers for centuries.

I raise these issues not to dwell on them, but because they were among the central debates of classical Muslim jurists and philosophers, and led to highly polemical works advancing the position of one side or the other. In point of fact, for our purposes, it suffices to note that this rather significant theological chasm does not lead to any real legal distinctions of note. This is because, to the disappointment of no small number of Shi'i Muslim reformists and liberals, jurists do not actually use reason at all to determine legal rules. The traditional Shi'i juristic position is that determinations derived through reason lack *ḥujjiyya,* or authority, and therefore cannot be relied upon.

3. SHI'ISM IN THE ERA OF OCCULTATION

As noted above, it is a core conception of Shi'ism that God would not leave humanity without an Imam to guide it. Yet, of course, the current Imam is, and has been, in hiding for over a millennium, thereby begging the question of what precisely humanity is to do in the meantime. To reduce matters considerably, the traditional Shi'i view consists of two core tenets. First, as to political matters, the doctrine urges a kind of patient Quietism, wherein the believer tolerates whatever illegitimate regime happens to be reigning, whether it be Umayyad tyrant, Abbasid despot, Ottoman autocrat, British colonial, or anyone else, pending the return of the Imam. As to religious matters, and legal ones, to the extent feasible, the jurists inhabit the role of the Hidden Imam as best as they can, attempting to determine God's Will and serving effectively as his fallible deputies.

The power this confers upon the jurists is significant. For example, through an expansive reading of a Qur'anic verse that appears to relate exclusively to war booty, Shi'i doctrine obligates believers to tithe one fifth of their earned profits after reasonable expenses. One half of this is supposed to be dedicated to the needy among the descendants of the Prophet Muhammad, and one half is referred to as the "Imam's share." During the Occulatation, pending the Imam's return, that share goes to the jurists, to be distributed by the jurists in their discretion. As a result, jurists are the recipients of significant revenue paid to them by the Shi'a devout throughout the world. While no jurist of note would, or could, use these funds to engage in ostentatious consumption and luxurious living, the power that such funds confer upon them is quite immense.

In addition to the conferral of power, there is an unmistakable theological component to the Shi'I conception of juristic authority that is less prevalent within Sunnism. Sunnism, as we have seen, traditionally invests the jurists with the authority to define the law, precisely as Shi'ism does during the Greater Occultation, because jurists are deemed to be more pious, less tempted by the profane temptations of this world, and in a better position to study holy texts and determine God's Will. However, within Shi'ism, juristic authority is grounded more deeply as a theological matter, because the jurists represent the Hidden Imam, the true leader of the community. The result is a more formalized seminarian structure, with scores of seminary students and aspiring jurists of varying levels studying, debating, and teaching religious law in those cities where the seminaries prevail. Currently, these are Najaf, in Iraq, and Qom, in Iran. The highest level of learning to be attained within the seminaries is the *Marja` al-Taqlīd,* or Source of Emulation. Perceptive readers might note that the term designating "emulation" in this formulation is *taqlīd,* the same word used in the Sunni tradition to refer to "imitation" of past rulings.

While the levels of juristic attainment and the structure of education within Shi'i seminaries are in some sense formal, the processes of determining which jurist has attained what level is not. In essence, a jurist rises to the level of being a Source of Emulation when the juristic community believes that the level has been attained. There is no certificate or ceremony to mark the occasion. The consequences of attaining this level, however, are quite significant. Specifically, all lay Shi'a are supposed to select one of the living sources of emulation to follow. This source of emulation also receives the Imam's share of the follower's tithe, creating some level of financial competition as between the high jurists for followers. It suffices to say that nothing quite so formalized, nor so demanding of unquestioned devotion, exists within Sunni doctrine.

There are two other features of Shi'ism as concerns the Imam's Occultation that are worthy of comment. The first is the inherent nature of doubt that pervades the jurisprudence. Obviously, within Sunni Islam, the fact that there are four schools of thought, and jurists taking varying opinions within them, is an implicit admission that it is difficult to know the Will of God in all instances. However, this uncertainty is more a feature of human limitation than it is a reflection on God's Will. In theory, if humans simply tried harder and thought more about it, they might ultimately come to consensus on all contested points of Islamic law and know perfectly the Mind of God.

This is not the case with Shi'ism. The reason that there is doubt in the jurisprudence is because God has chosen to place the Imam in hiding. The one with absolutely perfect knowledge of the Law, in other words, is present on this earth, and it is only because God is concealing him that we live in uncertainty respecting the complete content of God's laws. As such, the doubt in legal outcomes is itself the Will of God. The consequences of this are a jurisprudence in which uncertainty permeates and pervades the juristic tomes. Phrases like "the matter is not free from doubt," or "this may be problematic" are peppered in any compendium by any jurist, along with juristic indications that certain matters should be undertaken or eschewed as "an obligatory precaution." Hence, for example, Shi'i men are not permitted to marry non-Muslim women. However, juristic compendia do not describe such a marriage as a clear sin, but rather prohibit it as an obligatory precaution because of sufficient uncertainty attending to its permissibility. Attempting to translate such nuances into the language of the law of a modern state is no easy task.

Finally, because the central conception within Shi'ism is that the only legitimate state is the one led by the Infallible Imam, there is a remarkable dearth of scholarship in and consideration of public law, concerning the relationship of the state to the individual. That is, where Sunni scholars might consider where the caliph could or not issue edicts that would be binding on citizens alongside traditional Islamic law rules, Shi'i scholars showed no similar proclivity. In theory, though not always in practice, every edict of every regime not led by the Imam was an illegitimate one arising from an illegitimate authority. It was not until the start of the twentieth century that scholars really began to consider what role the jurists could or should play in the state in a more systematic fashion. In doing so, however, they lacked the same resources that their Sunni counterparts could draw upon. This has proved to be a problem that has lasted to this day.

D. BARRELING TOWARD MODERNITY

There is one important point with which this Chapter must conclude, and that must be internalized by anyone seeking to understand how Islamic law might work within the legal structure of a modern state, or in governing relationships between modern states. *The world in which Islamic law came into being, as a political, economic and sociological matter, no longer exists for all intents and purposes.* The caliphate ended in 1924, with the fall of the Ottomans. Around the same time, non-Muslim states initiated a series of colonial ventures within the Islamic world. Ultimately, what emerged in the Muslim world were a series of Westphalian nation-states with boundaries drawn by colonial powers, none of which could credibly claim to represent the entire Muslim community.

There have been a series of major consequences to these developments. Most important for our purposes, however, is a catastrophic loss of authority within the Sunni world of the juristic schools, which have all but ceased to exist. There are several reasons for this remarkable decline. Most obvious, perhaps, was that there was less need for them. If modern Westphalian states make law, then whatever rule the jurist was pronouncing was virtually irrelevant to how society would be governed. Accordingly, the sphere of the jurist's influence receded, to the point where their positions on matters outside of ritual, worship, and, to some extent, family and personal status law, mattered little. Even more importantly, states themselves came to view jurists as competing influences to place under greater control. States accordingly took over the charitable endowments, or *waqfs,* whose revenues were dedicated to seminary upkeep, thereby rendering the seminaries dependent on the state. The seminary leaders were also chosen by the state, thereby ensuring that they conformed to the will of the state, at great cost to their own legitimacy. These phenomena were not universal—Saudi Arabia's juristic classes are still in many ways independent—nor did they result in the total abolition or marginalization of the scholarly classes. They did, however, successfully democratize the articulation of Islam in the public sphere, so that the scholars have become only one voice among many on what Islamic law is, and how it is to be understood.

Shi'ism in many ways was able to resist some of these trends for a longer period of time. After all, if every state not led by the Imam was itself illegitimate, then the end of the caliphate and the onset of colonialism is not a cataclysm, but merely the replacement of one oppressor by another. Perhaps for this reason, the Shi'i juristic academies retain remarkably legitimacy and authority within the Shi'i world that their Sunni counterparts lack. It is a rare Shi'i figure who will challenge Grand Ayatollah Sistani, for example, on a matter of Islamic law.

Still, the realities of the modern era have affected the Shi'a as well. It is one thing to try to isolate a Shi'i community as much as possible from the reaches of a distant imperial power with nominal control over the territory the community inhabits. It is quite another to try to live in isolation of the law of the nation-state entirely. It is virtually impossible to do so. Accordingly, Shi'ism has had to adapt away from its traditionally Quietist positions, to legitimize broader juristic interventions into affairs of the state. The clearest effort in this regard, and the most theorized, is Ayatollah Khumaini's conception of the state as lying under the "guardianship" of jurists, pending the Imam's return. In other words, the role of the jurist during the occultation is not only to assume the Imam's lawmaking function, but also to assume his political role as well. The argument was quite revolutionary, and in fact undergirded the successful 1979 Islamic Revolution in Iran.

Iraqi jurists, for their part, have been more circumspect. After sporadic interventions in early Iraqi history, followed by a period of grasping tightly to the principle of Quietism through the reign of Saddam Hussein—out of survival if for no other reason—jurists have been more willing to involve themselves in state affairs since 2003. In some cases, as in *waqf* administration, their involvement is quite deep, almost as deep as it would be in Iran. In others, such as commercial and corporate law, the juristic role is dramatically reduced. For the most part, they oscillate between these two poles. It is fair to say that there is no deep theoretical conception that seems to undergird their forays into state affairs, which simultaneously legitimizes the state, in a manner that seems at odds with Quietism, while disclaiming any desire to rule over the state, in a manner that clearly conflicts with Khumaini's vision of juristic guardianship.

In any event, whether the Islamic law in question is of the Sunni or Shi'i variety, modern states seeking to insert Islamic law into their legal framework must address the very real dilemma that Islamic law was developed by authorities who no longer exist, in political and social contexts that no longer exist, to address problems that in many cases are quite different from those that modern societies face. To take a concrete example, while it is at least plausible to conclude that Islamic law bans interest on a loan, medieval jurists provide little meaningful guidance on how an interest ban might be achieved in a modern economy whose complexity they could not have possibly conceived of. Similarly, medieval notions of jihad are based on factual predicates that involve non-Muslim entities—the House of War—intent on annihilating the Islamic state and obliterating the faith. How these notions translate into a world of nation states purportedly based on the principle of mutual recognition is difficult to answer.

Finally, classical jurists of the Sunni variety might have some set of theories on what kinds of edicts an executive authority can or cannot issue. To take those ideas, and to insert them into a modern constitutional context, takes creativity and license, to say the least.

And yet, it is important to note, as impossible as the task sounds, it is one to which Muslim societies have dedicated themselves, with broad popular support. The fact is that Islam as a spiritual faith and as a form of social organization and constraint is deeply important to large numbers of Muslims around the globe, and they want to see their state reflect Islamic values and mores. Including Islamic law into the very fabric of the nation state, through the various means described in the Introduction, is one way to achieve that. The balance of this Nutshell will show how it is done.

CHAPTER 2
ISLAMIC FAMILY LAW

A. INTRODUCTION

There is a perfectly obvious reason to begin the substantive discussion of Islamic law with the law of the family—it is the primary area of law where the rules of the classical jurists continue to have the greatest salience in the modern state. Where Islamic procedural law, torts law, contract law, and criminal law, among others, have been largely supplanted in modern Muslim states by law transplanted from Western jurisdictions, family law remains firmly Islamic in most, though decidedly not all, Muslim majority nations.

Indeed, in many prominent states, including several that have adopted a thoroughly civilian model of law, with a high dependence on codes to supply the basis of decision in disputes, family law remains largely uncodified. Judges are in that field expected to issue their decisions according to the classical rules of a given school. Perhaps the most prominent example of this is Egypt. In other areas of law, the Egyptian codes serve as a template for other many other Arab states, and so it is quite striking that there is no comprehensive family law code. Instead, legislative interventions in the area are only sporadic and piecemeal.

Even in those states which have a family code or a personal status code, the influence of classical Islamic law is strong and unmistakable—certainly more prominent than it is in almost any other area of law.

That said, this reliance on the classical corpus creates some level of tension as well, because, quite ironically, it is in the area of family law where some of the ethical presuppositions of the classical jurists are in the greatest tension with the sensibilities of modern Muslims. Where much of classical Islamic contract law might seem to modern Muslims working in commerce and finance as quaint and potentially unworkable, it would be hard to describe it as offensive. The same is not true in the context of family law.

Thus, to describe, as we have, modern family law in most of the Muslim world as being framed in classical juristic terms is not to suggest that it is monolithic, irredeemably medieval, and not subject to evolution. None of these things are true. In the first place, the rich and pluralistic classical tradition provides ample flexibility to undertake reforms within its broad framework. Second, modern courts are willing in certain times and places to practice *'ijtihād,* and develop rules divorced from the classical tradition on the basis of their own readings of revelatory texts such as Qur'an and Sunna. Finally, there are times when particular rules seem so difficult, and so at odds with modern social expectations, that lawmakers and courts abandon them altogether in favor of alternatives that resemble those that might be found in developed jurisdictions. We will see each of these phenomena in this Chapter.

The Chapter is divided into three main sections. The first section addresses marriage. This section will show that the divergence as between classical rules and modern ethical understandings of Muslims begins with the very purposes of marriage, which is the bedrock institution on which family law is built. The section will further show the manner in which lawmakers and courts manage the tensions that arise as a result. The second section addresses marital dissolution, from the traditional right of the husband to end his marriage through oral pronouncement to the various ways that a wife may terminate a marriage. Finally, the third section addresses a matter of comparatively less concern to the classical jurists but of rather significant importance in modernity. This is the question of the custody and care of children. This final section will reveal most clearly that some of the tensions that inhere in Islamic family law extend well beyond the borders of the individual Muslim states, and give rise to conflicts as between many Muslim states on the one hand, and a broad global consensus on the other.

B. MARRIAGE

1. UNDERSTANDING THE MARRIAGE CONTRACT

To understand the problem of Islamic marriage law, it might help to begin with a quote from Kecia Ali, who summarized the matter quite well as follows:

[T]he overall framework of the [Islamic] marriage contract is predicated on a type of ownership (*milk*) granted to the husband over the wife in exchange for a dower payment, which makes sexual intercourse between them lawful. Further, the major spousal right established by the contract is the wife's sexual availability in exchange for which she is supported by her husband. This basic claim, which would have been accepted without controversy as an accurate portrayal of the legal dimensions of marriage by virtually any pre-modern Muslim jurist, is unthinkable today for the majority of Muslims, including those who write about Islamic law. [Kecia Ali, *Progressive Muslims and Islamic Jurisprudence: The Necessity for Critical Engagement with Marriage and Divorce Law*, in PROGRESSIVE MUSLIMS: ON JUSTICE, GENDER AND PLURALISM 163, 165 (O. Safi, ed. 2003)].

Before exploring the tension with modern expectations that Ali refers to above, her description of marriage in its broad terms among classical jurists—Shi'i and Sunni—deserves elaboration. Several salient characteristics in particular are notable.

First, marriage is a contract, rather than a sacrament. It is, fundamentally, an arrangement concluded by private parties that requires no specialized clergy to undertake. *Second,* the primary purpose of the contract is neither procreation nor companionship, but rather to render sex licit. *Third,* as with all contracts within Islamic law, the marriage contract is frequently analogized to the contract of sale. The man is effectively purchasing the right to the enjoyment of his wife's body (at times analogized to ownership of her genitalia) in exchange for a dower to be paid to her along with an obligation of continuing support.

To underscore Ali's point, all of this would be regarded as elementary and perfectly obvious to virtually any classical jurist of any school, though the schools would differ on some of the details. Hanafi jurists, for example, considered the dower the contractual obligation of the husband, while the obligation of maintenance towards his wife more akin to a gift. Similarly, Shi'i jurists were more hesitant to analogize marriage directly to sale given that analogy was not a source of jurisprudence in Shi'i Islam. As a final illustration, even in analogizing to sale, not every Sunni jurist envisioned a husband as owning his wife's genitals—many focused instead on a more abstract form of ownership of the marriage itself. Nevertheless, despite these differences the basic parameters of the arrangement remained the same—marriage was a contract wherein access to sex was traded for some form of material support.

Perhaps the most important to make respecting Islamic marriage law is that virtually every one of the fundamental precepts of the classical jurists, laid out above, is rejected in modernity among broad swaths of lay Muslims.

It is true that modern Muslims, whether scholars or pious lay people, will frequently indicate that marriage under Islamic law is a contract undertaken by private parties rather than a sacrament performed by clergy. However, the actual conduct of Muslims points to a very different set of social expectations. Muslims almost always resort to the use of clergy to solemnize a marriage contract. This rather odd discrepancy between the theory of Islamic marriage as contract and the practice of it as formal religious ceremony supposedly relates to a desire to adhere strictly to all procedural formalities, given the severe criminal consequences that attend to illicit sex, described in greater detail in Chapter Six.

This is no doubt true to some extent. However, it remains the case that much modern ceremony (recitations of the Holy Qur'an, speech by the clerical figure concluding the contract, in some cases practiced reticence of the bride to pronounce a marriage formula as a form of prescribed modesty) has nothing to do with procedural requirements of marriage. To explain these practices, one must take into account the influence of global practices on Muslim sensibilities. Muslims who marry expect a ritual led by clergy, as people the world over do, followed by a raucous (and costly) celebration. They do not expect or want a process that more closely resembles a contract closing, as would be customary in the context of the purchase of home.

The second discrepancy as between classical rule and modern Muslim expectation is even starker. The Qur'anic verse which most frequently is invoked in connection with Muslim marriages—printed on countless wedding invitations, recited at countless marriage ceremonies, and appearing in countless advertisements in bridal magazines—is the following:

> And of His signs is that He created for you from yourselves mates that you may find tranquility in them; and He placed affection and mercy between you. Indeed, in that are signs for a people who give thought. [Qur'an 30:21]

The purpose of marriage reflected in the verse, and very much internalized by modern Muslims, obviously relates to love and companionship rather than the permissibility of sex. Sexual obligations would obviously not be printed on a wedding invitation, nor made the subject of a wedding sermon by virtually any clerical figure of any standing anywhere in the Muslim world.

In addition, the association of procreation with marriage, while not as clearly identified with a single Qur'anic verse, is likewise extolled in any number of Islamic religious settings, from Friday sermons to satellite television talk shows hosted by popular clerics. The discourse in this context is usually sexist—used to justify why women serve better roles within the home than outside of it—and frequently homophobic—used to justify the self-evident absurdity (in the speaker's view) of same sex marriage. Overwhelmingly, however, the framing is far more Victorian than it is Islamic. Juristic rulings, when invoked in this context, are used to elaborate on a Western structure that entered the Islamic world in the colonial era more than reflect the ethical sensibilities of classical jurists.

Hence, for example, classical jurists did not seem particularly troubled by the idea of marriage of the *khunthā*—those individuals exhibiting both male and female anatomical characteristics—once their sex could be "properly" ascertained. (Various tests were established for this purpose). While it was thus important that a man marry a woman in order for the conception of marriage outlined above to function properly, the fact that the woman might lack a uterus was not itself particularly concerning. The point of marriage, after all, was sex, and not children.

Having laid out the core conceptions of marriage in the classical tradition, and the underlying tensions they create in modernity, the next several sections elucidate how all of this is managed in modern Muslim states in the context of the substantive rules of marriage. As with any contract, we begin with the rules and conditions that attend to its formation.

2. FORMING THE MARRIAGE CONTRACT

a. Age and Guardianship

i. *Classical Islamic Law*

It may seem obvious that once marriage is framed in terms of a contract, then it requires the agreement of at least two people to enter into it. The less obvious point concerns who the consenting parties must be. Within the classical tradition, much depended on the age and capacity of the parties.

Classical jurists within both the Sunni and Shi'i schools took the position that a child marriage was valid and enforceable if contracted by the guardians of the respective parties. The guardian, or *walī,* was usually the father or paternal grandfather, though other male relatives could serve in the role to the extent that the father or paternal grandfather were not alive or lacked legal capacity. A judge could appoint a guardian as well where there were no eligible relatives.

There was no expectation that a union of children would be consummated prior to each of them reaching the age of majority. Indeed, according to the Sunni Hanafi school, as well as the Shi'a, a bride who was contracted by her guardian into a marriage she did not desire had the power to repudiate it upon reaching the age of majority to the extent that the guardian was someone other than her father or paternal grandfather.

The more interesting classical questions concerned the extent to which to confer capacity upon adults to contract their own marriage. The rule across schools and sects was that adult, sane men were free to contract their own marriages.

With women, the matter was more complicated. On the one hand, an adult woman's consent could be quite relevant, depending on the school of thought, whether the woman had been previously married, and whether the guardian was a father or paternal grandfather (a so-called *walī mujbir,* or guardian with the power to compel). The details and differences across the schools are too complex and nuanced to discuss here.

However, even where the woman's consent to the marriage is necessary, it is not dispositive. This is because according to most of the Sunni schools, the *walī* was the only party who could actually contract the marriage. In other words, the *walī's* powers might be limited by the necessity of obtaining the bride's consent, depending on the circumstances, but the *walī* nevertheless concluded the marriage. The exception was the Hanafi school, which granted an adult, sane woman the power to conclude her own marriage. Shi'ism adopts a variant of this, permitting an adult woman to contract her own marriage, but only to the extent that she is not a virgin.

As the previous discussion shows, many of the questions surrounding consent and guardianship, for men and women, relate to whether a marrying party has reached the age of majority. This renders the question of when a person is deemed an adult a particularly important one for marriage purposes. Classical jurists did not settle on any set age, though they used a term, *bulūgh,* that is generally understood to signify puberty. Issues arose concerning when a person was deemed mature, or not mature, as a matter of law, irrespective of whether they showed signs of puberty. At one end, the Shi'a regarded a woman of nine lunar years to have reached the age of adulthood. The age could be lower in the (very unlikely) event that the girl had menstruated at an earlier age. As for boys, the age was fifteen, and again, signs of puberty such as wet dreams and pubic hair could give rise to an earlier age. Sunni schools varied. Generally, they regarded nine lunar years as a minimum age for girls, and fifteen to eighteen as a maximum age, with the minimum and maximum ages for boys the same or slightly higher.

ii. *Modern Legislation*

Given the nuances attending to the question of adult bridal consent within the classical tradition, most modern Islamic states find little difficulty in requiring the consent of an adult bride to any marriage conducted by her *walī*. Hence, even Sudan's 1991 Family law, which is remarkably conservative by almost any standard, requires in Article 34(1) that "the adult virgin female is married by her *walī* upon her permission and consent. . ."

The exceptions lie primarily in the states that adopt the Shafi'i school within Sunni Islam (primarily in Southeast Asia), given that the Shafi'is did not require the *walī* to obtain the permission of even an adult virgin bride. That said, courts in these jurisdictions tend to be sympathetic to women whose fathers contract them into marriage against their clear consent. An excellent example is offered in a 1959 case in Singapore, where a father from a prominent family of Arab descent sought to marry his daughter to a relative, where his daughter preferred instead to marry someone from a less prominent family of Malay descent. The father contracted the marriage over his daughter's objection, and she objected in very strong terms, going so far as to leave her home, report the matter to the police, and ultimately seek refuge in the family of the man whom she wished to marry. Moreover, the relative with whom the daughter had been contracted to marry showed no interest in continuing a marriage with a woman so clearly reluctant to marry him, and pronounced a divorce before a judge. The Court recited the Shafi'i rule that a father could marry his adult virgin daughter without her consent but further indicated that in this case, even if the husband had not divorced her, the court would have regarded it as "our duty . . . to assist the wife to take steps to terminate the marriage." The court justified this position on the basis of unspecified community interests, while taking pains to note that it had sympathies for the father. *Syed Abdullah al-Shatri v. Shariffa Salmah*, Sharia Court of Appeal No. 1/1959 Appeal Board of Singapore, decided May 16, 1959. Given its dicta, it is difficult to imagine a circumstance in which this court would have approved a marriage over a daughter's consent.

More problematic than requiring a bride's consent is the notion of an adult bride marrying without the consent of her *walī*. Sudan, as noted above, clearly adopts a view that such a marriage is not valid. Indonesia, relying on Shafi'i rules, indicates the same in Article 19 of its Compilation on Islamic Law. Iraq, by contrast, adopts the Hanafi view in Article 9 of its Personal Status Code, which states that any person who is of age may marry without a *walī*. Egypt also adopts Hanafi law and therefore the Egyptian Court of Cassation has been quite clear that a woman does not need a guardian to marry. As a Shi'i theocratic state, Iran unsurprisingly holds to the Shi'i view that an adult virgin female requires a *walī*, but an adult nonvirgin does not. It is hard to discern a prevailing practice in this area, and much depends on the school of Islamic thought that tends to predominate.

Far harder to reconcile with the classical corpus are rules establishing minimum marriage ages, given that the classical jurists permitted child marriage, and moreover deemed a party to have reached adulthood at a far younger age than modern societies do. Nevertheless, minimum marriage ages are fairly widespread. Article 7 of the Iraqi Personal Status Code, for example, sets a minimum age of marriage at 18, though in some cases it can be reduced to 15. Article 9 of the Code requires that a bride consent to her marriage, and indeed further indicates that no person can prevent an adult from marrying whomever they like.

Other countries follow similar practices. Egypt enacted a law in the year 2000 that indicates that no marriage could be registered or certified until both parties were 18. On the basis of pre-Partition colonial era legislation enacted in 1929, the minimum marriage age for females in Pakistan is 16, and for males it is 18. A similar approach is taken in Indonesia's 1974 Marriage Act, and in the Islamic Family Law Act of 1984 for the Federal Territories of Malaysia. Interestingly, however, the latter Act permits a sharia court to grant permission for a younger age "in certain circumstances." Neither the nature of those circumstances nor any minimum age below which they cannot be used to marry a couple are specified. Even Iran has amended its Civil Code to restrict marriage to the age 13 for girls, and 15 for boys, unless court permission is obtained. A *walī* who violates this rule is subject to imprisonment.

There are only a few exceptions to this general trend. Saudi Arabia, the country that adheres most closely to classical rules, has no minimum marriage age. The same is true in Yemen, though it did have such an age prior to 1999. Sudan sets a marriage age at ten years of age, and adopts the classical rules respecting the power of the guardian to contract the marriage for a virgin bride.

To be clear, the broad trends across the Muslim world prohibiting child marriages does not mean that the phenomenon of child marriage ceases to exist. Stories are replete in jurisdictions as disparate as Iraq, Egypt, Pakistan, Malaysia, and beyond of young children well under legal age limits being married in ceremonies presided over by clerics in remote villages with the approval of the guardians of the marrying parties. These marriages are not registered in state courts at the time that they are concluded. The rather ironic result is that a marriage age requirement at times has the potential of leaving child brides in some ways in an even worse position than they had been before the law had been enacted. Not only did the marriage law not protect them from the fact of the marriage, but it also had the effect of placing the marriage out of the purview of the state, and thereby deny the bride the ability to enforce whatever monetary rights she would ordinarily have in the context of the marriage. This is not to defend child marriage prohibitions of course, but only to suggest that efforts to put an end to the practice require far more than the enactment of legislation.

In the end, it is fair to say that while child marriage remains disturbingly common across the world, including the Islamic world, it is not as common as it once was. Across Muslim nations, there have been sufficient social and economic changes to render the practice rarer, less socially acceptable, and increasingly confined to ever more remote areas. This might well explain the willingness of states to innovate in this area of marriage law even as they are more reluctant to do so elsewhere, as the balance of this Chapter shows.

b. The Dower

i. *Classical Islamic Law*

One of the unique aspects of the Islamic marriage contract is the nature of the dower, or *mahr,* that serves as an essential element of the bargain. Simply stated, there is no marriage in the absence of a dower, paid by the groom or his family directly to the bride herself, and delivered to her in exchange for the surrender of her body to the husband for his sexual pleasure. To quote the 11th century jurist Sarakhsi, the common view among classical Sunni jurists was that "marriage is a reciprocal contract (*'aqid mu`āwaḍa*) with the dower, so if it is concluded properly, then the countervalue is due, as with a sale." While Shi'i jurists were not usually as explicit in their analogies to sale, the same general principle holds true. To quote from one of the more influential works of Shi'i law:

> [A wife] may refuse sex and the surrendering of her body until she receives her [immediate] dower ..., and the same is true for lifting her veil and other matters. This is because the marriage with the dower is compensation for these. She is not alone using these appropriate means. Every party to be compensated may refuse to surrender until they receive the compensation. 31 *MUḤAMMAD ḤASAN AL-NAJAFI, JAWĀHIR AL-KALAM FI SHARḤ SHARA`I AL-ISLAM* 41 (Abbas al-Quchani ed., 7th ed. 1981) (ca. 1841).

The dower may be paid in its entirety upon conclusion of the contract. However, it is both customary and permissible to divide it into two portions, one of which is paid immediately and one of which is delayed for a period of time not to last longer than the earlier of divorce or death.

Importantly, the failure to specify a dower does not result in an invalidation of the entire contract. Rather, the groom is obligated to deliver a "dower of equivalence" to the wife. The value of this dower is expected to be the same as one that a wife of a similar station would be entitled to receive, usually determined on the basis of what her female relatives would receive as dower. The factors commonly discussed by jurists to be taken into account include character, beauty, wealth, age, and virginity. The remainder of the classical rules relating to dower follow the logic of sale. Hence, for example, a man who divorces his wife prior to the consummation of the marriage owes only half the dower, the theory being that he has never actually received the benefit of that for which he contracted. Even more notable are the rules respecting the attribution of dower of equivalence in cases of rape. Most of the classical Sunni schools require a rapist to pay the dower of equivalence to his victim, and, where the victim is a virgin, Shafi'i jurists require additional payment for the rupturing of the hymen. The Hanbali Ibn Qudāma took issue with this latter ruling, arguing that the damage to the hymen was already compensated by the higher dower of equivalence that attends to a virgin woman relative to a nonvirgin. As for the Shi'a, their implicit recognition of the higher value attached to the virgin bride is reflected in the fact that a rapist's obligation to pay the dower of equivalence runs only to virgin victims. (Importantly, these rules are distinct from and additional to the imposition of any criminal penalties that relate to the rape, which are discussed in Chapter Six in the context of the Scriptural Crime of fornication.)

The nuances and distinctions among the schools deserve far more treatment than is reflected here. The point, for these purposes, is not to lay them out in detail but only to point out the manner in which they conceptualize the payment of the dower in fundamental contractual terms—a payment obligation of the husband in exchange for the countervalue of sexual access.

ii. Modern Laws and Court Practices

Broadly speaking, modern legislation and modern court practice replicate most of the classical rules of dower. Indeed, the dower is probably the one place where idea of marriage as contract retains the greatest salience among modern Muslims. Thus, the dower is an object of rather intense negotiations at times among the families of couples who seek to marry. Marriages are often not concluded precisely because the couple cannot come to agreement over the proper dower. As a result, it is almost never the case that the parties neglect to set forth a dower in their contract and thus need to rely on a dower of equivalence. Indeed, in most Islamic states, the Court would not even register the marriage unless the parties indicated what the dower was.

But if modern Muslims negotiate intensely over the dower in many social settings, and if they conceptualize an agreement to the dower amount as being an agreement by the bride to marry the groom, the primary purpose of the negotiation is not conceptualized so much as a capture of the vagina (as classical jurists would frequently indicate) but rather as a form of financial security for the wife in the event of divorce or death. For this reason, it is extremely common in modernity for much of the dower to be deferred rather than paid immediately. The concern is that the husband will either divorce his wife in the future or die prematurely. That a spouse of either gender has limited rights of inheritance, a matter discussed in Chapter 3, only makes the issue of the deferred dower even more salient.

Given the foregoing, there are comparatively few disputes over the amount or timing of dower as these are set forth in some detail in marriage contracts already. Where dower disputes arise, they are more often on ancillary matters. One common dispute relates to whether the parties had consummated the marriage prior to the husband pronouncing a divorce. (As noted above, the failure to consummate reduces the dower obligation by half.) An actual factfinding inquiry into the matter would prove awkward in a variety of circumstances, though courts have developed a variety of tools do deal with it. One is to use the Hanafi principle of "constructive consummation," where the seclusion of a husband and a wife under circumstances where sex is possible merits the payment of the full dower. Egyptian, Jordanian, and Syrian courts have ruled in favor of consummation in such circumstances. Another tool is to impose sanctions for vexatious litigation against husbands who claim that there has been no consummation years after the marriage was concluded. Iraq adopts this approach.

Even more pressing evidentiary disputes concern whether or not the agreed upon dower has actually been paid. While classical jurists wrote extensively about this issue, by and large modern courts pay little heed to their rules, and instead rely on their own procedural norms. Hence, for example, precisely because modern courts register marriages, and because the marriage contract almost always includes a reference to the payment of an immediate dower having been made, courts institute a presumption, difficult to rebut, that the immediate dower has been turned over to the wife. The reverse is true with respect to any deferred dower, given the lack of a writing. This would certainly not be classical practice, which would ignore the writing and focus instead on the testimony of witnesses. That courts in the modern world almost never do this demonstrates the extent to which in matters of legal procedure, Islamic law has become largely obsolete.

iii. Dower in American Courts

A very interesting set of questions arises as to the proper treatment of the dower in American courts. The basic problem is that as a legal concept the dower is not easily transferable into US marriage law. Compounding the difficulty is the fact that US Muslims do not take a great deal of care to ensure that their Islamic marriage contracts are written in terms that US courts can enforce, either because the contracts were written before the couple emigrated to the United States, or because the couple never considered the matter particularly worthy of their attention at the time they married. A few cases might help illustrate how courts manage to navigate these difficulties.

An early case that seems to have misunderstood rather fundamentally the nature of the dower agreement was *Chaudhry v. Chaudhry,* 388 A.2d 1000 (N.J. Super. Ct. App. Div. 1978). In that case, the court treated the dower as a form of prenuptial agreement, and held that the wife had essentially bargained away her right to a share of the marital estate in exchange for a deferred dower of $1500. The assumption in this analysis is that the deferred dower is part of an exchange where the countervalue is potential future property rights upon divorce from existing marital property. This is simply wrong as a matter of category. It is true that Islamic law does not recognize the concept of marital property, as discussed in the next section of this Chapter. As a result, wives in jurisdictions where Islamic law controls in matters of divorce usually have no expectation of receiving property upon divorce that was not theirs during the marriage. Concededly, the families of brides are aware of this when negotiating a deferred dower. This is all different from saying, however, that the deferred dower is a bargaining away from post divorce property rights. It is not, and indeed, in those jurisdictions as disparate as Egypt, Indonesia, and Iraq where wives do have limited rights to receive forms of property upon a husband's divorce, there is no question that such rights exist *in addition to* any deferred dower that the wife has contracted to receive. Indeed, there is a countervalue to the dower, as explained above, but it is not the relinquishment of property claims. It is instead the surrender of the wife's body to her husband. Imposing a second countervalue runs against the very conception of what the dower, and indeed the entire Islamic marriage contract, is supposed to be.

Fortunately, the result reached in *Chaudhry* has not been broadly replicated. Instead, courts have (correctly) come to view the dower promise as part of an enforceable contract that is independent of the marriage and therefore in addition to any other rights a wife might have upon divorce. One of the most influential cases adopting this approach, *Odatalla v. Odatalla*, 80 A.2d. 93 (2002), involved a claim by a wife against her husband for the deferred dower of $10,000 on the basis of a promise within the marriage contract to pay this amount as, to quote the agreement, "postponed" dower. The "prompt" dower had been set at one gold coin. Dispensing with the argument that enforcement of the dower constituted a violation of the Establishment Clause, the court invoked the Supreme Court case of *Jones v. Wolf*, 443 US 95 (1979) and held that it could apply "neutral principles of law" to enforce the dower agreement as a form of contract. It further held that the reference to "postponed" dower was not so vague as to be unenforceable given the testimony of the wife that by custom a wife would demand it only upon divorce or death, and that there was no violation of public policy inherent in enforcing the dower agreement.

By contrast, in the case of *In re Marriage of Obaidi & Qayoum*, 226 P.3d 787 (Wash. 2010), the court, citing *Odatalla,* reached a different result. Though the dower agreement was similar in form, setting forth an immediate dower of $100 Canadian dollars and a "long term marriage portion" of $20,000, there were key differences identified by the court that militated a different result. First, the negotiations were conducted in Farsi and the contract written in Farsi, a language that the defendant did not speak. Second, the defendant was unaware of what the dower even was until 15 minutes before the marriage ceremony. Third, the defendant was deemed to be under a form of duress because of the difficulty of failing to go through with the marriage ceremony once he learned of the dower, minutes before the ceremony was to begin.

While these facts make *Obaidi* distinct from *Odatalla,* the court in *Obaidi* also seemed more skeptical of the dower agreement for broader reasons relating to interpreting Islamic law. In particular, the court noted that there was no indication of when the "long term marriage portion" would be paid, and it seemed less willing than the *Odatalla* court to rely on parol evidence to determine that question. Whether this was due solely to its belief that parol evidence could not possibly have shed light on the defendant's intent respecting a contract term he could not even read, or whether the court's concern was that, at least in part, interpreting the timing of the payment would necessarily involve interpreting rules of Islamic law, is hard to discern. In any event, it seems rather clear that a more carefully drafted writing, in English, that the defendant had a more meaningful opportunity to negotiate and understand, would have helped ensure the enforceability of the dower agreement.

Some courts appear more overtly hostile to the idea of enforcing dower agreements under almost any circumstances, veering into language that borders on the Islamophobic while doing so. An excellent example lies in the case of *Soleimani v. Soleimani,* No. 11CV4668, 2012 WL 3729939 (Kan. Dist. Ct. August 28, 2012). In that case, there were ample grounds for the court to refuse to enforce the agreement. Most notably, there seemed to be no authenticated version of the dower agreement, which was in Farsi, nor was an official translation for it ever provided. Moreover, the payment of the dower, according to the translation provided, was subject to conditions (concerning who initiated the divorce, for example) that might require interpretation of Islamic law. The court discussed these matters, and then expanded its analysis from these narrow grounds to a far more troubling set of principles. It indicated that *any* agreement that purported to be an Islamic dower could very well be *per se* unenforceable, because they arise from "jurisdictions that do not separate church and state, and may, in fact, embed discrimination through religious doctrine." What follows is then a parade of horrors involving disparate elements of Islamic law pasted together in a Frankenstein-like manner that renders the Muslim faith, and indeed any adherent to it, seem positively ridiculous. Few of these rules bear any relationship to the case with which the court was dealing. For example, the court described the rules setting forth the dower of equivalence and how it is valued (noting in particular attributes of age, virginity, and beauty, described above) to point out the manner in which such valuations run contrary to core American legal principles of equal protection. Yet, of course, the existence of a dower of equivalence is predicated on the fact that there is *no* agreement as to the dower to be paid to the wife, in which case there would be no basis for its enforcement in a US court under any circumstances. By contrast, when there is an agreement as to the dower, both premodern jurists and modern US law would privilege the intent of the parties. They certainly would not subject that agreement to some sort of independent valuation based on the wife's attributes. The matter of equivalent dower was entirely irrelevant, and the discussion thus seemed more an attempt to malign Islamic law than to actually rule on the case before it.

The case is obscure, and given the rather unusual fact of an unauthenticated contract, much of its analysis might be dismissed as dicta with little influence on future cases. Aside from anything else, it is hard to imagine that an otherwise valid agreement between two parties involving the payment of a sum of money could be deemed per se unenforceable if based on an Islamic legal concept but not otherwise simply because of some unrelated rule in Islamic law that a US court might find objectionable. This on its own would seem to violate the Equal Protection Clause the *Soleimani* court claimed to be trying to respect. Moreover, such an approach would cast sufficient doubt on the enforceability of so many commercial arrangements involving various faith communities (including the Islamic finance industry, in which most major US financial institutions are significant stakeholders) that it would meet with broad resistance from elements far beyond America's rather small Muslim community. Nevertheless, the biases the *Soleimani* court reflects are certainly shared by a broad swath of the American public, as reflected in the plethora of anti-sharia legislation that has been introduced in states across the United States (the Kansas version of which the *Soleimani* court cited approvingly). It seems inevitable that such attitudes will continue to influence the outcomes in any number of cases involving American Muslims, in particular in contexts where Islamic law is potentially involved.

c. Polygamy

i. Classical Islamic Law

The final major element of marriage formation worthy of discussion is that involving polygamy. Classical Islamic law drew from the Qur'an to justify the permissibility of polygamy, and in particular verse 4:3, which reads as follows:

> And if you fear that you will not deal justly with the orphan girls, then marry those that please you of [other] women, two or three or four. But if you fear that you will not be, then [marry only] one or those your right hand possesses. That is more suitable that you may not incline [to injustice].

The verse itself seems rather grudging in its acceptance of polygamy, predicating it on fear that one will not otherwise deal justly with orphans, and then limiting the practice to four wives and further requiring monogamy to the extent that one is not just as between wives. When combined with a later verse, 4:129, which indicates that "you will never be able to do justice between wives, even if you should strive [to do so]", one could read, and indeed many modernist and reformist Muslims have read, polygamy to be deeply disapproved of, if not entirely forbidden.

Such an approach is an exercise of *'ijtihād,* or reading the original sources in a manner that derogates from what classical jurists understood. To the classical jurists, Qur'an 4:129 was not intended to restrict polygamy at all, but merely to admonish husbands that, try as they might, purely as a matter of affection, they would end up preferring some wives over others. As a result, across the traditional schools of Islamic law, polygamy was not disfavored and indeed, no small number of jurists described the practice as religiously recommended, in particular where a man found it difficult to derive sufficient sexual gratification from a single wife. Accordingly, the only restriction as to forming the marital contract in the premodern conception was that the man could not be at the time of the marriage already married to four other women. There were no other *ex ante* requirements associated with multiple wives, nor was there any notion that somehow the man could not marry another wife without the permission of his earlier wives.

To be sure, there were significant obligations imposed on a husband upon his taking an additional wife. Most importantly, he was obliged to support her, and in a manner equal to his other wives. Even if a husband would never treat his wives equally in terms of the affection he bestows upon them as per Qur'an 4:129, Islamic law could constrain how many resources he expended on any one wife relative to another, given the obligations of equal treatment imposed in Qur'an 4:3. Yet this obligation imposed after marriage is different from an ex ante condition necessary to fulfill before a husband is able to take a second wife.

Beyond financial obligations, classical jurists also imposed a series of elaborate rules respecting the amount of time a man was required to spend with each wife, so as to ensure an equitable distribution among the wives, again as per the Qur'an's requirement of equal treatment set forth in 4:3. Equality among wives, that is, was measured both in terms of resources and in terms of time. Jurists wanted to be sure that a wife would not somehow be neglected, financially or sexually, because her husband had taken a new wife. This is one of the many ways in which jurists recognized, explicitly, the reality of female sexual desire and sought to address it. In doing so, they are able to rely on ample revelatory material, primarily in the Sunna, which emphasize the importance of providing wives sexual pleasure. Jurists thus did not hold to some sort of notion that sexual pleasure was purely a male prerogative; indeed, the idea that women did not enjoy, and in fact need, sexual pleasure would have struck them as counterintuitive, even absurd.

At the same time, the patriarchal structures within which classical (almost entirely male) jurists were operating were sufficiently confining that they resulted in female sexual desire taking a decidedly secondary role in Islamic marriage law. Hence, within the classical tradition, a husband could marry up to four women freely, and a wife was limited to her single husband. Moreover, as is shown in the next major section in this Chapter, on marital dissolution, a husband wishing to end a marriage found it much easier to do so than a wife would. There were therefore far more ways for a woman to find herself sexually frustrated and legally constrained from being able to do much about it than there were for men.

ii. *Modern Legislation*

Broadly speaking, polygamy remains permissible across most Muslim societies that have not entirely rejected Islamic law, but the manner in which it is regulated varies widely. The personal status laws of the various states of the Gulf Cooperation Council, for example, do not seem to impose any restrictions on the practice, beyond the requirement that a man is not able to take more than four wives at once. Sudan takes a similar approach. In keeping with the classical rules, family law legislation in these states usually makes clear that a polygamous husband must treat his wives equally and must support all of his wives, but these are not understood to be ex ante restrictions on polygamy, so much as post hoc obligations.

At the other end of the spectrum, Tunisia bans the practice entirely in Article 18 of its Personal Status Code, claiming that in fact Qur'an 4:3 and 4:129 taken together render the lawful practice of polygamy impossible. A good number of jurisdictions fall somewhere between these two poles, permitting polygamy, but requiring *ex ante* registration of any polygamous marriage, and usually imposing additional restrictions as well. The following, for example, is the relevant language from the 1974 Marriage Act of Indonesia.

Article 3

(1) In principle, a man may have only one wife. A woman may have only one husband.

(2) The Court can give permission for a man to have more than one wife if it is desired by all concerned parties.

Article 4

(1) A husband wishing to have more than one wife as referred to in Article 3(2) of this Act is required to submit a petition to the Court in the region in which he resides.

(2) The Court referred to in paragraph (1) of this article shall grant permission for a husband to have more than one wife only if:

(a) his wife is unable to perform her duties as wife;

(b) his wife suffers from a physical defect or an incurable illness;

(c) his wife is not capable of bearing children.

Article 5

(1) To submit a petition to the Court under Article 4 of this Act the following requirements must be satisfied:

(a) the consent of [existing] wife or wives;

(b) an assurance that the husband is capable of supporting his wives and their children;

(c) an assurance that the husband will treat his wives and their children justly.

(2) The consent referred to in paragraph (1) line (a) shall not be required if it is impossible to obtain such consent and the wife/wives are incapable of giving consent; or if the whereabouts of the wife/wives have been unknown for a period of at least two years, or for other reasons accepted by the Court.

Some of these requirements, such as that the husband demonstrate financial capacity and provide assurance that he will treat his wives justly, have some roots in classical doctrines, though they have been transformed into conditions to enter into marriage rather than obligations arising from it. Others are modern inventions, among them the idea that the wife must accede to the second marriage, and that the court may only grant permission for a polygamous union if the wife is failing in her marital duties, cannot bear children, or suffers from some sort of defect or illness. Indeed, these innovations led to a constitutional challenge from a litigant who believed the restrictions breached constitutional provisions (i) describing the state as "based on belief in the One True God Almighty", (ii) granting citizens the right to adhere to their respective religions, and (iii) prohibiting discrimination. The Constitutional Court of Indonesia rejected the claim, describing polygamy as a form of social transaction (*mu`āmala*) that could be regulated by the state. Moreover, the Court indicated, because a defining feature of polygamy is "just" treatment between wives, the state has the obligation to ensure that justice is indeed done in marriages involving multiple wives. Decision 12/PUU-V/2007.

Other states impose requirements that are not necessarily as stringent as those of Indonesia. Iraq, for example, permits polygamous marriages if the husband can show he will treat his wives equally, he has financial wherewithal, and there is a "legitimate interest" that is vindicated in the second marriage. There is no requirement that the first wife consent to the marriage. The language is sufficiently broad as to result in wide variations across courts respecting permissibility to take a second wife. Hence, for example, a Personal Status Court in Baghdad in 2009 denied a petition from a husband who had obtained the consent of his first wife and who had sufficient means. The basis for the denial was that the husband's salary was largely based on danger pay and therefore subject to reduction if Iraq were to become more politically stable, and that the husband offered no particularly good reason for the second marriage beyond wanting more children and expressing a desire for more help in the housework. On the other hand, the personal status court in the city of Samarra' granted permission to a husband to take a second wife over the objection of the first wife where the husband was unable to identify any specific problem or impediment that existed in his existing marriage. That decision was upheld on appeal. Iraq Court of Cassation Case 2076/Personal Status Panel 1/2010.

Other states require court permission before a husband may practice polygamy, and grant a court some discretion in dispensing that permission, but lay out factors for a court to consider that are better defined than Iraq's exceedingly vague "legitimate interest." The 1984 Islamic Family Law Act governing the Federal Territories in Malaysia, for example, requires that the husband show "that the proposed marriage is just and necessary, having regard to such circumstances as, among others . . . sterility, physical infirmity, physical unfitness for conjugal relations, wilful avoidance of an order for restitution of conjugal rights, or insanity on the part of an existing wife or wives." As to the wife's consent, the same Act requires an inquiry into whether the proposed marriage would cause harm recognized under Islamic Law to the existing wife or wives, without specifically requiring her consent. Pursuant to a law enacted in 1985, Egypt takes a slightly different approach to the question of the first wife's harm. Like the Federal Territories, the Egyptian law requires that existing wives be notified and an opportunity to show harm. However, if they can show such harm, the second marriage is not disallowed, but rather, the first wife has the ability to end the marriage on the grounds that such harm is cause for a marital dissolution.

Whatever the standard, one common problem that arises in all states that impose ex ante conditions for polygamy is the extent to which they are in fact enforced. An illustrative example is offered in the case of *Suparman v. Tien,* Case 0450/2009, decided by the Islamic Court of Yogyakarta in Indonesia. In that case, the husband sought to register a polygamous marriage he had in fact already surreptitiously undertaken, and which had resulted in his second wife's pregnancy—indeed, 30 weeks pregnant at the time of the decision. Noting that the husband had financial capacity, that he promised to treat his wives equally, and that his first wife had consented to the union, the Court granted permission despite that fact that none of the presumed marital impediments listed in Article 4(2) of the 1974 Marriage Act were present. The first wife had a daughter with the husband, so she was capable of bearing children. She suffered no illness and, the Court specifically noted, was carrying out all of her marital duties. Nevertheless, the Court concluded, permission to take a second wife was warranted "in order to safeguard the interests and care for the child that is in [the] womb because of the actions of the [husband], and so as not to sacrifice the interests of the [first wife] by divorcing her but retaining her as his wife whose interests he is obligated to protect."

The problem in many ways parallels the continuing difficulties that exist as concern child marriage in the many jurisdictions that have sought to ban it. Once banned, parties simply continue to conduct themselves as they have—marrying second wives and arranging for the marriage of children—but they simply do not register the marriage. When it becomes necessary to register the marriage, for example, if the second wife becomes pregnant, the couple then approach the court. The pressure on the court, and on the first wife, to accede to the union is then intense, in particular given the difficulties that would attach to out of wedlock children in many conservative Muslim societies. The result, in the end, is a registered polygamous marriage.

Some societies have sought to address this problem through imposing penalties on husbands who contract polygamous marriages out of court. The 1984 Islamic Family Act of the Federal Territories in Malaysia, for example, requires that the husband pay his existing wives all delayed dower and other marital gifts owed to them and imposes a jail sentence of up to six months in prison for one who contracts a polygamous marriage outside of court. The Iraqi Personal Status Code imposes a potential jail sentence of up to one year for out of court polygamous marriages. It is difficult to know how often these provisions are used against husbands, though anecdotal reporting suggests high levels of underenforcement.

d. Competency

Classical juristic rules varied on the role of competency, or *kafā'a,* as a condition to marriage. This relates to the ability of a husband to marry a woman who is of a higher social class. (Men are always free to marry women below their social class.) The Shafi'i Sunni school gives extensive treatment to the idea of competency. The noted 13th century Shafi'i jurist Nawawī includes the following in his influential work *Minhāj al-Ṭālibīn*:

In order to determine whether the suitor is a good match, the following must be taken into consideration:

1. Absence of defects of body.

2. Liberty. A slave is not a suitable match for a free woman, nor an enfranchised slave for a woman born free.

3. Birth. An Arab woman makes a misalliance by marrying a man belonging to another nation; a woman of the Quraish does so if her husband is not of the Quraish; a woman who is a descendant of Hāshim or of 'Abd-al-Muṭṭalib, i.e., who is of the same blood as the Prophet, can make a suitable match only in the same family. In the case of marriages between persons belonging to different nations, like the Persians, genealogy must be taken in to consideration as in the case of Arabs.

4. Character. A man of notorious misconduct is not a suitable match for an honest woman.

5. Profession. A man exercising a humble profession is not a suitable match for a daughter of a man in a more distinguished profession. Thus, a sweeper, a barber, a watchman, a shepherd, or a servant at a bathhouse, is not a suitable match for the daughter of tailor; while the tailor in his turn is no match for the daughter of a merchant or a second-hand dealer, who in their turn are no suitable match for the daughter of a learned man or a judge.

The Hanafi school likewise has very elaborate rules concerning competency. Pursuant to such rules, an adult Muslim woman would not be able to marry someone who falls outside of her class without the permission of her guardian. As noted above, the Hanafi school is exceptional in its granting of permission to adult women to marry whom they wish without a guardian. These rules establish a significant restriction on that freedom.

On the other pole, the Shi'a reject the entire idea of competency as a condition of marriage, regarding it as a form of social stratification that runs contrary to Islam's otherwise egalitarian ethos. That said, as a matter of custom and practice, Shi'i women who are direct descendants of the Prophet rarely marry men who are not also such descendants.

The importance of competency has diminished in the modern era. Certainly, the rather elaborate stratifications by profession that Nawawi lays out are not adhered to. Indeed, some of them do not even make sense in most modern societies, as there is no reason that a tailor and a merchant should regard themselves as belonging to separate social classes by virtue of their respective professions. That said, competency does play a role in many jurisdictions as a basis to nullify a marriage. Bahrain's 2017 Family Law provides an illustrative example in Article 37, which reads as follows:

Competency according to Sunni fiqh:

a. A condition among others for the enforceability of marriage, and it is a right specially reserved to the woman and her guardian.

b. The defining factor in competence is piety in religion and all that is recognized in custom.

c. If a man claims competence, and then it becomes apparent that he is not, the wife or the guardian have the right to nullify (*haqq al-faskh*) the marriage.

d. The appropriate difference in age between the spouses is deemed a right for the wife alone.

In theory, the purpose of these rules is to prevent a groom from being able to misrepresent his piety, lineage, or professional training to the bride and her family. In practice, in most of the closely knit societies that predominate across the Islamic world, no groom could ever manage this. Marriages usually involve extensive negotiations between extended families, along with investigations of the respective bride and groom through mutual acquaintances. It is not hard to discover how often a man actually attends the mosque, or whether in fact he attended the medical school he claims to have attended, through such investigations. Family lineage is even easier to learn.

The more direct cause of the competency rules seems to be to limit female autonomy in cases where a woman might seek to marry someone her family opposes. As noted above, even in the classical era, the competency rules acted as a restriction on the right of an adult woman to marry without her guardian's knowledge or permission. Such rules have become even more salient now, as societies grow more mobile and women become more autonomous. The matter is especially salient in the nations of the Gulf Cooperation Council (GCC), including Bahrain. Hence, the reference to competency as determinable through custom in the Bahraini law is not one that derives naturally from classical juristic rules, and yet it appears with some frequency in the nations of the Gulf Cooperation Council. While it is often defended as being more copacetic and deferential to social realities than a strict hierarchy of professions and lineages, the rules also help to prevent women from being able to engage in "out-marriage" to the many men who are residents of Gulf states but not nationals of them. Any such marriage, even one the woman attempted surreptitiously, could swiftly be nullified by the woman's guardian given the capacious nature of what "local customs" might encompass and given the near certainty that a national court would conclude that a Gulf citizen marrying a resident who is an Egyptian, Iraqi, or Palestinian national would be violating such local customs.

e. Other Conditions of Marriage

Most of the other conditions of marriage imposed by the classical jurists tend to be less controversial and applied with some regularity across most of the Muslim world. Rules of consanguinity, for example, do not permit marriages to a person closer than a first cousin. (First cousin marriages are permissible and in some societies undertaken with frequency). A person cannot marry one of the parents of a current or former spouse, nor may a man marry two sisters concurrently. Those sharing a wet nurse as children are deemed equivalent to siblings and therefore prevented from marrying each other, or their respective near relatives. Hence, for example, a man cannot marry the sister, aunt, or mother of a person with whom he shared a wet nurse as a child. There are other restrictions pertaining to a husband remarrying the same woman multiple times, or marrying a woman who has been recently married to another person. These will be discussed in the context of marital dissolution below.

Finally, classical Sunni jurists did not permit a Muslim woman to marry anyone except a Muslim man. Muslim men, on the other hand, could marry women who were "People of the Book," meaning adherents to faiths who had also received Divine Revelations in the past. This primarily refers to Christians and Jews, though there are other groups, most notably the Sabians of Iraq, who are also mentioned in the Qur'an as enjoying this status. Most Shi'i jurists do not permit any Muslim to marry anyone except another Muslim.

Generally speaking, legislation in states where there are large numbers of both sects follows the Sunni rule, and permits marriages of Muslim men to non-Muslim People of the Book. Both Iraq and Bahrain, for example, adopt this approach. It has turned out to be relatively noncontroversial, even to the Shi'i juristic forces who seek more recognition of their rules in the law of the state as concerns marriage and divorce. After all, no Shi'i is prevented from following the traditional juristic rules by these more expansive legislative provisions.

Curiously, the Iranian Civil Code in Article 1059 appears to adopt the Sunni rule, and prohibit marriages only of non-Muslim men to Muslim women. However, through clarifications that the Ayatollah Khomeini has provided, Iran has followed as a matter of practice Shi'i tradition and will not register marriages between Muslim men and non-Muslim women. (These rules, it might be noted, apply only to permanent marriage. The Shi'i marriage known as the temporary marriage has different rules, and is discussed in detail below.)

3. MARITAL OBLIGATIONS

a. Maintenance

Under the classical rules, the primary obligation of the husband during the course of the marriage is to support his wife. This obligation is not based on need. A wife with substantial assets of her own is owed support from a husband of limited means, just as a poor wife is owed support from a rich husband. (As will be emphasized later, Islamic law has no conception of marital property, so that a wife with independent wealth maintains her assets separately from that of her husband). This lies in sharp contrast with a support claim that any other relative can make against a family member. Under the classical rules across schools and sect, a child making a claim against a parent, for example, or an elderly parent making a claim against a child, must demonstrate need in order to succeed on the claim.

While surprising to some audiences more accustomed to legal systems that establish a primary obligation of support running towards children from their parents, rather than husband to wife, the rules are perfectly compatible with the notion that the marital relationship is, in fact, a contractual bargain. The husband's obligation in the bargain is to support his wife and to pay her a dower. That the husband lacks means, or that the wife does not need the money, is as irrelevant as it would be in any other contractual relationship where one side agreed to undertake a series of pecuniary obligations. It is not a valid excuse for a buyer of a car to fail to pay the seller on the grounds that the seller does not in fact need the money.

Classical jurists agreed that the essentials of food, clothing, and lodging were included as part of a husband's marital obligation. In addition, a wife was entitled to a separate space where she could seclude herself from all but her husband. The specificities of the shelter and the total amount of the maintenance depended on socioeconomic class. Some juristic schools defined with precision what was owed to a wife in a given class—for example, whether she was entitled to a servant, or what types of meals she might expect. Others proved more flexible and willing to defer to custom and context to make such determinations.

Modern jurisdictions generally follow the basic principles outlined above. To quote the Jordanian Code at Article 59(a) "the maintenance of each person is from their own wealth, except for a wife, whose maintenance is from her husband, even if he has means." The same core concept is replicated in Codes and court practices across the Islamic world.

Modern jurisdictions similarly use the classical rules to determine what constitutes obligatory maintenance, at times updating them to take into account modern necessities, such as medical costs. The Jordanian and Iraqi Personal Status Codes, for example, both state that maintenance "includes food, clothing, shelter, her necessities, medical costs at generally recognized levels, and domestic help for a wife if [a woman] equivalent to her would have [it]." Indonesia's Compilation of Islamic Law makes reference to "support, clothing, and a place to live," which is deemed to include "household expenses, and the cost of medical care and medicines." Those states that do not codify their Islamic personal status laws routinely grant to wives similar sorts of expenses.

By far the most common source of litigation concerns the adequacy of the marital home. Quite commonly, the wife will either refuse to move into or leave the marital home, claiming it is inadequate. In that case, the court needs to determine whether the wife is failing in her marital duties by failing to deliver her body to her husband, or whether it is the husband who has failed by failing to provide the home he is obligated to provide.

In making this determination, courts follow classical examples and insist that a husband must supply a separate and secluded space apart from that of the husband's parents, relatives, or a second wife. Hence, for example, in an amusing 1977 case decided in the Islamic High Court for Surabaya, a wife refused to comply with her husband's extremely frequent demands for sex, described by the Court with some specificity. This led to a claim from the husband that his wife was not fulfilling her marital obligations. Drawing from a 16th century Shafi'i text that was itself a commentary on the highly influential *Minhāj,* the Court avoided ruling on this matter by pointing out that the wife had been asked to live with the husband's parents, and that this constituted a failure on the part of the husband to provide a proper marital home. Case No. 1 of 1977/ Islamic High Court of Surabaya. Therefore, her refusals were entirely justified by virtue of the fact that it was the husband who was failing in his own marital duties.

That same Indonesian court made reference to a home being "appropriate" for the wife, and certainly courts throughout the Islamic world have shown some level of flexibility in determining what a proper marital home is based on the socioeconomic position of the couple. In a 1969 case in Iraq, for example, the Sharia panel of Iraq's highest court of general appeal, the Court of Cassation, remanded a case where a wife had complained that the marital home consisted of a single room in a house occupied by others. The Court of Cassation indicated that it was incumbent upon the lower court "to ascertain if the couple was living in a separate home before their dispute and if their circumstances, in prosperity and difficulty, call for living in a separate room." This determination is necessary, the Court indicated, in order to fulfill the Qur'anic injunction respecting marital homes, which reads "lodge them of where you dwell out of your means and do not harm them in order to oppress them." [Quran 65:6]. Case 756/Sharia Panel/1969 Court of Cassation of Iraq.

Thus, according to the Court of Cassation, and indeed in courts across the Islamic world, whether or not a husband is unjustifiably oppressing his wife by asking her to live in a single room in a shared home, or whether he is providing proper maintenance by doing so, is largely a question of context. The same is true as concerns the maintenance obligation more broadly. A husband with ample means who seems to be acting out of some sort of spite to deny his wife that to which she is accustomed is failing in his maintenance duties, even if he is providing his wife with more than the bare necessities. By contrast, a husband who is from humbler circumstances, and marries a wife from the same socioeconomic class, does not have the same burdens placed upon him.

b. Non-Abstention

As noted earlier, classical jurists expected that a polygamous husband would spend an equal time with his various wives, and that he would not neglect one at the expense of another. A similar obligation pertains to monogamous husbands as well, less in the sense that a husband had some sort of obligation to spend a set amount of time with a wife, but more to the idea that he could not neglect her, or abandon her entirely. This type of abstention, known within juristic discourse (and Qur'anic verse) as *hajr*, had consequences attached to it. What those consequences were varied depending on the school and sect of Islamic law. This is another area of law where jurists paid attention to the sexual needs of women. However, these needs were of decidedly secondary importance. A husband's primary obligation related to support, not affection, and the idea of abstention usually only arises in classical texts in the context of the discussion of other matters, such as a polygamous husband's obligations of equal treatment or the right of a wife to seek a marital dissolution if her husband abandons her entirely.

c. Obedience

i. *Classical Rules*

The previous section explores the husband's obligation of maintenance in the marital bargain. This section concerns the wife's reciprocal obligations. Classical jurists tended to focus on two separate sources of countervalue for the maintenance the husband offers. Some emphasized the fact that the husband effectively takes possession of his wife's body and keeps her in the marital home, a concept frequently referred to by the Arabic term "confinement" or *iḥtibas*. Others focused less on the physical act of confinement and more on the sexual enjoyment that the husband receives from his wife.

The Arabic term used in the context of this latter obligation is *tamkīn,* or enablement.

Putting both obligations together encapsulates well the wife's core obligations within the marital bargain. She is to remain in the marital home, and she is to "enable" her husband to the sexual enjoyment of her body when he wishes.

Classical jurists took these twin obligations of wives extremely seriously. Numerous juristic texts point out that a woman on a nonobligatory fast (which involves the refraining from food, drink, and sex) was under a duty to break the fast should her husband desire sex from her. Likewise, as concerns the obligation to remain in the marital home, the expectation was that this was very broad in scope. The only exception approved by nearly all jurists involved the pilgrimage to Mecca. If a husband permitted his wife to undertake the pilgrimage, she would be out of his "possession" while traveling and he would not be able to enjoy her body during her absence. However, she had not failed in her marital duties and her husband therefore had a continuing obligation of maintenance toward her until she returned. The other major exception to a wife's confinement mentioned in the classical works involved visits to her parents.

A woman who fails in her marital duties, either by leaving a proper marital home, or by refusing sex, is deemed *nashiz,* meaning recalcitrant or rebellious. A husband is entitled to act against a rebellious wife, primarily by refusing to support her. A woman who remains in her husband's control and yet refrains from sex is also recalcitrant or rebellious and subject to other forms of discipline from him. The first of these is verbal admonition. If this fails, he may abstain from her as a means of discipline. Abstention in this context would include, for a polygamous husband, not spending an evening with her as he does with each of his other wives. If a husband is monogamous, the jurists took different views on what abstention meant, with some expressing concerns that a husband who avoids his wife and, consequently, refuses to have sex with her as a means to punish her ends up punishing himself as well. Accordingly, these jurists took the view that abstention in such cases meant refusing to speak with her or offer affection rather than refusing to engage with her sexually at all.

If abstention, however carried out, does not work, a husband is entitled to use moderate physical discipline against his wife for her rebelliousness. Much of this is defended by reference to Qur'an 4:34, which is traditionally translated as follows:

> Men are in charge of women by [right of] what Allah has given one over the other and what they spend [for maintenance] from their wealth. So righteous women are devoutly obedient, guarding in [the husband's] absence what Allah would have them guard. But those [wives] from whom you fear rebelliousness—[first] advise them; [then if they persist], forsake them in bed; and [finally], strike them. But if they obey you [once more], seek no means against them. Indeed, Allah is ever Exalted and Grand.

ii. Obedience in Modernity

In modern times, the idea of a woman never leaving the marital home at all, at least without a husband's permission, retains purchase in some limited and continually receding parts of the Islamic world—primarily in villages and more remote areas. It is also a defining feature of some particularly militant Islamist movements, from the Taliban to the Islamic State. However, even if courts continue to use the word *iḥtibas,* or confinement, for the most part what it precisely entails as a legal matter has been considerably relaxed away from what it seems to connote. The pressing concern of courts and codes is not whether a woman leaves the marital home to purchase goods or visit a friend, such practices being extremely common and socially acceptable across the vast majority of the Muslim world. The issues, however, concern more sustained departures, whether due to work or other reasons.

Some states, including Saudi Arabia, deny a woman the right to travel significant distances without permission from a husband if she is married. (This exercise of control is transferred to other male guardians if the woman is unmarried). Along the same lines, Syria prevents a woman from working outside of the home without her husband's permission.

Jordan's 2010 Personal Status Code is slightly more liberal. It does not permit a wife to work outside of the home without her husband's permission. However, once the wife obtains such permission, then the husband cannot rescind it unless he has a legitimate reason and the rescission will not cause his wife undue harm. Iraq adopts a rather curious variant of this in the context of travel. A married woman does not have the right to a passport unless her husband grants permission. Once the woman receives the passport, however, she is free to travel until its expiration without needing to demonstrate that her husband consented to any specific journey.

The broad consequence of this is that married women are often restricted as a legal matter from leaving the marital home for sustained periods of time, whether for work, international travel, or other purposes, and the extent of such restrictions depend on the jurisdiction. Courts almost never entertain claims, however, concerning a very brief departure from the home. That Arab codes, including those of Syria, Jordan, and Iraq, tend to use the root verb *taraka* when describing the prohibition against leaving the home, which connotes abandonment rather than temporary departure, helps courts reach this conclusion.

Indeed, most claims arise in court when a wife has left the marital home entirely, and the husband seeks an order that she return. Courts frequently issue such orders, though it would be exceedingly rare to locate a jurisdiction where a court order of this sort would be the subject of specific performance, such that a sheriff would arrive at the bride's location, place her into a police car, and return her to her husband's home. Forcible returns of wives may happen with depressing frequency in broad swaths of the Muslim world, but it is almost always a product of nonstate elements such as tribes exerting their own forms of legal order rather than the result of a state court order. Hence, the purpose of the court order, from the husband's perspective, is not to get his wife back, but instead to be relieved of his maintenance obligation towards her.

An illustrative case is a rather well known one involving The Most Exalted Tengku Muhammad Fahkry Ibn Sultan Ismail Petra, a prince in the Malaysian province of Kelantan, bringing suit against his estranged Indonesian wife, Manohara Odelia Pinot, whom he had met at a party in Jakarta when she was 14, and whom he married two years later. In essence, about nine months after they had married, the Tengku had taken a trip to Singapore with Manohara to visit his ailing father, and there, she left him with the assistance of the Singapore police and travelled back to Indonesia. She then initiated a rather embarrassing high profile campaign against him, alleging physical and mental abuse, claiming she was a virtual prisoner in the palace, and alleging private conduct on his part that can only be described as sadistic. The Tengku denied all of this and insisted the entire matter was part of a broader publicity campaign orchestrated by Manohara, who later became a fairly well known model. He went to court in Malaysia in order to seek an order for his wife to return to him.

Perhaps unsurprisingly, the Malaysian court sided with the Malaysian prince and against the Indonesian juvenile, citing at length various Prophetic statements that referenced a wife's obligation to obey her husband and make herself available to his sexual desires even if (to cite one Prophetic report, quoted in the case itself) "she is in the kitchen baking bread." The court also referenced a second Prophetic report concerning remaining in the marital home, which reads as follows:

> The rights of husbands over their rights (responsibilities of wives to their husbands) that wives may not leave their husbands' bed without permission, receive with grace what their husbands give them, obey their husbands' commands, and not leave the house without permission and not allow those whom their husbands hate enter.

The Court referenced a husband's obligation of support as well, and cited to ample Prophetic statements and Qur'anic verse obligating men to treat their wives with kindness. As concerns the material obligations, the Court pointed out the rather luxurious marital home in which Manohara was residing, and the comfortable circumstances in which she found herself more generally. The Court also dismissed as unproven any suggestions that the Tengku had mistreated his wife and therefore determined the following:

> There is no longer any reason for the defendant, as the plaintiff's lawful wife according to both the sharia and statute, to refuse to submit to and obey the plaintiff, and begin anew a life together filled with love and happiness, peace and tranquility, like grass sprouting after rain following a long period of drought. The plaintiff,

who has been a faithful husband to the defendant since their marriage on August 26, 2008 and has well and truly discharged his responsibilities toward the defendant, is entitled to demand that the defendant return to him. If the defendant fails or refuses she is deemed disloyal and obstinate causing her to lose her support and rights from the plaintiff.

The Court then ordered Manohara to return to her husband within 14 days and, "if [she] fails to comply with the order to return she is deemed disloyal and obstinate and loses her maintenance and other rights from the plaintiff." Unsurprisingly, Manohara did not return to her husband, and her husband was then free not to support her any longer. *Y.A.M. Tengku Muhammad Fakhry Ibn Sultan Ismail Petra v. Manohara Odelia Pinot*, Case No. 03001-0062-0971/2009, Shariah High Court, Kota Bharu, Malaysia.

While this case was prominent, it is not atypical of the manner in which a sizable number of cases involving the issue of the wife's marital obligations is litigated. At times, the husband raises the claim, as occurred in *Manohara*. At other times, if a wife leaves the marital home, the husband simply stops supporting her. She might raise a claim for support, in which case the husband then raises as affirmative defense that his wife is recalcitrant. The Court must then determine whether the wife's absence from the husband is justifiable (most clearly, if the husband has not supplied a proper marital home or has failed to pay the immediate dower), or whether it is not. If her absence is justified, the husband's obligation to support remains intact. If it is not justified, then the court proceeds to issue an order to the wife to return and, if she does not, she loses her right to the support she instituted suit for.

Such was the result in a case decided in 2008 in a trial court in Baghdad by a fairly well known trial judge operating in the Hayy al-Sha'ab district. The wife had left the marital home, claiming that her husband had "impugned her honor", and steadfastly refused to return. The husband had attempted mediation, but, when it failed, he stopped supporting his wife and child, as a result of which the wife brought suit. The Court described at length a wife's obligation to enable her husband to enjoy her body, and noted that the wife had failed to do so in this case. It also pointed out the obligation, set forth in Article 25 of the Iraqi Personal Status Code, that a wife not leave the marital home without permission. Given the essential nature of this obligation, the impugning of the wife's honor on a single occasion was not sufficient justification to refuse to return to the husband's home in the Court's view, in particular after the husband had attempted mediation. Personal Status Court, Ḥayy al-Sha`ab, Baghdad [unnumbered], decided August 24, 2008.

The above discussion focuses largely on the wife's obligation to remain "confined" in some broader sense in the marital home, and touches only tangentially on the issue of the wife's obligation to submit herself to her husband sexually. This reflects what I have seen in court dockets generally, which are replete with cases concerning marital homes and not with sexual obedience, perhaps for obvious reasons. It is comparatively rare for a husband to bring suit against a wife present in his marital home for refusing to have sex with him, though exceptions certainly exist.

That said, the sexual obedience obligations, and more saliently, the husband's deemed right to exercise physical discipline on a recalcitrant wife who denies him sex, can have important legal effects. Most particularly, it tends to complicate considerably the prosecution of husbands for spousal battery. To be clear, courts in much of the Islamic world will not excuse a husband who beats a wife severely. Hence, in a 2001 case in Kadhmiyya, one of the most conservative cities in Iraq and a Shi'i holy site, a man was ruled to have acted far beyond religiously permitted forms of discipline when he beat his wife with a car belt, sold her furniture over her objection, attempted to drown her in a bathtub, and threw her against a sink so severely it caused the sink to break. Not only was the physical harm more severe than that which courts understand to be permissible, but it also had nothing to do with his wife's alleged recalcitrance, which is the only justification to exercise discipline in the first place. Case No. 2601/2001, Personal Status Court of Kadhimiyya.

That said, in many state courts, criminal prosecutions of husbands for wife battery are rare. Some of the problems are social—a certain lack of sympathy for battered wives, and in particular those who leave the marital home, and a pervasive belief that the matter of abuse is best resolved within the family. Some, however, are legal. A man in many jurisdictions is able to raise as defense the fact that his abuse, when not as shockingly severe as it was in the case relayed above, was in fact intended as physical discipline to induce his wife to obey him.

To end this section on marriage on a hopeful note, there are growing trends toward a prohibition of husbands striking their wives for any reason. Primarily, this is through narrowing the right to such an extent that, coupled with increased penalties towards husbands who strike their wives, the right effectively becomes impossible to exercise. An increasing number of clerics and jurists are calling for laws against physical abuse and emphasizing the fact that the Prophet himself never struck any of his wives. More radical voices suggest that the Qur'an's reference to "striking" in 4:34 has been misinterpreted by jurists operating under patriarchal norms and that it requires reappraisal. Even the most conservative of jurists emphasize limitations on physical discipline far more extensive than those of earlier jurists, suggesting that the trends run across all groups. Undoubtedly, such changes have already affected courts addressing the problem of spousal abuse, and there is no reason to expect that they will not continue to do so—in all likelihood slowly and gradually—over the years and decades to come.

4. THE TEMPORARY MARRIAGE

Before continuing to the subject of marital dissolution, it is important to examine one final area of marital law relevant to the modern world, and this is the peculiarly Shi'i doctrine of the temporary marriage. The principle of a temporary marriage is one in which the temporal period of the marriage term is predetermined by the parties themselves at the time of the marriage. There are no limits to the time period itself, so long as it is long enough to render sexual enjoyment possible, and short enough to be plausibly less than the expected lives of those entering into it. When the term ends, the marriage has come to an end. Any children born during the marriage are treated as the children of any marriage would be, with custody rules being no different than they would be if the couple had divorced. (These rules are discussed at the end of this Chapter).

As with a permanent marriage, the man must offer a dower to the woman in exchange for her willingness to submit herself to his sexual enjoyment. Unlike a permanent marriage, a temporary wife may limit her husband's access to her—to certain times of the day, for example, or certain types of intercourse. Moreover, the husband has no obligation to support a wife during the marriage, nor is he limited in the number of temporary wives he can take at any given time. Hence, while a husband may not dissolve a temporary marriage unilaterally as he can a permanent marriage (the subject of the next section), he may release his temporary wife from any obligations on her part for the remainder of the marriage period. This effectively achieves the same result, given that a husband has no obligations in the temporary marriage vis a vis his wife beyond the payment of the dower.

It is not hard to discern the reasons that the temporary marriage has developed something of a negative reputation in many modern Muslim societies. The idea of a man paying a woman a "dower" in order to "marry" her for a period as short as an hour sounds rather unambiguously like a contract for prostitution. In theory, this is tempered by the fact that the woman must wait two menstrual periods between temporary husbands, though it is difficult to see how in practice this is much of a constraint against men, who can usually plausibly claim ignorance on the point. That married men at times engage in temporary marriages in brothels only fortifies the position of its detractors, who view it as religiously legitimizing the most sordid forms of adultery practiced in the modern era.

Two qualifications to these entirely justifiable conclusions are warranted. First, while the temporary marriage is clearly an exchange of sex for money, the same is largely true of the traditional marriage within Islamic law, as shown above. That in the modern world some modern Muslims may profess shock at the temporary marriage and the manner in which it commodifies marriage through dower only demonstrates the extent to which modern Muslims are unaware of the treatment of marriage doctrine in the classical texts. As noted above, the jurists regarded as self evident that marriage was a contract, and that the countervalues to the contract were, on the one hand, dower and maintenance and, on the other, sexual obedience and confinement of the wife's body to the marital home. Limiting the time period of the marriage renders the nature of the contract more transparent, and therefore harder to disguise in modernity, but that does not somehow render sex more central to the exchange. Hence, while a married man looking for sexual enjoyment outside of his current marriage has a broader set of opportunities with the institution of temporary marriage in place, the idea that somehow classical Sunni jurists viewed a married man with means taking another wife for sexual pleasure as abhorrent and treacherous to his existing wife is simply wrong. As noted above, in many juristic accounts, Sunni and Shi'i alike, polygamy is described as a recommended practice.

Even more saliently, in particular among those who do not view the temporary marriage with such a negative connotation, the temporary marriage can, but does not have to, resemble a contract for prostitution. A dower does not need to be set at any given amount, after all, meaning that it does not actually have to be a countervalue for sex. If, for example, a young couple find themselves without means to marry, or perhaps wishing to engage in a trial relationship before a final marriage, the temporary marriage may serve as a useful vehicle. The dower may be set at some trivial amount, the "wife" may limit her husband's access to her in whatever way she wishes, and a form of relationship thereby initiated that might resemble modern courtship elsewhere in the world. In particularly conservative societies where the mixing of the sexes is strongly disfavored, including Iran, this vehicle therefore serves an important social purpose having nothing to do with the purchase of sex.

In any event, whether used as a means to legitimize prostitution, or to engage in some form of premarital relationship that would otherwise be strongly disfavored, the need for legal recognition of the temporary marriage is quite muted. To the contrary, the preferences of those engaged in it would almost surely be against some sort of state registration or licensing. Accordingly, the temporary marriage is simply not part of the law of almost any state. Iraq's Personal Status Code, for example, has long been interpreted to recognize only the traditional marriage unlimited by time, and even efforts to codify Shi'i rules for the Shi'i population omit mention of it. Bahrain's recently enacted family law code for its majority Shi'i population likewise does not reference the temporary marriage. Even Iran, where in theory Shi'i juristic rules run supreme, in particular as concerns the law of the family, legal recognition of the temporary marriage is quite limited. The temporary marriage only needs to be registered if the contract specifies as much, or there are children that arise from it. Thus, while the sociological import of the temporary marriage is a matter of some debate, there is little doubt that as a legal matter, it is of minimal significance.

C. DIVORCE

1. *ṬALĀQ*

a. Basic Contours of the *Ṭalāq*

In conceiving the marital bargain, classical jurists viewed the parties within the relationship somewhat differently. As the one who was effectively the "buyer" in marriage, in the sense that his obligations were financial in nature, the husband "owned" the marriage. As the marriage owner, he was therefore free to repudiate it for any reason or for no reason. This right of the husband is referred to in Arabic as *ṭalāq*.

Carrying through with the same logic, the *ṭalāq* does not require the permission, or indeed even the presence, of the wife. All that is required is an oral pronouncement on the part of the husband that he wishes to repudiate the marriage. Precisely what type of oral pronouncement was required to give effect to the repudiation was the subject of contention among classical jurists. Hence, for example, the Shi'a were quite exacting in the procedural formalities attending to a valid *ṭalāq*. They demanded that the word *ṭalāq* or a variant derived from its root be pronounced by the man, and that it be clear precisely whom he is divorcing. The Shi'a also required that two male Muslim witnesses hear the pronouncement, and invalidated a *ṭalāq* if pronounced in anger, under duress, or while drunk. Finally, a *ṭalāq* to which a condition is attached ("you are divorced through *ṭalāq* if you leave the home tonight") is invalid among the Shi'a, though permissible under the rules of the four Sunni schools.

Classical jurists within the four Sunni schools varied in precisely what was required to perform a *ṭalāq*. Generally, the position was that use of the word *ṭalāq* met the requirement of repudiation. However, if a party used a different word, then there needed to be an investigation into intent. A notable implementation of this classical Sunni principle in modernity occurred in a 1993 Malaysian case when a husband used the Malay word *cerai* rather than the Arabic *ṭalāq*. The meanings of the two words are similar, in that both refer to a divorce (though *cerai*, unlike *ṭalāq*, can also mean to separate in contexts having nothing to do with marital relations). The court determined that because the husband had not used the Arabic *ṭalāq*, the court needed to effect an investigation into the pronouncement to determine intent, and that the husband's intent was not clear given the surrounding context in which he made the pronouncement. Accordingly, it deemed the putative *ṭalāq* invalid. *Mohamed bin Mohd Ali v. Roslina binti Mohd Yusoff* [(1993) 8 JH 275].

Another source of division between the sects concerned the timing of *ṭalāq*. The rule across the sects was that the proper way to effect a *ṭalāq* (the so-called "sunna" form) was when a wife was between menstrual periods, and the husband had not had sexual intercourse with her following her most recent menstrual period. Both Sunni and Shi'i jurists operating within the rich classical tradition broadly dismissed any *ṭalāq* performed in violation of this rule as a form of innovation not supported by Prophetic example and therefore impermissible.

The main difference between the Sunni and Shi'i jurists related to the effectiveness of the religiously impermissible *talāq*. In other words, what legal effect attaches to a husband who pronounces a *talāq* during his wife's menstrual period. According to the Shi'a, the attempted *talāq* is simply invalid and ineffective. (Certain exceptions exist where men who have lived apart from their wives for some significant period of time, rendering it impossible for them to know when precisely their wife's menstrual period transpires). According to the Sunni schools, though religiously impermissible, such a *talāq* is nevertheless effective.

One final note respecting the *talāq* is worth some exposition in this introductory section. While the wife does not "own" the marriage in the same way the husband does, a wife can at the time of the marriage contract be designated as her husband's irrevocable agent or delegee for purposes of effecting the *talāq*. The creation of such an agency or delegation does not limit the husband's ability to pronounce *talāq*, but it does effectively vest the same power in the wife. In other words, a wife who wishes to have the equivalent right of her husband to effect a divorce can simply insist that the contract designate her as agent or delegee, in which case she is free to declare a *talāq*, and, acting as her husband's agent, end her marriage at a time of her choosing. It is fair to say, however, that for the vast majority of Muslim women alive today, such an unencumbered right is more theoretical than it is real. In most of the Muslim world, the social taboos against a wife demanding a right to end the marriage prior to its initiation are strong, and few are willing or able to extract such a concession from their husbands as a result.

Given the comparative complexity of rules and procedural formalities respecting what types of *ṭalāq* are valid, and what types are invalid, who can pronounce the *ṭalāq*, and how a *ṭalāq* might be performed in a religiously permissible fashion, husbands who actually wish to divorce their wives through *ṭalāq* rarely attempt to do so on their own. They almost always procure the assistance of an intermediary, whether that be a judge in a state sharia court or a cleric unaffiliated with the state. Their failure to do so would almost certainly result in the *ṭalāq* being subject to challenge, should a party find it in their interest to so challenge it. One example of this is *Mohamed bin Mohd Ali*, described above, where the husband's use of a Malay word helped lead to invalidation of his *ṭalāq*. An even more interesting example lies in a 2010 case decided by a panel of Iraq's Court of Cassation. Before the lower court, a daughter sought to disinherit her mother from the estate of her father, claiming the mother was not entitled to the spousal share because her father had repudiated the marriage. The mother refused to testify under oath that the *ṭalāq* had not occurred, leading the lower court to draw the adverse inference that it had, and on that basis, it disinherited the mother. The Court of Cassation reversed, noting that the question of whether or not a valid *ṭalāq* had occurred was not purely a factual matter, but also a legal one. Therefore, it was inappropriate to ask the mother to testify to the existence of a *ṭalāq* between her and husband in the first place. It would not prove a *ṭalāq* occurred. The Court therefore reinstated the wife's inheritance portion, on the grounds that a *ṭalāq* had not been proven. Case 3888 of 2010/Personal Status I/Iraq Court of Cassation.

b. Effect of *Ṭalāq*

If a *ṭalāq* is pronounced in a manner that accords with Prophetic example as described above (meaning between menstrual periods where the husband has not engaged in intercourse with his wife since her last menstrual period), the classical rule is that the *ṭalāq* is revocable by the husband at his option for three menstrual periods. (For women in menopause, this period is three lunar months, and for women in childbirth, it is through the birth of the child). During this time, the husband remains responsible for supporting his wife in the marital home, and the wife remains obligated to remain there, and be sexually available for the husband. The husband is then empowered to revoke the *ṭalāq* either by word or through engaging in sexual intercourse. Some jurists emphasize that the wife during this period is not only permitted, but indeed encouraged, to dispense with the modest dress requirements normally imposed on women when her divorced husband is in the marital home. The principle seems to be that the resumption of marital relations following a *ṭalāq* is a matter to be actively promoted.

Following this three month waiting period, if there has not been a resumption of the marriage, then under the classical rules across sect and school, the parties are formally separated in what is known as a lesser irrevocable divorce. Neither of them has any obligations towards the other, though they are free to remarry with a new contract and a new dower if both parties (and, where applicable, the bride's guardian) agree to the union. Where a wife exercises a *talāq* as agent or delegee, the immediate effect is a lesser irrevocable divorce, rather than a revocable one. This is only logical, as it makes no sense to vest a power to divorce in the wife, and then suggest the husband could somehow revoke it at his option for three months. Within the Sunni schools, the forms of divorce that are impermissible but effective (for example, a divorce during a menstrual period) also result in an immediate lesser irrevocable divorce.

Finally, and most commonly known outside of the Islamic world, there is the triple *talāq*. The proper manner in which a triple *talāq* is pronounced is one where the husband pronounces the *talāq* once in the approved manner described above, and then repeats that *talāq* a second and then a third time after each of his wife's successive menstrual periods. Throughout the entire three month period, the husband should not engage in sexual intercourse with his wife. Another manner in which the triple *talāq* can occur in a permissible fashion is one where the husband divorces his wife permissibly, and then revokes the *talāq,* and resumes marital relations. During a subsequent time between subsequent menstrual periods, the husband pronounces an approved *ṭalāq* again, and again resumes the marriage. After a third, approved *ṭalāq*, a permissible triple *ṭalāq* takes place. The effect of any of these, across school and sect, is that the couple are separated in what is known as a greater irrevocable divorce. They may not remarry unless the wife marries another and that marriage dissolves. Under Shi'i rules, this entire process can only be repeated three times, so that the couple could theoretically be married nine times, with each three divorces separated by an intervening marriage. This latter, exclusively Shi'i, rule is of extremely limited relevance given the rather unusual fact scenario it envisages.

The form of triple *ṭalāq* with which most Western audiences are familiar, and the subject of near caricature across popular media, is one where the husband pronounces the *ṭalāq* three times in a row rather than across several menstrual periods, in the manner described above. The first point to note is that the classical jurists across school and sect dismissed this sort of marital dissolution as an impermissible innovation and a departure from the practices and traditions of the Prophet Muhammad. The divergence among them was not on this point, but rather on the effectiveness of the triple *ṭalāq*. As with other religiously impermissible forms of *ṭalāq*, the four Sunni schools generally took the position that the pronouncement was effective, and therefore resulted in a greater irrevocable divorce. Shii jurists, and a subset of late jurists within the Sunni Hanbali school, disputed this. They regarded such a triple *ṭalāq* as being a single, revocable *ṭalāq*. (Indeed, some early Shi'i jurists regarded the triple *ṭalāq* as invalid and ineffective altogether, rather than a single *ṭalāq*. However, over the course of history and certainly by the modern period, the Shi'i consensus was in favor of the triple *ṭalāq* acting as a single, revocable *ṭalāq*.)

Thus, while there is some truth to the caricature that a triple pronouncement of *ṭalāq* is a means by which a husband ends his marriage to his wife, it is absolutely not the case that this is the normal means by which a marriage is dissolved within the Islamic tradition. To the contrary, it is a religiously impermissible and disapproved way to do so, understood to depart from the Sunna. The reforms that arise as a result of this ethical conclusion are discussed in the next subsection.

c. Modern Reforms and State Court Practices Pertaining to *Ṭalāq*

i. *Limited Scope of* Ṭalāq *Reforms*

Even leaving aside the misrepresentations and distortions attaching to *ṭalāq*, there is no doubt that, as classically conceived, it can be exercised in a manner that is detrimental to the interests of women. Nonetheless, states overwhelmingly have retained the basic contours of the doctrine and not sought to abolish it altogether. Thus, it remains the case that in most states, an effective divorce is achieved through an oral pronouncement on the part of the husband (with two male Muslim witnesses present within Shi'i societies), at which point a woman enters into the three menstrual cycle waiting period during which the husband can unilaterally revoke his decision to repudiate the marriage and resume the marriage. There are some states where some core aspects of this doctrine is altered in a fundamental fashion. Perhaps most notable is Indonesia, where, under prevailing Supreme Court precedent, a husband must demonstrate a reason to pronounce *ṭalāq* for it to be valid, and a wife has the right to contest those grounds. *Yaneta Binti Hakam v. Syafnil Bin Ahmad*, Case No. 51/1981, Supreme Court of Indonesia. This proved so controversial that for years following the establishment of the rule in 1981, many lower courts simply ignored it prompting the Supreme Court to issue an admonishing circular to the lower courts about this in 1985.

The Supreme Court of Indonesia has also interpreted Article 6(1) of the 1974 Marriage Law, which requires the consent of the parties to a marriage as a condition of its validity, to apply when a husband seeks to *revoke* a *ṭalāq*. Case 29/K/AC/AG/1980, decided June 24, 1981. This means that the husband's revocation following a single *ṭalāq* is not unilateralt. Again, however, this is exceptional in the context of the broader Muslim world. More common is the example of Iraq, whose Personal Status Code plainly requires that parties consent to a marriage, but whose Court of Cassation has repeatedly held that a wife's consent is not necessary for a husband to revoke a *ṭalāq* during the three menstrual cycle waiting period that follows a pronouncement of *ṭalāq*.

As a partial explanation for the durability of *talāq* doctrine, it is important to note that *talāq* is not necessarily problematic in many, indeed perhaps most, instances where it is deployed in modern, state court. Couples who wish to end their marriages consensually very often find it easier to do so through a *talāq* pronounced by the husband rather than trying to locate a different basis for marital dissolution that might prove more cumbersome and expensive. In these contexts, the *talāq* serves the role of a no fault divorce with an Islamic imprimatur. The husband pronounces the *talāq*, before a judge or a religious officiant, with members of the wife's family present, pays the deferred dower, and the wife then enters the three menstrual cycle waiting period without any real expectation that there will be a revocation.

This may be why states generally see no purpose to disturbing the *talāq* as a concept, but instead seek to curb abuses that arise out of some of its application. Perhaps the most fundamental of such abuses is that the wife who is being divorced through *talāq* plays no necessary role at all in the process—indeed, she does not even need to be aware of it when it is taking place. We begin with this, and then turn to other major concern, which is post marital support. Finally, we conclude with the triple divorce and reforms associated therewith.

ii. Notification and Registration of Ṭalāq

While a wife does not need to be notified of a *talāq* under the classical rules for it to take place, there tends to be a rather easy way in which at least this aspect of the doctrine can be reformed in the modern era, and it is one that Muslim states have broadly adopted. This is the requirement that a husband perform any marriage dissolution, including a *talāq*, in court, or, in some cases, register it after the fact within a certain limited period of time. This requirement is a logical corollary to the requirement that marriages be registered. After all, if modern states within and beyond the Muslim world require marriage to be performed or registered in court for any number of reasons, including allocating state benefits and granting spouses and children particular rights they would not otherwise have, then surely the state needs to know if the marriage has ended.

Notification to the wife follows naturally. The reason is that across the Muslim world, rules of procedure in family law courts applying Islamic law are often taken from a transplanted Civil Procedure Code that would operate in any civil dispute involving contract, tort, or property, almost none of which are adjudicated according to Islamic law. Every such code would have elaborate rules (familiar to lawyers in non-Muslim jurisdictions as well) to ensure that both parties were notified of any court proceedings taking place. Courts would be quite accustomed to applying those rules. Hence, for example, in 2010, Iraq's Court of Cassation was faced with a circumstance where a husband performed an out of court divorce and was filing to register it in court. The lower court registered the *talāq*, but the Court of Cassation remanded, on the grounds that the husband could only show that he had served process on the wife's brother, rather than the wife. The Court required a demonstration that the wife's brother lived with the wife, and a showing that the service as so effected in fact met with the service of process rules of Iraq's Civil Procedure Code. Case 3403/Personal Status Panel 1/2010.

In addition to the procedural rules themselves, substantive notice provisions are often inserted into legislation requiring that a wife be notified of the *ṭalāq*. Given broad deference to modern procedural rules and norms, these provisions are rarely controversial. Hence, for example, in 1985 Egypt enacted a family law reform act imposing a requirement that a wife be notified within 30 days of any *ṭalāq*. While various parts of this 1985 law have been the subject of much debate, this provision has largely escaped attention.

It might be noted that notification of the wife does not usually mean that the wife can contest the actual *ṭalāq* if a husband chooses to pronounce it. (Again, as noted above, Indonesia is the exception). Some limitations exist in modern personal status codes to invalidate a *ṭalāq* pronounced in extreme anger, on a deathbed, or while drunk, largely on the basis of patching together limitations derived from the various schools of Islamic law, and a notified wife might seek to make use of one of them to render a *ṭalāq* ineffective. This is of marginal value, however, to a wife whose husband is intent on pronouncing *ṭalāq* and willing to do so in court. After all, even if the wife convinces the court that the initial *ṭalāq* was pronounced in anger, if the husband truly wishes to carry out a *ṭalāq*, he can merely pronounce it again before the judge.

In some cases, however, a wife might be able to make use of mandatory mediation processes imposed by courts prior to registering *ṭalāq*. Article 88 of Syria's Personal Status Code, for example, reads in relevant part as follows:

(1) If a *ṭalāq* proceeding is initiated before the court . . . the judge will delay it for a period not to exceed one month in hopes of reconciliation, and he may during this period seek support from those selected from the relatives of the couple or one of the centers of family reconciliation.

(2) If the husband insists on the *ṭalāq* after the period expires . . . the judge will call the parties and hear their dispute and attempt to end it and achieve the continuation of marital life.

(3) If the efforts do not succeed, the judge will register the *ṭalāq*, and the *ṭalāq* will be effective from the date it is pronounced.

Algeria's Family Code has a similar procedure in Article 49. These provisions do not prevent the husband from carrying out the *ṭalāq*, but they do slow the process down, often to the wife's advantage.

Finally, if it achieves nothing else, notification to the wife is important because it enables a wife to know to assert her material rights upon *ṭalāq*, chief among which is the deferred dower.

The next salient question that arises in the context of these reforms is precisely what consequences attach to a husband who fails to pronounce a *ṭalāq* in court or fails to register it for a long period afterwards. After all, the reforms outlined above are only useful to the effect that the state is aware that a *ṭalāq* has taken place.

States vary widely in their practice. Indonesia and Tunisia adhere to the progressive practice of deeming the *ṭalāq* invalid until registered. Most states are not willing to go this far, simply because if the *ṭalāq* meets Islamic law requirements, and is officiated by a cleric, courts do not feel empowered to declare it somehow not a *ṭalāq*. Some impose minor criminal sanctions instead. Jordan, for example, adopts this approach in Article 97 of its Personal Status Code, as does Syria in Article 93. The extent to which such sanctions are actually applied in practice is a matter of some dispute.

For its part, Iraq requires that a husband pronounce a *ṭalāq* in court. The husband may register it after the fact if it was infeasible to pronounce in court, and even then only within the wife's waiting period. There is no criminal consequence for failing to do so. Given the lack of sanction, husbands ignore these provisions with some frequency and register *ṭalāqs* months and at times years after the fact, without consequence. While the Personal Status Code suggests that this could subject the husband to a support claim from a wife for the period the *ṭalāq* was not registered, such claims on the part of wives are comparatively rare.

The final consequence of an out of court divorce in some states is that a court could, upon reviewing it, deem it to be a "capricious" *ṭalāq*. Material consequences would attach to that determination, as explored in the subsequent section.

iii. Post Marital Support and the Capricious Ṭalāq

As noted earlier, a husband's obligations to a former wife end when her waiting period ends. It is at this time that he is no longer obliged to offer her shelter or support, and she is likewise under no obligation to submit to his sexual demands. In some circumstances, and in particular those where a wife's family has negotiated a deferred dower of significant size, this presents no problem to the wife given her right to that dower upon the pronunciation of *ṭalāq*. Indeed, in some cases, the deferred dowers demanded can be sufficiently high as to deter a husband who might otherwise wish to divorce his wife from declaring *ṭalāq*. Iraqi courts, for example, are inundated with claims from husbands who seek a marital dissolution on the basis of cause rather than *ṭalāq*. The only reason a husband would ever go through the time and expense of such proceedings when he could simply pronounce *ṭalāq* is in the hope that the court will find the wife at fault for whatever problem exists in the marriage and in so doing, relieve him having to pay all or part of the deferred dower. This is discussed further below.

That said, not every wife or wife's family is willing or able to extract a significant dower at the time of marriage, and, when she is not, she might find herself in significant financial hardship upon *ṭalāq*. Moreover, even in circumstances where a wife has negotiated a decent deferred dower, there is a social stigma associated with divorcees that persists with some force in much of the Islamic world that causes real harm. That a husband can effect such harm by a mere oral pronouncement is a source of some concern, and various states have tried to take actions to limit these burdens, with modest success and much controversy.

The most common method to do this is through legislation that permits a wife to make a claim against her husband for a lump sum payment when he pronounces a *ṭalāq* in a fashion that the court deems to be "capricious" (in nations such as Jordan, Iraq and Algeria) or "unwarranted" (in the case of Egypt). Egypt, Iraq, and Jordan calculate this sum based on maintenance payments that would otherwise have been made absent the *ṭalāq* for a period of years, depending on the extent of the capriciousness. Algeria, by contrast, establishes the amount on the basis of the harm done to the wife through the capricious *ṭalāq*.

On the basis of these provisions, husbands who pronounce *ṭalāq* through text message, at a wife's place of work, or on social media, have had significant support requirements levied upon them. These are in addition to any deferred dower due. While it is certainly not the case that every *ṭalāq* performed out of court is deemed capricious, the *talāqs* that are found to be capricious are almost always performed out of court.

The provisions obligating post marital support need not necessarily be controversial from the perspective of Islamic law. To be sure, they impose liability on a husband in a manner that Islamic law did not historically contemplate. Yet the same might be said of virtually any rule of private law in the areas of contract or tort, where Islamic law plays almost no role in most Muslim states. Hence, for example, modern laws in almost every Muslim state permit a plaintiff to recover damages for defamation, and Islamic law did not historically recognize moral harm as a basis for recovery. If a modern, legislatively mandated wealth transfer on the basis of harm to reputation is not controversial, there would seem to be no reason to believe that a modern, legislatively mandated wealth transfer to a wife harmed by her husband's capricious divorce constitutes some sort of core violation of Islamic law.

It is probably a demonstration of the deep patriarchy that prevails in Islamic societies that while the tort of defamation is quite popular, even if it does not exist in the classical texts, post marital support of wives is controversial, because it does not exist in the classical texts. In Iraq, the capricious divorce provision was one of the first to meet with a constitutional challenge, on the theory that it lies against the settled rulings of Islam. In Egypt, when originally introduced, the comparable provision was widely derided and the law in which it was embedded was referred to dismissively (and misogynistically) as Jihan's Law, after President Sadat's wife, who, critics alleged, was the real force behind the law. Of course, the laws have their supporters as well, and they remain very much on the books in a significant number of Muslim states, primarily within the Arab world.

Where post marriage maintenance has been most controversial, however, has been in India, in particular following the famed *Shah Bano* case decided by the Supreme Court of India in 1985. In that case, a 62 year old woman named Shah Bano was divorced by her husband after 43 years of marriage and five children. (In the intervening period, the husband had taken a second wife as well). Shah Bano made a claim for maintenance under Section 125 of the Code of Criminal Procedure, and the question before the Court was whether that provision applied to Muslims, given that Muslims were governed by their own separate personal law. The Supreme Court of India decided that it did. According to the Court, Section 125 only imposed maintenance in situations of genuine need, and therefore did not violate the general rules of Islamic law, which did not address such exceptional circumstances. Moreover, the Court argued, the Qur'an itself imposes a requirement of support on divorced wives, thereby rendering Section 125 largely consonant with it. Finally, the Court lamented that Article 44 of the Indian Constitution, which called for a uniform civil code to apply to all Indians in family law matters, had not yet been put into place. *Mohammad Ahmad Khan v. Shah Bano Begum,* 1985 SCR(3) 844.

The reaction was swift and strong, so much so that the Indian Parliament effectively overruled *Shah Bano* the next year in the ironically named Muslim Woman (Protection of Rights on Divorce) Act 1986. That Act required that all maintenance payments be made during a wife's waiting period, as the classical rules contemplate. A decade and a half later, long after the controversy had dissipated, the Supreme Court cleverly interpreted the 1986 Act as requiring actual maintenance payments be made within the waiting period, but permitting them to be made in amounts that constituted support well beyond it. *Danial Latifi v. Union of India* (2001) 7 SCC 740. In this way, Indian law has come to resemble that of many of the Arab states described above, in that it permits a wife to make a claim for marital support over the course of years, calculates the amount due to the wife, and then awards that amount in a lump sum payment paid immediately.

iv. The Triple Divorce

Perhaps the greatest divide within modern states in terms of reform of *ṭalāq* lies in the treatment of the triple divorce. The point of agreement concerns a valid third *ṭalāq* pronounced after successive waiting periods, at times with periods of reconciliation, and at times without them. In such cases, overwhelming state practice is that the husband has initiated a greater irrevocable divorce and that as a result, the marriage cannot be resumed unless the wife marries another husband first, and that marriage comes to an end. This is clearly in keeping with classical rules.

The more controversial form of triple *ṭalāq*—where the husband pronounces *ṭalāq* three times successively in one sitting—is not as well received in modern states. Article 4 of Egypt's Law 25/1929, states that "a divorce executed in multiples, in words or by signal, does not occur except once." Indonesia, Iraq, Jordan, and Kuwait have instituted similar rules. While this reform is by no means universal—Syria for example continues to regard a triple *ṭalāq* as a greater irrevocable divorce to the extent that the husband intended it as such—it is fair to say that a rising proportion of the states in the Muslim world has found no difficulties putting an end to the practice as a legislative matter.

This is not to say that social practice has followed as closely. Professor Nasir in his research on religious courts in Indonesia tells the story of a husband on the island of Lombok in Indonesia who divorced his wife through a triple *ṭalāq* in a fit of anger. While the couple reconciled and the husband insisted he had not intended the *ṭalāq*, life in their village proved unbearable given that witnesses had heard the *ṭalāq* and deemed them to be living in sin. The wife was forced to return to her home village, marry another man, have him divorce her, and then marry her original husband again with a new marital contract before they could resume marital relations.

That said, with the increased focus on the triple *ṭalāq*, the broad social campaigns initiated against it, the rather defensive apologetics offered by opponents of change, and the legislative interventions, all of the elements seem to be in place toward a gradual receding of the practice, at least for the indefinite future. It is unlikely that it will disappear entirely any time soon, but it is similarly hard to believe that the trends against it will somehow reverse themselves.

2. OTHER MARITAL DISSOLUTIONS

As the previous section makes clear, men had the unilateral power to end their marriage through *ṭalāq* for any reason, or for no reason. The same was not true for wives. That said, the classical jurists did establish rules pursuant to which a wife could end her marriage if she wished, in some cases over her husband's objections. Modern jurisdictions have built upon these foundations to expand a wife's right to seek a marital dissolution—in some cases, quite substantially. This section lays out some of the primary forms of dissolution that are relevant in modern Muslim jurisdictions.

a. Conditional or Delegated *Ṭalāq*

It was noted in the previous section that while a husband could theoretically irrevocably delegate his right to *ṭalāq* to his wife while still also retaining it himself, broadly speaking, across the Islamic world in the modern era, this is rather rare. There are social stigmas attached to a wife demanding such an unconditional right, and even states seeking to reform *ṭalāq* are more interested in finding ways to limit its abuse rather than extend it. That said, there are important states and regions where the *ṭalāq* is deployed an instrument of more limited female empowerment. This is usually achieved through what is known as a conditional *ṭalāq*.

In some parts of the Arab world, the notion of the conditional *ṭalāq* is viewed with some disfavor. In these areas, the primary conception of it is one where aa husband threatens a wife with a *ṭalāq* during an argument if she takes a particular action he disfavors. Most modern Muslims find distasteful the idea that a marriage would dissolve because, for example, in a fit of anger, a husband tells a wife she is divorced if she leaves the home that evening, and she does.

It is for this reason that in Article 36 its Personal Status Code, Iraq has long adopted the Shi'i rule that conditional *ṭalāq* is invalid. Arab Sunni states such as Jordan and Syria do not prohibit conditional *ṭalāq*—indeed, Article 88 of Jordan's Personal Status Code makes clear that a *ṭalāq* dependent on a condition is valid. However, such states try to curb abuses of the practice of the type set forth above. They do this primarily through a provision that indicates that if the intent of any conditional *ṭalāq* is not in fact to effect a marital dissolution if a condition is met, but only to discourage a particular act or omission in strong terms, then a *ṭalāq* does not occur upon the satisfaction of the condition.

In stark contrast, in parts of the Muslim world beyond the Arab world, the idea of a conditional divorce is thought of, at least in part, as a means of female empowerment. Consider, for example, the following conditional *ṭalāq* from a 1990 decision by the Sharia Appeal Board in Kuala Lumpur:

> Every time I do not give my wife named Aisny binu Mohamed Daris such maintenance for her as is sufficient according to the custom for four months or more, my wife can make a complaint to the sharia judge. If the complaint is proved before the sharia judge, she will be divorced by one *ṭalāq*. Every time I revoke the *ṭalāq* without her consent, one *ṭalāq* will be effected. Appeal 5/1989, Sharia Appeal Board (Kuala Lumpur).

Clearly, in this case, the conditional *ṭalāq* is not one where the husband is threatening to terminate his marriage if the wife does not adhere to his wishes, but rather one that a wife might be expected to negotiate, as a means to ensure that her husband continues to support her. Indeed, a multitude of conditions are routinely inserted into marriage contracts in certain parts of the Muslim world that will bring about a *ṭalāq* for mistreating a wife. These include a husband choosing to take a second wife, physical abuse (at least when taken beyond the bounds permitted by the jurists), and the departure of the husband for extended periods of time. Such conditions do not carry social stigmas in many jurisdictions, including, for example, Indonesia, Malaysia, and Iran, and indeed in some places are deemed to be something of a norm.

In theory, the conditional *ṭalāq* is a matter of private negotiation between the husband and the wife and their respective families, and therefore requires no state support or intervention. However, states do take steps to facilitate negotiations to the wife's benefit. The most important of these is a legislatively imposed limitation on the right of the husband to unilaterally revoke the conditional *ṭalāq* after he has pronounced it. Without this limitation, the negotiation with the wife is pointless, as whatever the husband agreed to in the conditional *ṭalāq* could be instantaneously be erased by its subsequent unilateral retraction. While classical jurists across the Sunni schools thought a husband could always revoke a conditional *ṭalāq*, as he could a *ṭalāq*, modern states from Jordan to Indonesia have inserted provisions into relevant laws and regulations that do not permit such a revocation.

The second means of state facilitation is through the insertion of text in state marriage contracts that lists various conditions pursuant to which a *ṭalāq* occurs, which the parties are free to accept or reject in part or in whole. There is nothing per se objectionable to this as a matter of Islamic law, as whether or not the conditions are inserted is ultimately up to the parties themselves. Nevertheless, such text makes it easier for parties to come to agreement because they do not need to then draft such provisions on their own. This method also provides the court with language with which it is accustomed and which it can adjudicate in a predictable and efficient fashion. Finally, model language closes potential loopholes that might otherwise arise. A wife negotiating a condition for a *ṭalāq* might overlook the fact that there needs to be a mechanism to ensure that the husband does not return his wife following such a *ṭalāq* during her waiting period, for example. Legislative text, as existed in the *Aisny* case above, wherein an attempt to return the wife itself constitutes another *ṭalāq* helps to address this problem.

Creating a default wherein such conditions are automatically included in the contract unless the parties exclude them enhances a woman's rights even further. A husband seeking to remove such conditions is then put into the awkward position of explaining why it is he wants to change a state marriage contract that only enables his wife to divorce him if he takes actions that are objectionable on their face.

One final note on conditional *ṭalāq* requires elaboration. As noted earlier, the Shi'a generally reject the idea of any sort of *ṭalāq* with conditions, thereby rendering a conditional *ṭalāq* one that is difficult to put into effect in Shi'i dominated societies such as Iran. Shi'i jurists do permit, however, a husband to appoint his wife his agent for the purposes of declaring a *ṭalāq* upon the establishment of certain conditions. While the process is different (in that the wife under the Shi'i rules must first establish that the conditions were met, and then must herself pronounce the *ṭalāq* as empowered agent of the husband), the legal effect is the same. A wife is under this mechanism able to ensure that certain forms of mistreatment will provide her an avenue to exit the marriage.

b. Compensated Divorce (*Khul`*)

A separate form of divorce available to a wife is known as the *khul`*, or compensated divorce. The compensated divorce is on the basis of Qur'an 2:229, which instructs believing husbands as follows:

> And it is not lawful for you to take anything of what you have given them unless both fear they will not be able to keep [within] the limits of Allah. But if you fear they will not keep [within] the limits of Allah, then there is no blame on either of them concerning that by which she ransoms herself. These are the limits of Allah, so do not transgress them. And whoever transgresses the limits of Allah is among the wrongdoers.

The reference to sin are notable. As the noted Hanbali scholar Ibn Qudama states:

> If a wife despises her husband for his looks, his character, his religion, his age, his weakness, or something similar and she is afraid that she will not fulfill the rights of God in obeying him, she may divorce him with compensation that will ransom herself from him.

While not all jurists adopt precisely this formulation (Shi'i jurists, for example, indicate that more than a mere personal despising of looks or character are necessary), the basic structure and justification are the same; namely, that the basis for the compensated divorce is that if it is denied, the wife might disobey her husband, and, indeed, the limits of God. The latter phrasing strongly suggests the possibility of fornication. One commonly cited Prophetic report deals with a wife fearing that she will fall into disbelief if she remains with her husband. Thus, rather than succumb to physical desire and fornicate with another, the *khul`* provides an avenue for a wife to extricate herself from the marital bond through a ransom of sorts.

Pursuant to the *khul`*, a wife agrees to pay her husband a sum of money in order to induce his agreement to effect a *talāq*. Precisely how much this is depends on the school of thought prevailing in a given location as well as local custom. Generally, however, a wife is expected to waive her deferred dower. Often, she must also pay back her immediate dower as well as any other gifts given to her in the marriage. Some schools permit a husband to demand more, and in some cases, a wife is willing to accede to more. Where the state law adopts such an approach, the potential for extortion deepens. Wives in Iraq for example quite frequently receive demands from husbands that are many times larger than their dower in exchange for a divorce, and often accede to them if desperate enough to wish to exit the marriage.

As a doctrine with deep classical pedigree, the compensated divorce is recognized and adjudicated regularly in almost every jurisdiction that purports to apply Islamic family law. It is rarely the source of much contention in its purest form, as most adjudications of merely involve the court confirming the arrangement of the parties as concerns the dissolution of the marriage.

The main issue that arises with respect to the *khul`* in modernity is whether or not the husband need consent, in particular if the wife is willing to return everything she ever received by way of gift or dower from the husband to ransom herself free. Classical jurists generally answered this question in the negative, the theory being that the *khul`* as set forth in Qur'an 2:229 is a bargain, and a bargain requires the consent of two parties.

That said, a significant number of jurisdictions, from Pakistan to Egypt to the Kurdistan Region of Iraq, expressly permit a wife to obtain a compensated divorce if she is willing to give up her entire dower along with other gifts received from her husband, and if a mediation process involving members from both families fails to reconcile the parties. In Egypt and the Kurdistan Region of Iraq, this is managed through legislation passed in 2000 and 2008, respectively.

In Pakistan, the result came much earlier by way of a 1967 Supreme Court case that resolved inconsistent earlier decisions in the lower courts. Specifically, the Supreme Court in that case deployed *'ijtihād* to interpret Qur'an 2:229 in an entirely different way that the classical jurists had. Classical jurists had read the provision "if you fear they will not keep [within] the limits of Allah, then there is no blame on either of them concerning that by which she ransoms herself" to refer to a consensual bargain between the parties. In this reading, "you" obviously refers to husbands, who fear that their wives will not fulfill their marital obligations, thereby precipitating the arrangement reached for the wife to ransom herself. According to the Court, however, a better reading of the verse than that offered by the classical jurists is to understand "you" to refer to a court itself. This is because, in its words, "it is significant that according to the Qur'an she can 'ransom herself' or 'get her release' and it is plan that these words connote an independent right in her." In other words, the verse is not reflecting a bargain, but a court proceeding wherein a wife successfully convinces the judge that she so despises her husband that she will fall into sin if she is not released from her marital bond.

The Court was aware that it was interpreting Qur'an 2:229 in a manner that diverged sharply from a virtual unanimity of classical jurists, and it made clear that it did not care. Specifically, the Court stated as follows:

> The opinions of Jurists and Commentators stand on no higher footing than that of reasoning of men falling in the category of secondary sources of Muslim law, and cannot, therefore, compare in weight or authority with, nor alter the Qur'anic law or the [Sunna]. If the opinions of the jurists conflict with the Qur'ān and the Sunna, they are not binding on Courts, and it is our duty, as true Muslims, to obey the word of God and the Holy Prophet. *Mst. Khurshid Bibi v Muhammad Amin* PLD 1967 SC 97, 141.

In the broader context of modern Muslim jurisdictions applying Islamic family law, the Pakistan Supreme Court's candid deployment of *'ijtihād* to dispense with juristic consensus is rare. Few courts are willing to be so outspoken, and few legislatures are willing to even implicitly challenge classical understandings of Qur'anic verse. As such, dispensing with the husband's consent for a compensated divorce remains the exception in most Muslim jurisdictions rather than the rule. Where states have started to make it easier for wives to obtain a divorce without fault, such as in Morocco and Indonesia, they have done so through other forms of dissolution sanctioned by at least some classical jurists, as discussed further below.

c. Cause

i. *Classical Rules*

Within the classical framework, the above forms of marital dissolution require the consent of the husband, either *ex ante* in the case of the delegated or conditional *ṭalāq*, or *ex post* in the case of the compensated divorce. Not all marital dissolutions require such consent, however. Classical jurists across all schools of thought maintained that there were some circumstances pursuant to which a wife could petition a court to end a marriage under a doctrine known as *faskh*, and that a court could order such a dissolution, whether or not the husband consented.

The most obvious of the grounds concerned bodily defects about which the wife or her marriage guardian were unaware at the time of contracting the marriage. A husband who was castrated or simply impotent would be the paradigmatic case. Clearly if the jurists took any cognizance of a woman's sexual needs at all, as they did, then this conclusion seems natural. Other examples listed by some jurists include communicable diseases common in medieval societies such as leprosy and tuberculosis.

It is important to note that husbands also had a right to invalidate the marriage on these grounds, and might do so in order to avoid payment of a dower. While these sorts of invalidations seem akin to annulments in the US legal system, as a result of which the Arabic term *faskh* is often translated as annulment, they are different in one important sense. In a *faskh,* he marriage is deemed, even *ex post*, to be valid and effective from the time it is entered until the time that the court orders a *faskh*.

Jurists differed across the schools and sects respecting the extent to which a wife could petition for marital dissolution, through *faskh* or otherwise, if a husband failed to fulfill his marital obligations. The most common examples are a husband abstaining from his wife, disappearing entirely, causing his wife harm beyond the moderate physical discipline that jurists maintained was sanctioned by Qur'an 4:34, or failing to maintain his wife. The Maliki school permitted a wife to dissolve a marriage in any of these cases, though in the case of a missing husband who has left her assets from which she derives maintenance, she must wait four years before she is able to do so. In the case of harm, a noted number of Maliki jurists proved quite flexible, encompassing within it virtually any type of mental or physical abuse as determined by the custom of the place and the time.

The Malikis used the term *ṭalāq* to describe dissolutions imposed where a husband refused to fulfill his marital obligations. The procedure usually included as an initial matter offering the husband the option of promising to fulfill his obligation or pronouncing *ṭalāq*. If he failed to do either, the court would pronounce the *ṭalāq*. The Shi'a adopt a very similar approach to the Malikis, and permit dissolution on very similar grounds.

The Hanafi school was the strictest among the classical schools, denying a wife the ability to petition to dissolve her marriage on the grounds of abstention or failure to maintain. The two remaining Sunni schools, the Hanbalis and the Shafi'is, were more permissive than the Hanbalis but less permissive than the Malikis.

ii. Modern State Practice

Modern jurisdictions commonly weave together these disparate rules into one large legislative fabric that gives a wife the right to petition for a marital dissolution whenever she is able to show any of the causes recognized by any classical school of thought. As Chapter Five will show, this sort of patching, known in Arabic as *talfiq,* is quite common in Islamic finance and, while rarer in family law, certainly is the norm as concerns a wife's right to dissolve her marriage. Hence, for example, in Iraq, Kuwait, Jordan, Egypt, and Syria, where Hanafi rules traditionally apply, and in Indonesia and Malaysia, where Shafi'i rules apply, a wife can petition for dissolution on the grounds of harm, a failure to maintain, abstention, imprisonment, disease, among other grounds. By way of illustration, relevant provisions of the Kuwaiti Personal Status Code are supplied below:

Article 120

(a) If a present husband refuses to maintain his wife, and he does not have obvious means, nor is his financial difficulty established, his wife may petition for *talāq*. The judge will divorce them forthwith and the husband may stop the *talāq* by paying her required support from the date that the suit began.

(b) If the husband can prove financial difficulty, or he was absent in a known place or imprisoned, and he has no obvious means, the judge will grant him a respite of not less than a month, nor more than three months ... to satisfy the referenced maintenance, and oi he does not, [the judge] will issue the *talāq* against him.

(c) If the husband is absent in an unknown place, or missing, and he has no obvious means, the judge will issue the *talāq* without a respite.

Article 121

The *talāq* of the judge for failure to maintain is a revocable one. The husband may return his wife during the waiting period if he can show to the court that he has means to continuous maintenance and is ready to support her.

Article 122

If the suit for a lack of support is raised more than twice, and the wife petitions for a *ṭalāq* for harm, the judge will issue a lesser irrevocable *ṭalāq*.

Article 126

Either of the spouses before consummation or after may petition for dissolution for reasons of the harm of the other, by word or deed, in a manner that renders the continuation of married life for one of their station impossible.

Article 127

The court shall use its efforts to reconcile the couple. If it is unable to do so and the harm is proven, it shall dissolve them by a lesser irrevocable *ṭalāq*. . . .

Article 136

If a husband is missing for a year or longer without an acceptable excuse, the wife may petition for dissolution if she is harmed by his absence even if he has means to support her.

Article 137

If an absent person can be notified, the judge shall grant him a time period, and shall inform him that he will issue a *ṭalāq* against him if he does not make an appearance and reside with his wife, send for her, or divorce her. If the time period elapses and he does not act nor is an acceptable excuse apparent, the judge will dissolve the marriage by a lesser irrevocable *ṭalāq*.

If the absent person cannot be notified, the judge will dissolve the marriage without excuse or warning.

Article 138

If a husband is imprisoned by a final sentence by a punishment that limits freedom for three years or more, his wife may petition for a lesser irrevocable *ṭalāq* after a year of his imprisonment, even if he has means to support her.

Article 139

Each of the spouses may petition for *faskh* of the marriage if there is a deep rooted defect in the other that is repulsive, harmful, or of the type that denies [sexual] fulfillment, whether or not the defect was present before the contract or occurred thereafter. The right of *faskh* to each of them is invalidated if they knew of the harm before the contract, or clearly accepted if afterwards.

Article 140

As an exception to the foregoing rule, the right of a wife is not invalidate to petition for *faskh,* because of a defect in the man which denies [sexual] fulfillment, such as impotence, congenital or unexpected, even if she clearly assented to it.

Article 141

If the referenced defect is not capable of ending, the court shall issue the *faskh* forthwith and if it is capable of ending, the case will be extended for an appropriate period. If it does not end during this period, and the applicant insists on the *faskh,* the court will issue it.

The language is relatively clear and relatively representative of much legislation across the Islamic world in its broad references to marital defects and *faskh,* its willingness to grant dissolutions more readily to wives who are not supported by absent or missing husbands relative to those who are so supported, and its acceptance of harm as a ground of dissolution. Virtually no provision above lacks classical support, but it would be difficult to find a single jurist who would include all of them.

There are two additional items of note. First, both as a matter of legislation, and as a matter of practice, courts are unwilling to invalidate a marriage if a husband is not fulfilling his marital duties without at least warning the husband that they will do so. Hence, for example, Article 120 of the Kuwaiti Code, quoted above, permits a husband to end a divorce petition for failure to support simply by starting to pay the maintenance. He can also do so during the waiting period and then return his wife. Under Article 137, if he is absent, the court is expected to try to reach him to warn him not to abstain from his wife before issuing a *ṭalāq* against him. Such provisions are taken very seriously. Hence, for example, the Iraqi Court of Cassation has remanded cases where a dissolution was ordered for failure to maintain under a comparable provision to that of Article 120 in the Kuwaiti Code, even though the lower court did warn the husband to pay the maintenance. The reason was that the warning from the lower court was in the form of an order to pay maintenance, but it did not specify that his failure to pay would result in a judicially ordered dissolution. This probably reflects a bias, inherent in the classical doctrine, that absent overt bodily defects, a dissolution ordered against a husband should be a form of last resort. The preference is to either get the husband to fulfill his marital duties, or to issue the *ṭalāq* himself.

This bias often transfers over to the area of harm as well, where it can prove rather problematic. Kuwait, and Egypt in its parallel legislation, only permit a wife to dissolve a marriage for harm where such harm makes the continuation of married life impossible for one of her social standing. Egyptian courts in the past have taken note of this, and reported in dicta that moderate physical discipline of a peasant wife might be customary and therefore not interfere with married life in the manner that the beating of the wife of a judge does.

Even in states where language respecting social standing does not exist, as in Iraq, Jordan, and Syria, or where it is not remarked upon, as is common in more recent Egyptian decisions, the fact that the harm must be of the sort that renders life intolerable tends to be understood by the courts to require a high level of severity. That husbands commonly cite to Qur'an 4:34 to justify their physical discipline of their wives only complicates matters. This frequently induces courts to at least attempt to reconcile the couple, as per Article 127 of the Kuwaiti Code, quoted above, and numerous parallel provisions across the Muslim world. However appropriate such reconciliation efforts are in other contexts, they hardly seem fitting in cases involving harm. It is disheartening indeed to witness a patently abused wife being coaxed by a judge to return to her husband, with the same judge seemingly willing to do little more to the husband than sternly lecture him on proper Islamic behavior and, in connection therewith, the importance of being kinder to his wife.

Aside from severity and social standing, there is the quite serious matter of proof. In nearly all of the relevant Codes, the Court may order a dissolution only if it can prove the harm. Courts in much of the Arab world in particular tend to regard questions of harm as being primarily about criminal conduct, and thus defer consideration of any dissolution petition pending the outcome of criminal proceedings associated with the same conduct. This is precisely how civil courts in the Arab world have long treated tort claims where there was a parallel criminal claim proceeding. therein citing to such provision, courts seem to reflect an implicit belief that there is no difference between, on the one hand, a victim of a tort awaiting a criminal proceeding outcome before making a compensation claim, and, on the other hand, a wife claiming abuse awaiting a criminal proceeding outcome before being relieved of her obligation to obey her husband's sexual demands.

d. Irreconcilable Differences (*Shiqāq*)

It has become increasingly common to find a provision in the Personal Status Codes of Muslim countries that enables either party to petition for a marital dissolution on the grounds of an irreconcilable difference. While such provisions are often described as creating a form of "no fault divorce," in fact this is something of a misnomer. It is clearly the case that pursuant to these legislative innovations, either spouse is able to seek a marital dissolution without having to identify some sort of defect or specific cause. However, the relevant legislation almost always initiates a process specifically designed to identify who is at fault as concerns the marital discord, and then to attach financial consequences to that determination, primarily through potential reduction of the deferred dower to the extent that the fault is that of the wife. In other words, the law not only presumes fault, but also mandates a process to determine whose fault the dissolution is.

Legislation that establishes *shiqāq* as a form of dissolution is taken from a set of jurists within the Maliki school, who developed it from Qur'an 4:34. That verse reads as follows:

> And if you fear dissension [*shiqāq*] between the two, send an arbitrator from his people and an

arbitrator from her people. If they both desire reconciliation, Allah will cause it between them. Indeed, Allah is ever Knowing and Acquainted [with all things].

Obviously, the verse is focused more on reconciliation than dissolution, but at least some Maliki jurists have suggested it can authorize a dissolution where, after attempting to bring a couple back together, the court finds differences between the parties to be deep rooted and irreconcilable. The process these jurists set forth was for the court to appoint arbitrators, and, where the arbitrators could not reconcile the couple, they could either declare *ṭalāq* or *khul`*. They would declare *ṭalāq* where the husband was at fault for the continued discord, thereby obligating him to pay the deferred dower. They would order *khul`* where the wife was at fault, thereby relieving the husband of any deferred dower obligation.

In relevant legislation in some states, such as Syria and Kuwait, the *shiqāq* automatically follows a claim for dissolution on the grounds of harm. In such states, if a spouse makes a claim for harm, and the harm cannot be proven, then the *shiqāq* process is initiated. The theory seems to be that in a marriage where one of the spouses is accusing the other of abuse, there is a need to attempt some form of reconciliation, even if the allegations are not true.

In Iraq and Indonesia, the *shiqāq* process stands alone. Once deployed, however, its procedures tend to be broadly similar across jurisdictions and largely congruent with the Maliki approach. Article 41 of

Iraq's Personal Status Code is illustrative. It reads as follows:

(1) Each of the spouses may request a dissolution on the grounds of a difference between them, whether before consummation [of the marriage] or after it.

(2) The Court must investigate the reasons for the difference. If it is established as present, the Court shall an arbitrator from the wife's family and an arbitrator from the husband's family—if present—to look into reconciliation. If no family members are available, the court shall charge the spouses to appoint two arbitrators and if they cannot agree on their appointment then the court will appoint them.

(3) The two arbitrators shall make efforts toward reconciliation, and if they are unable, they return the matter to the court, making clear the party who is at fault. If they do not agree, the court shall appoint a third to join them.

(4) (a) If it is proven to the court that the difference between the spouses continues and it cannot reconcile them, and the husband refuses to divorce, the court shall order a dissolution between them.

(b) If the dissolution is after consummation [of the marriage] the deferred dower is cancelled if the fault was from the side of the wife whether she was plaintiff or defendant. If she has already received all of the dower, she must return no more than half. However, if the fault is from both parties, then the delayed dower is divided between them based on their proportion of fault.

(c) If the dissolution is before consummation and the fault is on the side of the wife, she must return what she has received by way of immediate dower.

From this and parallel provisions across the Muslim world, three observations are worthy of note. First, in terms of process, the *shiqāq* is not altogether different from the *khul`* in those states where a wife may seek a *khul`* without a husband's consent. There are, however, some important differences. In the *khul`*, there is no inquiry into fault. Instead, the wife is offering to give up at least her deferred dower and potentially her entire dower as well as other gifts given to her in order to be free of her marriage. She only needs to demonstrate to the court an intense dislike of her husband that causes her to question her ability to adhere to the limits of God, which is independent of whether or not he has done something specific to cause marital discord. By contrast, in the *shiqāq*, there is a much deeper inquiry into who is at fault in causing the marital discord, and the deferred dower and potentially other amounts are then distributed accordingly. Almost by necessity, the proceedings are contentious and bitter.

Second, also unlike the *khul`*, either spouse may petition for a *shiqāq* in almost any jurisdiction that recognizes the practice. Husbands quite frequently resort to it rather than merely pronounce *ṭalāq* because they are convinced that wives have caused marital discord, and, as a result, they should not have to pay the deferred dower. (That husbands would choose to enter into this sort of intensely combative process rather than pay a deferred dower and free themselves of the marriage as a matter of routine demonstrates that at least in some important contexts, the deferred dower serves its purpose in deterring the exercise of capricious forms of *ṭalāq*.)

Finally, the extent to which wives are actually able to use these provisions to free themselves from a marriage in which they are unhappy is a matter of some debate, and varies broadly from jurisdiction to jurisdiction. There is significant evidence that in Indonesia, wives are able to make liberal use of *shiqāq* to obtain a divorce from their husbands. By contrast, in Iraq, the matter is far more constrained than the legislation cited above would seem to suggest. In particular, the Iraq Court of Cassation has read the term "difference" *(khilāf)* in the Code to mean, in its words, a "deep-rooted" *(mustaḥkam)* difference, and it has ruled that this standard is met in very few cases. At times, the Court's position approaches the absurd. In a notable 2011 case, a husband described his wife's mother as promiscuous, her sisters as prostitutes, was frequently drunk, joked about wishing to butcher his wife, and did all of this in such an open and conspicuous fashion through his mobile phone and elsewhere that members of the wife's family instituted suit against him for defamation of character. The wife also petitioned for a dissolution on the grounds of *shiqāq*. The lower court granted the petition, but the Court of Cassation reversed and remanded, holding that in fact defamation of character was a civil claim that a putative victim could settle at any time. Therefore, it was not clear that this was in fact a truly "deep-rooted" difference that could give rise to dissolution, and further reconciliation efforts were merited. Case 5916/2011, Personal Status Panel, Court of Cassation of Iraq. In other cases, the Court of Cassation does not even remand because it deems the difference to be *per se* not deep rooted. Examples include a dispute over the vaccination of a child and one over whether a wife would continue to work after the birth of their child. To the Court, all of these are reconcilable and not a cause for marital dissolution. Indeed, the only clear deep rooted differences the Court recognizes with regularity are those where a spouse is guilty of committing some sort of crime vis a vis the other spouse. Yet, in such cases, the *shiqāq* rules seem superfluous, in that the victim almost certainly had alternative grounds for dissolution in the form of harm. Iraqi court practice in this area thus seems to reflect a bias against forms of marital dissolution that are of more limited classical pedigree, and, in so doing, reveal the continued hold that classical doctrine has had and indeed continues to have in the field of Islamic marriage and divorce law.

D. CHILD CUSTODY

As with much of Islamic family law, the child custody rules developed by classical jurists come into some clash with international expectations and prevailing international treaties. In particular, classical Islamic law in this area lies in some tension with the Convention on the Rights of the Child, November 20, 1989, 1577 U.N.T.S. 3, and the Hague Convention on Jurisdiction, Applicable Law, Recognition, Enforcement, and Cooperation in respect of Parental Responsibility and Measures for the Protection of Children, October 19, 1996.

That said, there has been significant evolution of child custody norms in modernity, for two primary reasons. First, the classical rules set up a rather elaborate matrix of rights and responsibilities that, precisely because of its complexity, is easier to adjust over time to meet modern demands. Second, the international expectations in this area have led to more sustained difficulties across jurisdictions in child custody disputes. This has put pressure on courts in Muslim majority states to use internationally accepted norms in their adjudications. This subsection lays out the evolution by first describing classical rules, and then showing the very different modern state practices.

1. CLASSICAL PRINCIPLES

Classical jurists within the Sunni and Shi'i schools usually only approached the question of custody in the context of marital dissolution, it being assumed, for the reasons explored above, that in all other cases, the wife would be residing in the marital home provided by the husband, and the child would be raised there. If a wife had abandoned the marital home during the marriage and was thereby in breach of her marital obligations, she could hardly demand that her children be given to her. This was a point so obvious to the classical jurists that they rarely found the need to make it. The same would be true of a husband who had disappeared and abstained from his wife for a period of years. A question arose as to whether a husband on legitimate, lengthy travel away could demand that his children accompany him. The answer was largely no. Thus, in sum, during a marriage, the children remained in the marital home, and the spouse who chose to leave it would do so without the company of the children.

Upon dissolution of the marriage, the jurists divided rights of custody into two parts. The first was known as the right of guardianship (*wilāya*) and the other the right of "rearing" (*ḥaḍāna*). The matter of guardianship is easier to address. It included not only the power to enter a child into a marriage, as discussed earlier in this Chapter, but also the primary right to education and discipline of the child. In addition to these forms of "guardianship over the person", the guardian had certain rights that could be exercised with respect to the ward's financial affairs, which were collectively described as guardianship over property.

Guardianship devolved exclusively to men, and those connected to the ward on the man's side. Obviously this meant the father first, and then the paternal grandfather. Following this, guardianship passed to other men from the father's family. A mother could never be a guardian, except through a testamentary assignment (*wiṣāya*) from a guardian. Hence, for example, a father could assign a right of guardianship to a wife in the context of a marital dissolution, and she would then have the same rights as the father by assignment. Recent scholarship suggests this was common in the Ottoman era, in particular in the context of a compensated divorce.

The matter of "rearing" was more complicated. The universal view, informed by the patriarchal norms that pervaded the classical era, was that in a child's youngest years, females offered the child the love and affection that a child needed more than males did. Accordingly, it was the mother who enjoyed priority in rearing at the younger ages. Thus, in the case of an infant upon a marital dissolution, the mother would take physical custody of the infant to rear the child, but important decisions such as marriage, education, and disposition of assets would remain with the father, as guardian. If the mother was unfit or dead, custody would transfer to the next person in priority. For the Shi'a, this is the father. The Sunni schools vary, though all of them privilege female ascendants of the mother over the father. Some also privilege other female relatives in addition to ascendants, such as the sister or maternal aunt of the mother.

The length of time that a child remains in a mother's physical custody for purposes of rearing varied according to sect and school. The Maliki school extended the mother's right until puberty for a boy, and marriage for a girl. On the other end, the Shi'a granted a mother the right to physical custody only until the age of two for a boy, and seven for a girl. The other Sunni schools fell between these two poles. For the Hanafi school, the relevant age for a boy was seven, and for girls it was puberty. The Shafi'is focused instead on a largely undefined age of discernment, which they estimated to be around the age of seven or eight. The distinction in ages as between boys and girls was not universal—neither the Hanbali nor the Shafi'i school adopted one—but was easy enough to explain in context. If the prevailing, patriarchal idea was that females showed more tenderness and affection, and males more discipline and rigor, then it would be natural to expect that jurists would extend the time that females remained in the custody of other females, where, presumably, their tendencies of tenderness and affection would be enhanced. In fact, the main reason girls were given over to the physical custody of their fathers at all was that as the enforcers of discipline, the father and his male relatives were assumed to be in a better position to ensure a girl's continued chastity pending marriage.

Following early childhood, at whatever age it ended, the schools diverged sharply. The Shafi'i school permitted either a boy or a girl to decide with whomever the child would rather reside after the period ended. However, a boy would need to spend days with his father even if he chose the physical custody of his mother, so that the father could ensure his proper education. The Hanbalis also permitted a boy to decide with whom to reside, though they did not extend this right to a girl, the risks to her chastity being deemed too great if she were to remain with her mother. The other schools permitted no choice, and automatically transferred physical custody of the child to the father at the end of the early childhood period. (The sole exception was the Maliki school, where the girl remained with her mother until marriage, at which point she would move to the marital home).

In terms of rights of visitation, the parent with physical custody was not permitted to deny the other parent access to the child. Details respecting how the process of visitation would be implemented are scant in the juristic literature, with the matter largely left to judicial discretion and custom.

While these gender driven rules are obviously at odds with modern, global norms and expectations outside of the Muslim world, where the paramount focus is on the best interests of the child, it is worth noting that the interests of the child are not entirely ignored. For one thing, there is the rather obvious fact that the Shafi'i school permits a child to select the parent with whom they will reside upon reaching an age of discernment, and the Hanbali school does this for boys. Moreover, both this right of election, as well as the rules respecting the parent with whom a child will reside, are subject to the qualification that the most fundamental interests of the child—food, clothing, and shelter—will be met. If the parent exercising a right of rearing or guardianship is not going to safeguard these interests, then the right transfers to the next person in priority.

Even some rules that are decidedly patriarchal in nature are usually justified by classical jurists on the basis of a child's interests. Hence, for example, a mother's ability to exercise physical custody terminates with her remarriage to another man. Though in modernity there are suggestions among some scholars that this serves as some sort of chastisement to the woman for marrying again, classical jurists certainly did not view the matter in this manner. They did not suggest that remarriage was prohibited, or even disfavored, as a matter of Islamic law. Rather, to them, the problem was that the new husband would presumably be hostile to the stepchild in the marital home, and the mother would not protect that child's interests given her marital obligations of obedience to her new husband.

Hence, the notion of custody within classical law was based on a complex matrix of rights and obligations involving three different sets of participants. The first were the male dominated guardians, who made the most important decisions respecting the child. The second were the custodians, initially at least female dominated, who exercised physical custody. Finally, there was the child as well, whose interests played some role in the application of the rules.

Having laid out classical rules, the next section demonstrates the extent of modern legislative fealty to those rules, and further sets forth where the greatest evolution has been.

2. MODERN STATE PRACTICE

As noted above, classical Islamic law is in some contrast with broadly accepted international instruments in the matter of child custody. Most prominent among these instruments is the Convention on the Rights of the Child, ratified by ever nation in the world except the United States. Article 3(1) of that Convention indicates that "[i]n all actions concerning children, whether undertaken by public or private social welfare institutions, courts of law, administrative authorities or legislative bodies, the best interests of the child shall be a primary consideration."

For its part, Article 23(2) of the 1996 Hague Convention permits courts in states that are party to it to refuse to enforce judgments issued by courts in other states party to it to the extent that such judgments are "manifestly contrary to the public policy of the requested State, taking into account the best interests of the child."

In other words, there is an overwhelming international sense that custody determinations are supposed to be in a child's best interests, nearly exclusively. This is in some tension with rules that automatically assign a child to one parent or the other based on sex and age. By and large, Islamic states have not resolved this tension, simultaneously ratifying the Convention on the Rights of the Child (in some cases, with reservations where the provisions conflict with Islamic law) while continuing to have legislative provisions applied in domestic courts that are largely informed by classical Islamic rules.

Nevertheless, it would be incorrect to suggest that social changes in the Muslim world in combination with international pressures have had no effect on child custody rules as they apply across the Islamic world. Indeed, child custody is perhaps the area of family law where there has been the most flux over the past several decades, and evolution continues in this field. The balance of this chapter describes the changes, and the manner in which they bend, but do not break, the framework set by classical Islamic jurists centuries ago.

3. GUARDIANSHIP

Muslim states by and large continue to adhere to the division of custody into the two classical categories of guardianship on the one hand, and rearing on the other. The former category has seen the least evolution. While there are exceptions, with the reliably progressive Tunisia being the most obvious, most Islamic states continue to rely on classical Islamic conceptions respecting who may act as guardian for a child, vesting that power exclusively with the father and other male relatives within the father's family. Hence, for example, only a child's father will be able to represent the child in court, grant permission for the child to marry (to the extent such permission is legally required), and dispose of the child's assets.

That said, there is some obvious overlap as between the role of the physical custodian of the children, who rears them, and that of the guardian. Hence, for example, in theory the guardian is responsible for the education and discipline of the children. Yet the parent rearing the child obviously has an important role in these areas as well, as the one who sees the child on a daily basis and does the most work raising the child. This overlap has allowed courts to extend the rights of the parent with physical custody, which is presumptively the mother in the child's earliest years, at the expense of the guardian. For example, Article 57(4) of Iraq's Personal Status Code gives the father the right to "review" the raising and education of the child while in the mother's custody. The term "review" suggests a decidedly secondary role for the father, as guardian, in matters relating to the education and upbringing of the child in the child's earliest years.

4. REARING (*HADANA*)

There has been far more evolution in matters relating to the physical custody of children through the doctrine of rearing. The major change has been through extending the age at which a mother's presumptive right to physical custody ends. This has not been difficult, largely because the juristic schools were never in agreement on a relevant age, to the extent they even sought to specify one, as opposed to relatively vague references to an "age of discernment." States have used this uncertainty to extend the age of physical custody well beyond what at least most of the traditional jurists envisioned.

Hence, for example, Indonesia has extended the date at which a mother's physical custody ends to twelve. Iraq has extended it to ten, Qatar to thirteen for boys and fifteen for girls, the United Arab Emirates to eleven for boys and thirteen for girls, and in Egypt and Jordan, the relevant age is fifteen for both sexes. Similar trends exist across the Islamic world. These changes have been advocated for by women's rights organizations, which is understandable, given the interests many mothers have in retaining physical custody of their children following a marital dissolution. At the same time, the suggestion that the changes somehow accord with the Convention on the Rights of the Child, which regards the best interests of the child as paramount, requires a patriarchal assumption that is quite controversial; namely, that women are presumptively better nurturers and caregivers of young children than men are.

Islamic states have also been willing to take somewhat greater cognizance of the child's best interests. Many of the states within the Gulf Cooperation Council, for example, permit judges to vary rules on which spouse retains presumptive physical custody to the extent that the presumptive rule is not in the child's interests. Indonesia's Compilation of Islamic Law does the same. By contrast, Iraq only revokes a mother's presumptive rights until the child is ten if harm will come to the child. However, from the age of ten to the age of fifteen, the determination of custody is based on the child's best interests. In those states where mothers have presumptive rights of custody until fifteen, such as Egypt and Jordan, a child's best interests are in the normal case irrelevant. The child remains with the mother until fifteen, and then chooses which parent to stay with, irrespective of what the court might believe the child's best interests to be.

The other major area of reform has been with respect to a mother's remarriage. Where classical rules generally terminated a mother's physical custody upon her remarriage, many Muslim states no longer do so. Modern laws quite often permit a mother to retain custody of the children in these cases so long as it is in the best interests of the child. Examples of this include Qatar, Morocco, and Iraq, and case law in both Egypt and Jordan support similar results.

5. EXCEPTIONS

Finally, it might be noted that there are states where Islamic law rules have been completely reformed in a manner that focusses squarely on the best interests of the child. The most obvious examples are Tunisia and Pakistan. Tunisia is perhaps relatively unsurprising, in that its family law rules stand apart as a model of Islamic progressivism. This helps to explain why there is so much literature on it. Pakistan is more interesting, in that as a state it is not necessarily known for its progressivism in the area of Islamic law—indeed, it is unusual in its codification of Islam's Scriptural Crimes, the subject of Chapter Six. Nevertheless, taking advantage of ambiguous text in a colonial era nineteenth century law known as the Guardian and Wards Act of 1890, along with the broad common law tradition, Pakistani courts have been able to concoct an entire legal doctrine relating to custody and guardianship that focuses on the paramount interests of the child first and foremost, and refers to Islamic law principles only secondarily, to the extent they are not in conflict with such interests. The result is that Pakistani court judgments on custody are routinely upheld in other jurisdictions, including the United States, simply because in reasoning and outcome they accord with the expectations of the broader global community. This has not led to broad opposition, certainly relative to other aspects of Islamic law, which are the subject of more heated public debate. While some of the Pakistani transformation depended on unique circumstances relevant to Pakistan alone, the example does show the extent to which Islamic law, even its family law, is subject to significant evolution over a relatively short period of time. Subsequent chapters will show even more dramatic evolution in other fields of law.

E. ADOPTION

Finally, in concluding this section, a few words on adoption within the context of Islamic law are warranted. This is because of the longstanding Islamic law prohibition on adoption, endorsed by all relevant Islamic law schools and supported by ample revelatory text. The prohibition creates some tension with modern needs and expectations, but they have been managed to a large extent, as explored further below.

The prohibition against adoption is perhaps clearer than many others in Islamic law precisely because adoption was practiced in pre-Islamic Arabia. Indeed, the Prophet himself adopted a son, Zayd. Three separate Qur'anic verses later prohibited the practice, two of them relating to the specific case of Zayd. One indicated that the Prophet was not father to the believing men [Qur'an 33:40]. Another stated that people should be called the sons of their biological fathers [Qur'an 33:5]. A third verse specifically legitimized the marriage of the Prophet to Zaynab, the ex-wife of Zayd, "in order that there not be upon the believers any discomfort concerning the wives of their adopted sons" [Qur'an 33:37]. There is also Sunna specifically discontinuing the pre-Islamic adoptive practices.

The third of the Qur'anic verses referenced above, concerning the marriage of the Prophet to the ex-wife of his once adopted son, has led detractors of Islamic law to suggest that the reasons for the Islamic law prohibition were driven more by libido than reasoned discourse. This is extremely difficult to justify. From the biographers of the Prophet to the accounts of the early jurists, the concern with adoption did not relate to marriage, but exploitation by adoptive fathers. Specifically, the concern was that clans would seek to enrich themselves through adopting orphans from other, richer clans. The practice would in such cases be socially disruptive as exploitative, as clans fought over who might be able to adopt any given orphan child.

At the same time, the desire of the childless to raise children is not purely a modern phenomenon, and even classical jurists seemed to respond to the sociological needs of their era by narrowing precisely what the Prophet was putting an end to, and substituting another form of adoption in its place. Specifically, the classical jurists came to actively encourage a practice known as *kafāla*, literally translatable as "sponsorship". Under the *kafāla*, an adult, and usually a family member, acted as a guardian of a child, raising them, providing for them, and exercising all supervisory care that a parent would, with two primary distinctions. First, the child would be known as son or daughter of their biological father, and not their guardian. (Hence, Zayd, the once adopted son of Muhammad, is historically known as Zayd, son of Harithah, rather than Zayd, son of Muhammad.) Moreover, the inheritance links to the biological family remain intact in a *kafāla*, thereby preventing adoption as a means to increase wealth as opposed to care for an orphan.

As might be obvious, the distinction between the permitted forms of sponsorship and the prohibited forms of adoption were not great, but they were amply justified. After all, while the Qur'an does seem to prohibit adoption, it also repeatedly refers to care and concern for the orphan as the quintessential act of charity, and a lack of such concern being the quintessential characteristic of the hypocrite whose prayers are purely for the sake of appearance.

The fine juristic distinctions have proven to be of vital importance in the modern era. The most traditional form of the Islamic rules may not mesh particularly well with traditional "closed" adoptions, where the link as between biological parent and child is severed entirely, but there have been adaptations and evolution both in Islamic law and adoption law to bring the two fields closer together. Hence, modern Muslim jurisdictions have proven somewhat flexible in their treatment of the adoption rules in the area of inheritance. While a child with a guardian through *kafāla* may not inherit from the guardian as a matter of Islamic law, the guardian is permitted to bequeath property to the child of up to 1/3 of the estate. In some jurisdictions, including Indonesia, this sort of bequest is rendered obligatory by the law of the state. (The same treatment is given to orphaned grandchildren, as the next Chapter makes clear).

At the same time, on the other end, the traditional closed adoption has given way in many jurisdictions to systems wherein the connection between an adopted child and the biological parent is not permanently severed. In such jurisdictions, the ability to manage the divide between Islamic law and prevailing adoptive rules is all the easier. The divisions between Islamic law and the law common in other jurisdictions then collapses into nomenclature, concerning what the child is called and whose last name they carry, rather than one over the respective rights and obligations of the guardian and the child.

CHAPTER 3
INHERITANCE LAW

Islamic inheritance law is similar to family law in that most modern Muslim states have continued to use it. In fact, most modern Muslim states frequently refer to inheritance law and family law together as belonging within the single legal category of personal status law, and they apply Islamic law more assiduously in this field than in any other. Hence, though many Muslim majority states have developed their own civil codes, modelled on the Continental European templates, that govern almost all private law, these codes almost always exempt issues of personal status from their purview, specifically to preserve the primary role of Islamic law in both inheritance and family law.

As with family law, those many contemporary courts that apply Islamic inheritance law largely use the classical corpus as part of a continuous tradition that has not been radically disrupted with the onset of modernity. Of course, there have been important changes over the centuries, as was the case with family law. These changes have arisen because of changing conceptions and expectations of Muslim peoples. Modern Muslims live in very different family and societal structures than those that dominated seventh century Medina, or 10th century Baghdad for that matter, and hence they have different views on who should be entitled to inherit their estates and why. Modern states have tried to grapple with this while remaining faithful to the core features of the classical system, as this chapter will show at length.

In this regard, the parallels between this chapter and the previous one on family law will be easy to identify.

Yet despite all of these similarities to family law, the law of inheritance is also unique in Islamic law in two important ways. First of all, inheritance law is the one area of law where a significant portion of the rules come directly from Qur'anic verse. This is one of the reasons it tends to be harder to displace in modern states. This is not to suggest, to be clear, that workarounds are not possible among those dissatisfied with Qur'anic distributions. They are quite possible, and indeed some have long pedigrees that precede the modern state. However, it is harder for lawmakers and judges to justify a conclusion that seems directly at odds with Qur'anic verse, as opposed to one that addresses subjects on which the Qur'an has little to say. As a result, as this chapter will show, the areas of Islamic inheritance law that have seen the most evolution have been with respect to matters where the Qur'an is either silent or ambiguous.

Inheritance law is also unique because of the significant differences in approach between the Sunnis and the Shi'a. As was noted in Chapter One, the deep theological divide between the sects does not always reflect into a deep legal one. Inheritance provides a stark exception to that rule, however.

These two features of inheritance law seem somewhat contradictory to one another. If, that is, the Qur'an's detailed verses are the basis of inheritance law, and if the Sunnis and Shi'a accept the same core Qur'anic text, how can it be that they have such different rules? In the answer to this question, laid out in the context of this chapter, much is revealed about the important gaps that exist in the Qur'an as concerns inheritance law, the role of Sunna in filling in such gaps, the predispositions and assumptions prevailing within each sect on what inheritance law is intended to do, and, perhaps most broadly, the role of both text and lived experience in giving life to the law.

A. ROLE OF QUR'ANIC VERSE

The source text from which the classical jurists developed inheritance law appears in the Qur'an primarily in the three following verses, from the fourth chapter, entitled "The Women":

Verse 11. Allah instructs you concerning your children: for the male, what is equal to the share of two females. But if there are daughters, two or more, for them is two thirds of one's estate. And if there is only one, for her is half. And for one's parents, to each one of them is a sixth of his estate if he left children. But if he had no children and the parents inherit from him, then for his mother is one third. And if he had brothers, for his mother is a sixth, after any bequest he [may have] made or debt. Your parents or your children—you know not which of them are nearest to you in benefit. [These shares are] an obligation [imposed] by Allah. Indeed, Allah is ever Knowing and Wise.

Verse 12. And for you is half of what your wives leave if they have no child. But if they have a child, for you is one fourth of what they leave, after any bequest they [may have] made or debt. And for the wives is one fourth if you leave no child. But if you leave a child, then for them is an eighth of what you leave, after any bequest you [may have] made or debt. And if a man or woman leaves neither ascendants nor descendants but has a brother or a sister, then for each one of them is a sixth. But if they are more than two, they share a third, after any bequest which was made or debt, as long as there is no detriment [caused]. [This is] an ordinance from Allah, and Allah is Knowing and Forbearing.

Verse 176. They request from you a [legal] ruling. Say, "Allah gives you a ruling concerning one having neither descendants nor ascendants [as heirs]." If a man dies, leaving no child but a sister, she will have half of what he left. And he inherits from her if she [dies and] has no child. But if there are two sisters [or more], they will have two-thirds of what he left. If there are both brothers and sisters, the male will have the share of two females. Allah makes clear to you [His law], lest you go astray. And Allah is Knowing of all things.

The verses address some important questions, while leaving important gaps. The specific questions the verses answer relate to specific inheritance portions for the following individuals:

(i) daughters (one half of the estate for one daughter, and two thirds for two or more),

(ii) spouses (1/2 for a husband if the decedent had no children, and 1/4 if she had children, with this reduced by half for wives), and

(iii) parents (1/6 to each parent if the decedent had children, but if there are no children, then 1/6 for a mother if the decedent had brothers, and 1/3 for the mother if the decedent did not have brothers).

The verses also seem to suggest that males should inherit at a rate that is twice the amount of similarly situated females (hence a husband receives double what a wife would), and that these proportions are obligatory.

While many Muslims thus regard the verses therefore as clear, comprehensive, and determinative, in fact this is far from the case. The verses leave far more questions than they do answers. Among the more obvious gaps to be filled in are the following:

First, if a daughter inherits one half of an estate, and a similarly situated male is supposed to inherit twice what a female does, then what does a son inherit? Obviously it makes no sense to suggest the son inherits twice that of the daughter in such a circumstance, as the son cannot inherit the entire estate and the daughter half of it at the same time.

Second, why is the inheritance portion of a son not precisely delineated, precisely as a daughter's is?

Third, what is the logic of granting each of the father and mother a specific portion of 1/6 if the decedent had a child, but seeming to give the mother the father's share, so that she receives 1/3, if the decedent does not have a child? And then, in turn, what is the logic of limiting the mother to 1/6 of the estate if the decedent had brothers? What possible relevance could the existence of the decedent's brothers possibly be to the mother's inheritance portion?

Fourth, if the apportioned amounts in the Qur'an lead to a fraction of the estate less than one, where does the balance go? For example, if a decedent leaves behind a wife (1/8 of the estate), two daughters (2/3), and no other relatives, this adds up to 19/24 of the estate. What should be done with the rest? In reverse, if the apportioned amounts in the Qur'an lead to a fraction of the estate greater than one (i.e. two daughters (2/3), a mother (1/6) and a husband (1/4), which adds to 13/12), then whose shares are to be reduced?

Fifth, is there any limitation on these principles for a decedent who wants to bequeath some property to a third party, for example a charity? Or is a person, no matter how wealthy, unable to direct any of his property to any person other than legal heirs?

As the next two sections will show, these questions are answered differently depending on the sect in question. We will begin with the Sunni rules before turning to the Shi'a.

Before doing so, however, there is one immediate matter of interpretation, rather than gap-filling, that should be addressed here. This is how to resolve the direct conflict as between 4:12 and 4:176 on the inheritance rights of siblings. Verse 4:12 refers to siblings receiving 1/3 of an estate (or 1/6 if there are two or fewer of them) equally and without regard to gender when there are no ascendants or descendants. Verse 4:176 speaks of sisters, but not brothers, earning 2/3 of an estate if there are more than one, or 1/2 if there is only one, when there are no ascendants or descendants. Obviously these two different rules cannot both be applied to the same people.

The general juristic interpretation of this is that the references in Verse 4:12 are exclusively to maternal half-siblings. That is to say, brothers or sisters of a decedent by virtue of a common mother, but not a common father. The reference in Verse 4:176, by contrast, is to full or paternal sisters. This of course begs the question of how full and paternal brothers are supposed to be treated, who are under this interpretation not mentioned at all, except, seemingly, in the context of limiting the inheritance share of a mother. The answer to this constitutes part of the broader discussion below respecting filling the gaps created by the Qur'anic verses.

B. SUNNI INHERITANCE

1. THE AGNATES AS PRIMARY RESIDUAL HEIRS

Within Sunnism, across the four Sunni schools, the primary explanation for the gaps in the Qur'anic verse is that the Qur'an was not intended to create an entirely new system of inheritance, but rather to amend an existing one. Pre-Islamic Arabian custom privileged the male members of the tribe known as the `aṣaba, or agnates, who were themselves related to the decedent through men. Hence, for example, the son of a decedent is one of the agnates, as is the father, and full and paternal brothers. The maternal brother, or the grandson of a decedent through a daughter, however, is not an agnate. Though each of these relatives is a man, his connection to the decedent is through a female, rendering him what is known as a "uterine heir" rather than an agnate.

The Sunni conception of inheritance law is one wherein the Qur'an imposes limited reforms of the agnatic system, primarily in favor of closely related women and spouses, who would otherwise receive nothing. The balance of the estate is then to be distributed to the closest of the agnates in accordance with pre-Arabian custom.

The exegetical basis of this approach is a Sunna from the Prophet Muhammad, which reads as follows:

> Give the Qur'anic shares to those entitled to receive them, and whatever remains to the closest male agnate of the deceased.

This is reported in several of the major Sunna compilations broadly accepted by Sunni jurists as canonical. As we shall see, it is categorically rejected among the Shi'a.

It might be noted that the Sunna accords well with Sunni juristic biases and predispositions. As the first chapter showed, Sunnism in many ways privileges the preservation of community authorities across the point of the Prophet Muhammad's revelation. Hence, for example, it is the tribal elites who ultimately settle on the identity of the rightly guided caliphs. The idea that the Qur'an was intended to usher in limited reforms to an otherwise satisfactory system supports this fundamentally conservative outlook.

In any event, once the Sunni assumptions are inserted, the gaps in the Qur'an prove relatively easy to fill. It is easiest to demonstrate this through an example. Imagine that a decedent leaves behind a daughter, a wife, and a father. Under the Qur'anic verses, the daughter receives one half of the estate, the wife receives 1/8 of the estate, and the father receives 1/6, as a Qur'anic heir, because the decedent left children. This leaves 5/24 of the estate. This would devolve to the father, as the closest male agnate, and he would receive this share in addition to his Qur'anic share.

If, on the other hand, the decedent had left a wife, a full sister, and a father, then the wife would inherit

1/4 and the sister would inherit 1/2, because the decedent had no children. The father would have no Qur'anic share, but he would be entitled to receive the balance of the estate of 1/4 as a male agnate.

These examples help to demonstrate the manner in which the Qu'ranic reforms were primarily intended to include women, who otherwise would not inherit at all. Hence, in pre-Islamic Arabia, the father would inherit the entire estate in both of the examples laid out above, while the Qur'an devolves more than half of the estate onto female relatives. The Sunni presumptions also help to explain why the presence of a full or paternal brother limit a mother's share to 1/6—the brothers are agnates and therefore have an interest in the residue after the mother receives her share.

There are additional complexities, described below, but one additional feature of the Sunni system is important to lay out preliminarily. This is the process of what is known as *ta`ṣīb*, or "agnatization." As alluded to above, the Qur'anic verses on their own cannot work if one imagines a son alongside a daughter because one verse indicates the son is entitled to twice the share of the daughter, and a separate one indicates that the daughter is entitled to one half of the estate. The resolution of this dilemma by medieval jurists was, unsurprisingly, to privilege men by reading the first of these commands to the derogation of the second. This is achieved through rendering the daughter into an agnate when the decedent has a son, such that the daughter no longer receives a Qur'anic share but rather half of the share of a son.

Again, a hypothetical might help to clarify. Imagine a decedent leaves behind a husband, a son and a daughter. The husband receives 1/4, given that the decedent had children. The daughter no longer receives a Qur'anic share. Instead, she is rendered into an agnate, alongside the son. They share the remaining 3/4 as agnates, in a 2:1 ratio. In this case, the daughter would receive 1/4 of the estate, and the son would receive 1/2.

A similar result would hold if the decedent had left no children, but instead a husband, a full brother and a full sister. In such a case, the husband would be entitled to 1/2 of the estate, because there are no children, and the brother and the sister would share the remaining half as agnates. This would leave 1/6 for the sister, and 1/3 for the brother.

While the above helps lay out the core features of the Sunni inheritance scheme, some questions obviously remain. Chief among them is how one is to determine who the nearest agnate is. Conversely, what is to be done when there are no agnates, and the Qur'anic fractional shares do not add to one? Finally, how should distributions occur when the sum total of the Qur'anic heir fractions exceed one? Each of these will be discussed in turn.

a. Determining the Nearest Male Agnate

The determination of the nearest male agnate is calculated on the basis of what is known as Jabari's rule, which is itself divided into three parts. The first part of the rule creates classes or relatives. Class I agnates are male descendants through the male line (sons, grandsons of sons, great grandsons of grandsons of sons, and so forth. Class II relatives are male ascendants of the decedent, again connected through the male line (i.e. fathers, paternal grandfathers, fathers of paternal grandfathers, and so forth). Class III are agnatic descendants of the decedent's father (meaning brothers and paternal half-brothers) and their descendants (i.e. nephews and grandnephews through the male line). Class IV are agnatic descendants of the decedent's grandfather (paternal uncles) and their descendants (cousins through the male line). In theory, the classes extend ad infinitum, such that Class V would be great uncles, first cousins once removed, second cousins, and so forth. At some point, of course, the relationship becomes exceedingly difficult to prove as a practical matter.

Each class excludes the former class. Hence, for example, if a decedent leaves behind only a son (or a grandson of a deceased son) and a father, then the son (or grandson) excludes the father as agnate. Similarly, the father excludes the full brother, the full brother excludes the paternal uncle, and so forth. This helps to explain why the Qur'anic verse 4:11 grants the father a Qur'anic share if there are children, but does not grant him one if there are no children. In the absence of children, the father serves as the nearest male agnate and will inherit in that capacity, and so her requires no Qur'anic share. If there is a son or a grandson of a predeceased son, however, the father is not the nearest male agnate and so will inherit only the Qur'anic share of 1/6, with the remaining 5/6 going to the son (or grandson) if there are no other Qur'anic heirs. (As noted above, if the decedent leaves a daughter and a father, then the father inherits in two capacities. He inherits 1/6 because the decedent left children—namely, a daughter—and he inherits the residue after the distribution of the daughter's share as the nearest male agnate.)

The second part of Jabari's rule relates to degree, where the nearer exclude the former. Hence, a son excludes a grandson, a grandson excludes a great grandson, a father excludes a grandfather, a grandfather excludes a great grandfather, and so forth. While this might seem rather arcane, in fact the consequences of this are rather significant in the modern world, in particular in the context of orphaned grandchildren. If a decedent leaves behind a son and a grandson who is the child of a different predeceased son, then, according to the principle of degree, the orphaned grandson is excluded from inheriting entirely. This conclusion does not seem to accord with the preexisting preferences of modern Muslims generally, who consider their orphaned grandchildren to be the most in need and therefore the individuals for whom they are most concerned with making provision.

Finally, the third part of Jabari's rule relates to the strength of the blood tie. This means that a brother excludes a paternal half-brother because the brother is the nearest kin. The basis of this is a Sunna that indicates that "kinsmen by the same father and mother shall inherit before kinsmen of the same father only." Note, however, that a full brother does not exclude a maternal half-brother under Jabari's rule. This is because, as outlined above, the maternal half-brother is deemed not an agnate subject to Jabari's rule, but a Qur'anic heir by virtue of Verse 4:12. He is therefore entitled to inherit 1/6 of the estate on this basis, before the agnatic distributions are made, so long as there are no children. While the result seems puzzling, it does not arise frequently. The only situations where it can be relevant are those where there are no sons or other agnatic descendants, no father or other agnatic ascendants, and yet there are full brothers, and maternal and paternal half-brothers. (For a rare and puzzling case along these lines, see the Case of the Donkey, described in further detail below)

A few examples might help to illustrate how the three principles described above apply in actual circumstances. In the interests of brevity and clarity, the Nutshell confines itself to three basic examples, and leaves those interested in more elaborate permutations to other source material, which discusses the matter of Sunni inheritance law in much more exhaustive detail.

Example 1: A decedent leaves behind a daughter, a full brother and a husband.

Spouses are usually the easiest to calculate first. The husband receives 1/4 of the estate, because the decedent had a child. (He would receive 1/2 in the absence of children). The daughter receives 1/2. The remaining 1/4 goes to the brother, as the nearest of the agnates.

Example 2: A decedent leaves behind two daughters, a grandson from a predeceased son, a father, and a wife.

The wife receives 1/8 of the estate, because the decedent had children (she would receive ¼ if the decedent had been childless). The daughter receives 2/3. The father receives 1/6, as a Qur'anic share because the decedent had children. This adds to 23/24, leaving 1/24 of the estate to the grandson of the son as the nearest agnate, because descendants (such as a grandson) are nearer in class than ascendants (such as a father). It is worth noting that this leaves the grandson in a considerably worse position than his father would have been had his father, the decedent's son, survived. This is because the son would have "agnatized" the two daughters, who would then no longer receive 2/3 of the estate, but instead be rendered into agnates alongside the son. Together, they would have shared in 17/24 of the estate, with the son receiving twice the amount of the daughters.

Example 3: A decedent leaves behind ten grandchildren of his full brother, five of whom are male and five of whom are female, and three cousins of his paternal uncle.

The ten grandchildren of the full brother are entitled to inherit the entire estate, because they are closer in class than the cousins. Class III are descendants of the decedent's father, which includes the decedent's full brother and any descendants of his. An uncle, and his children, the decedent's cousins, are not descendants of a decedent's father, but rather of a grandfather, which is class IV. The ten grandchildren of the brother divide the estate in a 2:1 ratio favoring the males, such that each of the male grandchildren receives 2/15 of the estate, and each of the females receives 1/15 of the estate.

The facts in the last example were taken from a 1976 adjudication in Denpasar, Indonesia, on the island of Bali.

b. Uterine Heirs

Relatives who are not Qur'anic heirs, and not agnates, are described in Arabic as *dhul-raḥm,* or "uterine heirs." The name arises because in most cases, it is the interpolation of a woman connecting the heir to the decedent that results in the classification of the heir as "uterine." Hence, for example, the son of a decedent's son is an agnate while the son of a decedent's daughter is a uterine heir. That said, a paternal aunt, related to the decedent through the decedent's father, is also a uterine heir. Also, technically speaking, a maternal brother is a uterine heir, because connected to the decedent through a common mother, and yet he can inherit as a Qur'anic heir.

For purposes of this Nutshell, it suffices to note that uterine heirs inherit with extreme infrequency. This is because they are lower in priority to any living agnates. The result in some cases seems rather jarring to modern expectations. A good example is provided in a 1955 case by an Islamic court in Tangerang, Indonesia, where a decedent's grandchildren through a predeceased daughter, the decedent's only child, were not permitted to inherit because they were uterine heirs. Receiving the estate instead, in its entirety, was the decedent's paternal uncle, who was a Class III agnate under Jabari's rule. *Estate of H. Sapinah,* Islamic Court for Tangerang, Indonesia, decided July 20, 1955.

2. ADJUSTING THE QUR'ANIC SHARES

The fact that Qur'anic shares are distributed first, and the residue is given to the agnates, can result in some rather unusual permutations. For example, consider a case where a decedent leaves behind a husband and two parents. Technically speaking, the husband should receive a Qur'anic share of 1/2, and the mother should receive 1/3, as there are no children. This leaves 1/6 for the father, as the closest agnate. This seems to contort the patriarchal logic of the system, given that it results in a mother receiving twice the portion of a father. While Shi'i jurists let this result stand as a necessary consequence of Qur'anic verse, the second Sunni caliph reversed the result, arguing that the mother is entitled to only 1/6, and the father 1/3, on the theory that the mother's portion in this circumstance (and no other) is calculated after distribution to the husband.

An even more interesting and more unusual permutation involved the famed "Case of the Donkey" wherein the decedent was survived by a husband, a mother, two full brothers and two maternal brothers. Under Qur'anic verse, the husband was entitled to 1/2 of the estate, and the mother 1/3. The two maternal brothers were entitled to a Qur'anic share of 1/6 under Verse 4:12. This exhausted the estate, and left the full brothers with nothing. Pressing their case to the second caliph, the full brothers argued, inter alia, that they should be entitled to share equally with the maternal brothers because they had the same maternal link. Had their father been a donkey, their argument went, they would have been so entitled, because they would then also be maternal half-brothers of the decedent. It made little sense, therefore, that they would not be entitled to inherit if their father was a man, and indeed the same man who fathered the decedent. The second caliph was persuaded by this curious reasoning and awarded them an equal share to that of their maternal brothers.

The Case of the Donkey raises for consideration a hypothetical circumstance that arises with more frequency, which is how to treat a situation where the Qur'anic shares *more than* exhaust the estate. An example would be a decedent who is survived by a husband (1/4), a mother (1/6) and two daughters (2/3). This adds to 13/12, or more than the value of the entire estate. In such an instance, under the rules of all four Sunni schools, the shares of each heir is proportionally reduced, so that each of them receives 12/13 of their Qur'anic share. It should be noted that such a circumstance never arises when there are sons. This is because the only Qur'anic heirs who may inherit in such a case are parents (or ascendants in their place), at a total amount of 1/3, and a husband, at 1/4 of the estate, for a total Qur'anic share distribution of 5/12. All siblings and further agnates are excluded by the presence of a son, and the daughters, who receive a considerable Qur'anic share when there are no sons, are "agnatized" when there are sons.

The other situation that can arise at times is one where the shares equal less than one, and there are no agnates or uterine heirs to whom to distribute the residue. Here, the Sunni schools differ in result. According to the Hanafi school, the Qur'anic shares are increased proportionately. Hence, for example, if a decedent leaves a daughter and a mother, their respective shares are 1/2 and 1/6. If there are no other relatives that can be located, then they share in the remaining 1/3 in a 3:1 ratio favoring the daughter. This is because the daughter's Qur'anic share is three times the size that of the mother's share.

In sharp contrast, the Maliki position is that the public treasury of the Islamic state is an heir as well (albeit one lower in priority than the agnates and uterine heirs), and therefore the Qur'anic shares are never increased. Rather, the residue escheats to the state. Adopting a middle position are the Shafi'is, who adopt the Hanafi rule but do not extend it to spouses. Hence, if there are no agnates or uterine heirs, but there are Qur'anic heirs other than a spouse whose portions add to less than one, then those heirs inherit the residue in the proportion of their Qur'anic shares, as with the Hanafis. This would apply, for example, in a case where a decedent left behind only a single daughter.

However, as the High Court of Singapore decided in 1960 in the case of *Re Mutchilim Alias Ashrhin,* 1 MLJ 25 [1960], if only a wife survives the decedent, then under Shafi`i rules, she receives no more than her Qur'anic 1/4 share, and the balance goes to the state. The Shi'a, for their part, adopt a variant of the Shafi'i rule whereby they prohibit a wife, but not a husband, from sharing in residue. All other Qur'anic heirs receive residue if there are no other heirs according to the Shi'a. Indeed, this right of residue, proves to be a key feature of Shi'i inheritance law, as shown below.

It is important to note that situations involving increasing Qur'anic shares or inheritance escheating to the state might be expected to be extremely rare. After all, if a relative of any sort, agnate or uterine heir, is present and able to demonstrate their relationship to the decedent, then the residue will flow to that person rather than to a Qur'anic heir or the state. In fact, however, the situation of a decedent with no heirs other than Qur'anic ones arises in the modern world with more frequency than might be expected. At times, this is because of emigration that has separated a decedent from more distant family members. At other times, it is because the decedent is a recent convert to Islam, and there is a prohibition against non-Muslims inheriting from Muslims. In such cases, there may well be no eligible heirs to whom to distribute residue other than close family members who are often Qur'anic heirs.

3. WILLS

A separate, important matter that deserves exposition is the extent to which a person is able to vary these inheritance rules through a will. In other words, are the inheritance portions divinely mandated and therefore not subject to alteration of any kind, or are they merely default rules that a person is able to adjust through some sort of declaration? With some limitations, Sunni jurists generally adopt the former approach, in reliance on two reports of the Prophet Muhammad. The first is from one of the Prophet's companions, Sa`ad bin Abi Waqqaṣ, and it reads as follows:

> I was stricken by an ailment that led me to the verge of death. The Prophet came to pay me a visit. I said, "O Allah's Messenger! I have much property and no heir except my (only) daughter. Shall I give two-thirds of my property in charity?" He said, "No." I said, "Half of it?" He said, "No." I said, "One-third of it?" He said "(You may do so) though one-third is also too much, for it is better for you to leave your offspring wealthy than to leave them poor, asking others for help. And whatever you spend (for Allah's sake) you will be rewarded for it, even for a morsel of food which you may put in the mouth of your wife...."

The second report of the Prophet is one where he is supposed to have stated that there may be no bequests to an heir.

Taken together, what these mean is that under the Sunni rules, a person may bequeath up to one third of the estate, but that the bequest cannot benefit someone who is already entitled to inherit by law. Hence, to draw on an earlier case example, if a decedent leaves behind a paternal uncle and grandchildren through a predeceased daughter, then the decedent could, while alive, have drafted a will to bequeath up to 1/3 of the estate to the grandchildren. This is because, as uterine heirs, they would not otherwise be entitled to inherit any of the estate. Similarly, a husband with a non-Muslim wife could leave her up to one third of his estate by bequest.

However, more controversially in modernity, among the Sunni schools, is that a husband with a Muslim wife and two children could not leave his wife with more than the 1/8 of the estate to which she would otherwise be entitled via bequest. Similarly, again to draw on an earlier example, if a decedent leaves behind two daughters, three grandsons from a predeceased son, a father, and a wife, then the decedent cannot leave his grandsons more than the 1/72 of the estate to which each is entitled. This is because they are each formally heirs, and an heir cannot have their share supplemented by bequest.

4. OTHER LIMITATIONS

Several other limitations as concerns Sunni inheritance should be described in brief. First, in keeping with the Islamic prohibition on adoption, inheritance does not run to adopted children. The adopted child inherits from, and is inherited by, their own blood relatives.

Second, the Sunni schools do not permit Muslims to inherit from, nor to have their estate inherited by, non-Muslims. This is particularly relevant in two contexts. The first concerns the estates of converts, who might have a sizable number of non-Muslim relatives. The second concerns non-Muslim wives.

Third, a nonmarital child has no inheritance rights as against the father, but the child has a potential claim as against the mother.

Fourth, Islamic law contains its own version of the common law's "slayer rule," which prohibits a person from inheriting from another whom they have killed. The schools differ as to the minimum *mens rea* necessary to disinherit the heir.

Fifth, and finally, a wife whose marriage is repudiated by her husband via *ṭalāq* (a process described in ample detail in Chapter Two) continues to enjoy inheritance rights under circumstances where that pronouncement took place on the deathbed. In other words, a husband cannot at the end of his life disinherit his wife by repudiating his marriage. The schools differed among themselves on precisely what constituted a deathbed sickness and how near death the husband must be before this rule applies.

Having summarized inheritance law among Sunni jurists, the Chapter turns next to the rules that prevail within Shi'ism, before describing how modern states apply and, in some cases vary, these rules.

C. SHI'I INHERITANCE

As noted earlier, the Shi'a begin with the same Qur'anic verses as the Sunnis do in determining the contours of Islamic inheritance law. This is unsurprising, given that both sects operate on the core theological presumption that the Qur'an is the received word of God from the angel Gabriel. The result of this is a convergence of rules that is not insignificant. The Qur'anic shares of daughters, parents, spouses, full sisters, and maternal siblings are precisely what they are in Sunnism, and require no repetition here.

Still, if these create important areas of convergence, there are also quite important differences. Where the Sunnis stress continuity with the past, and preservation of communal and tribal authorities and privileges, the Shi'a seek to extricate the pre-Islamic system from its roots. As with Sunnism, there are ostensibly exegetical bases for the distinctions, but there are also historical ones as well that deserve exploration.

As to the exegetical distinctions, the Sunnis credit a report of the Prophet Muhammad told by Ibn 'Abbas that the residue of an estate after distribution of the Qur'anic share goes to the nearest male agnate. The Shi'a dispute the validity of this report, largely on the basis of a second report from Qariyat ibn Madrab, who hails from the generation succeeding the Prophet Muhammad. According to the Shi'a, Qariyat indicated that he questioned Ibn 'Abbas about this very Prophetic tradition, and that ibn Abbas told him he never reported it. Later, Qariyat questioned the famed Ṭāwus ibn Kaysān, who reported near all of the Sunna originating from Ibn 'Abbas. Ṭāwus denied angrily that he had ever reported such a thing from Ibn 'Abbas, insisting instead that the devil had put it in the mouths of those saying it. The stridency of this denial is then reflected in the Shi'i tradition in the form of a report from the Infallible Sixth Imam, Ja`far al-Ṣādiq, the eponym of the Shi'i school of Islamic jurisprudence, who states that under Islamic law, to the agnates is left dust in the teeth.

This contempt for the agnatic system, and for the traditional centers of power within pre-Islamic Arabia, are of little surprise in the context of Shi'ism, given the historical assumptions that are core to the sect. It was, after all, communal authorities who betrayed the express will of the Prophet Muhammad himself respecting his chosen successor, the first Imam, Alī ibn Abi Ṭalib. Traditional authorities further denied Alī's wife and the Prophet's daughter Fāṭima her due inheritance, and killed Alī's son, who was also the Prophet Muhammad's grandson, at the fields of Karbala. The idea that these authorities, their hierarchies, or the remnants of their legal system, were to serve as a continuing source of God's law was, to the Shi'a, absurd on its face.

If the pre-Islamic system is to be discarded, this begs the question of precisely how the gaps inherent in the Qur'an's inheritance verses are to be filled. The answer to this is supplied in the next subsection.

1. THE INHERITANCE RIGHTS OF KIN

As explored above, Shi'ism is dramatically contemptuous of the prerogatives of the pre-Islamic Arab tribes and focused on the claims of the Prophet's family, including very much his daughter, on a variety of matters, very much including inheritance. It is therefore unsurprising that the sect ultimately credited a series of reports from the Prophet and the Imams that called for an inheritance system based on the notion of kinship, or degree of blood affiliation to the decedent, as opposed to agnatic link. A primary consequence of this is that the right to inheritance runs equally along male and female lines, meaning that the daughter of a daughter is as entitled to inheritance as the son of a son. In other words, the Sunni concept of the "uterine heir" who is distinct from an agnate in terms of category is obliterated in Shi'ism. As a second primary consequence, Shi'ism clearly privileges nearer relatives, such as a daughter, over more distant ones, such as a brother, by denying the latter inheritance upon the presence of the former.

On the other hand, Shi'ism engages in a process similar to that of Sunnism's agnatization, where a daughter is transformed from a Qur'anic heir into one who receives residue with the presence of a son, and a full or paternal sister is likewise transformed from Qur'anic heir into one who receives residue with the presence of a brother. In each case, as with Sunnism, the resulting similarly situated heirs inherit in a 2:1 ratio favoring the males. What this means is that while the son of a son and the daughter of a daughter, have an equal *right* to inherit, the *amount* they inherit varies significantly. The daughter of a daughter receives one half of one half (i.e., one quarter) of what a son of a son receives.

The result is a very different system conceptually, albeit one that in some common cases replicates the results of Sunnism closely. The concepts and results are laid out in further detail below.

2. CATEGORIES OF KIN AND CAUSE

As with Sunnism, the most obvious question that arises after a conceptual foundation for inheritance has been established (agnatic in the case of Sunnism, and kin-based in the case of Shi'ism), is how priority is to work within the system. As with Jabari's rule, the Shi'a have created an elaborate system of priority to determine who inherits an estate's residue after Qur'anic shares have been distributed. The actual system is quite different from that of Sunnism, however.

Specifically, the Shi'a establish three classes of priority. The first class consists of the parents, and the children and their descendants, however distant. The second class are the parents of parents, and their ascendants, as well as siblings, however far descending. Third are uncles and aunts, however far ascending, and their children, however far descending. Each class excludes the one beneath it.

The result of these rules is that the presence of a father, a son, a daughter, or a grandchild preclude a grandfather, a brother, or a nephew from inheriting.

Similarly, the presence of a grandfather, a brother, or a nephew preclude an uncle, an aunt, or a cousin from inheriting. The one exception is a mother, who is limited to one sixth of the estate if the decedent was childless and had brothers, but not otherwise. This means that it is conceivable that brothers will inherit if there are no Class I heirs except a mother. This is necessitated by virtue of Qur'an 4:11, quoted above, which indicates that a mother inherits only one sixth in the presence of brothers.

The result of the Shi'i rules is that Qur'anic heirs often receive more than their Qur'anic shares. Imagine, for example, a circumstance where a decedent was survived by a mother, a daughter, and a brother. In that circumstance, the brother, as a Class II heir, will not inherit. The mother will only inherit one sixth, because of the presence of the brother. The daughter will inherit her Qur'anic share of one half, and then, in addition, she will inherit the remaining 1/3 as residue given the absence of any other Class I heirs. This leaves her in a much better position than she would be under Sunni rules. By contrast, if the decedent was survived by a father, a daughter, and a brother, then under both Sunni and Shi'i rules, the brother is left with nothing—in Sunnism, because the father is the nearest agnate and in Shi'ism, because the brother is a Class II heir. However, in Sunnism, the father would receive the residue after the Qur'anic shares are distributed. In Shi'ism, the father and the daughter would share in the residue in proportion to their Qur'anic heirs, meaning the daughter receives three times the residue that the father does. The father is thus not at all privileged by virtue of his agnatic status. Indeed, his small Qur'anic share in relation to his daughter suggests he is at greater distance from the decedent and therefore entitled to considerably less residue than she is.

Beyond the daughter's inheritance portion, the examples above also reveal the oddity of the mother's inheritance rights under Shi'ism. If the decedent had no brother, then the mother would inherit 1/6 as Qur'anic share, but would be able to share in the residue alongside the daughter based on their respective Qur'anic proportions. It seems counterintuitive to deny the mother that same right to receive residue when there is no daughter but only a brother. Despite the seeming illogic, Shi'i jurists are reluctant to disregard clear Qur'anic verse limiting a mother to 1/6 when there are brothers and no children, and hence limit the mother's inheritance portion accordingly.

Separate from kin is a concept known as cause, which also gives rise to a right to inherit. With one major and one minor exception, cause is irrelevant in modern Shi'ism, for two reasons. First, it is usually the basis for inheritance only when there are no eligible kin. Second, it includes categories—such as the manumitter of a slave, or the guarantor of blood money—with little to no relevance in the modern world.

The major exception to the irrelevance of kin is the spousal share, which is distributed on the basis of cause in the proportions dictated in the Qur'an, before distribution to kin. This means that in effect, spouses inherit identical amounts among the Sunnis and Shi'a alike. However, because they inherit by cause, spouses never receive more than their Qur'anic share unless there are no kin who are eligible to inherit. Even then, the right to residue runs only to husbands, but not wives.

The other way in which cause may be relevant in the modern world is that when there are no heirs by kin or cause, or where a wife is the only heir, the residue reverts to the Infallible Imam. In modernity, with the Imam in hiding, this means it reverts to the jurist to whom the decedent pledged fealty, in a process described more thoroughly in the Introduction. This is a rare occurrence, but not altogether unheard of.

One final complexity deserves mention at this stage. This is that, as with Sunnism, within Shi'ism, nearer generations exclude further ones. Thus, within Class I, the presence of a child excludes the grandchild, and the presence of the grandchild excludes the great grandchild, and so forth. This creates the same problem of orphaned grandchildren as exists in Sunnism, though it manifests itself in slightly different ways. In particular, Sunnism only excludes orphaned grandchildren when there are predeceased *sons,* where Shi'ism excludes them whenever there are *children* of either sex. On the other hand, Shi'ism does not exclude grandchildren through daughters as uterine heirs, but places them at the same level of priority as grandchildren through sons.

To illustrate how these rather abstract concepts apply in practice, I provide specific examples below.

Example 1: A decedent leaves behind a daughter, a son, a wife, a father, and a brother.

The wife inherits 1/8 by cause. The father inherits 1/6 as Qur'anic heir, but receives no residue. The brother does not inherit because he is a Class II heir. The daughter and the son share in the residue in a 2:1 ratio because the daughter no longer has a right to a Qur'anic share once there is a son. This leaves 17/72 for the daughter, and 17/36 for the brother.

It might be noted that this result is the same as it would be in Sunnism. This is almost always the case in situations where there is a living son. The reason is that the son is both closest agnate, and closest kin. Hence, he converts the daughter into a closest kin alongside him, and he prevents any other Qur'anic heirs from inheriting beyond their Qur'anic shares.

The more interesting cases involve those where no son is left alive, as more fully explored below.

Example 2: A decedent is survived by a husband, a daughter, and a father.

The husband receives 1/4 by cause, his Qur'anic share, when there are children. The daughter receives 1/2 as Qur'anic share, and the father receives 1/6 by Qur'anic share. This leaves 1/12 of the estate. In Sunnism, this would go to the father as the nearest agnate. In Shi'ism, it is divided among the Class I heirs—the father and the daughter—in a 3:1

ratio favoring the daughter, because her Qur'anic share is three times that of her father.

Example 3: A decedent is survived by a daughter, a grandson from a predeceased son, and a mother.

The mother receives 1/6 of the estate. The daughter receives 1/2. The grandson is excluded from inheritance because further in relation to the decedent than the daughter. Therefore, the balance of the estate is shared between the mother and daughter in a 3:1 ratio favoring the daughter.

In this case, Shi'ism's rules prove more deleterious to the grandson than Sunnism would. In Sunnism, the grandson would have inherited the residue after distribution of the Qur'anic shares because he was the closest agnate to the decedent.

Example 4: A decedent is survived by a wife, and a daughter of a predeceased daughter, and a paternal uncle.

In this case, Shi'ism proves more helpful to the grandchild. This is because the granddaughter is Class I kin, running through the female line. Accordingly, she inherits 7/8 of the estate, after payment of the 1/8 to the wife by cause. She excludes the paternal uncle, who is Class III kin. In Sunnism, the granddaughter is a uterine heir and therefore entitled to nothing so long as there is an agnate. In this case, there is an agnate, a paternal uncle, and he excludes her.

The facts of this example were taken directly from a documentary division undertaken under the supervision of the Personal Status Court of Kadhmiyya, Iraq.

3. OTHER FEATURES OF SHI'ISM

As with Sunnism, Shi'i doctrine contains other rules pertaining to inheritance, though these do not differ quite as radically from those of the Sunnis. As with Sunnis, Shi'is do not permit one who intentionally kills a decedent to inherit from that decedent, nor do they permit inheritance on the basis of an adoptive link. In contrast to Sunnism, Shi'ism permits Muslims to inherit from non-Muslims. However, like Sunnism, it does not permit non-Muslims to inherit from Muslims. Nonmarital children have no claims against a father, but they do against a mother, as with Sunnism. A wife retains inheritance rights if the husband pronounces a divorce on his deathbed, again in a manner that is not dissimilar from the Sunni schools. These rules are only important at the margins, for the most part.

Two features of Shi'ism stand out and require more extensive exposition. The first involves the distribution of the estate when the Qur'anic shares exceed the sum of the estate. An example would be where the decedent is survived by two daughters (2/3), both parents (1/3 total), and a husband (1/4), for a total of 5/4. Within Sunnism, each person's share is proportionally reduced. Within Shi'ism, it is the daughters whose proportion is reduced exclusively, so that they receive 5/12 of the estate. The same would be true as concerns sisters, in situations where the decedent had no child.

The result is that daughters are treated precisely as sons would be treated in a like situation. That is, if the decedent was survived by two *sons*, both parents, and a husband, then the husband would receive his 1/4 share, and the parents would receive their 1/3 share, without reduction of any kind, for a total of 7/12. The sons would then receive the residue of 5/12, as the nearest agnates.

Finally, as concerns wills, and as shall prove relevant in the next section, Shi'ism *accepts* the principle that no more than 1/3 of an estate can be bequeathed, but *rejects* the Sunni position that no bequest can be made to an heir. Under Shi'ism, a person can bequeath to an heir, and holds that any reports from the Prophet to the contrary are unreliable or fabricated. This means that, for the most part, a person wishing to leave equal proportions of their estates to their children can do so under the Shi'i rules, merely by drawing up a will. For example, if a decedent is survived by a husband (1/4) and a son and a daughter, the son and the daughter would theoretically be entitled to 1/2 and 1/4 of the estate, respectively. However, under Shi'ism, the decedent could draw up a will and award one quarter of the estate to her daughter by bequest, and thereby equalize the portions received by the son and the daughter. Despite its permissibility, such a practice is comparatively rare.

D. MODERN STATE PRACTICES AND INNOVATIONS

1. GENERAL COURT PRACTICE

This chapter has not cited a great deal of case law, but instead focused extensively on the classical doctrine. This is because, in most cases, court decisions are a rather straightforward application of the classical rules. The process usually involves little more than a mechanical series of calculations often undertaken by a specialized unit working under court supervision. The court merely stamps its approval on whatever conclusions the unit makes, and the conclusions are rarely contested.

Classical juristic rules are therefore largely a description of modern court practice in most Muslim jurisdictions. This is subject to the important caveats set forth below, however.

First, there are often factual disputes that arise in connection with the division of the estate. These include disputes over the value of particular properties when a court seeks to actually distribute the estate, or claims from creditors over contested, preexisting debts, which would have to be deducted from the estate before distribution to heirs. (The most common of these is the wife's deferred dower, to the extent that the husband has not paid it.)

The more intriguing factual disputes that arise in connection with inheritance concern the marital status of the decedent. There are two common circumstances where this can be factually ambiguous. The first arises when a spouse—invariably a wife—claims an Islamically marriage that has not been registered with the state. The lack of registration might arise because the wife is underage, the marriage is secret and polygamous, deliberately being concealed from the first wife, the parties never bothered to register the marriage because they lived in a remote area far from a courthouse, or for a combination of these and other reasons. As the previous Chapter indicates, courts treat such marriages as valid and legal (albeit entered into in a manner that contravenes the law), but there is always a problem in proving their existence. This problem is particularly salient upon the death of the alleged husband. A decedent husband with an alleged secret, second wife, who appears to make a claim on the estate on behalf of herself and her children is almost surely going to meet resistance from the husband's acknowledged family. The acknowledge wife is very likely to deny that her husband ever entered into a second marriage.

The second circumstance where factual ambiguities arise over marital status is where it is not clear whether a husband has pronounced a valid *ṭalāq* ending his marriage to his wife, and, if he did, whether or not the *ṭalāq* was issued on his deathbed, thereby depriving him of the ability to disinherit his wife. Often, these issues are intertwined. For example, in the well known case of Pakistani Supreme Court Case of Nazar Muhammad v. Shahzada Begum (PLD 1974 SC 22), a wife argued that her husband, who had died on November 10,

1959, had pronounced *ṭalāq* against his other wife nine months earlier. To demonstrate this, she relied on a document dated November 6, 1959 which related these facts. The Court thus had to decide three separate things. The first is whether the husband had repudiated his marriage at all, the second was, if he had, when he had done so, and the third was whether or not such a repudiation was a deathbed divorce. The Court ultimately decided that the *ṭalāq* had taken place, but that it was not proven to have taken place until November 6, at which point the husband, gravely ill and only four days from death, was certainly on his deathbed. Hence, both wives and their children could inherit from the decedent. No doubt informing the court's decision was the fact that the putatively divorced wife had a child, who would have been deemed nonmarital if the first wife's claim of a much earlier *ṭalāq* had succeeded.

2. INNOVATIONS

Notwithstanding the frequent application of classical law in modern courts in the area of inheritance, there are important areas of divergence which deserve extrapolation. These generally arise for one basic and perhaps obvious reason—divisions of an estate that might have seemed sensible in 7th century Medina appear antiquated, or even offensive, in much of the Muslim world today. There would be very good reason to keep resources preserved within an agnatic structure in a system in which such agnatic bonds formed the basis of social organization. In such circumstances, a result such as a daughter receiving half of an estate, and a son of a paternal cousin receiving the other half, seems to strike an appropriate balance between rights of family and rights of tribe. For the same reasons, there is good reason that spouses receive comparatively little of an estate. After all, they have their own tribes to fall back upon for support in times of need.

Many people today do not know the sons of their paternal cousins particularly well, if at all, and they certainly would not regard them as being entitled to an equal inheritance portion to their daughters. Few people think of seeking support from a tribe if their spouse dies. As such, some of the rules from the classical Islamic system have come under strain, and courts and legislatures in modern Muslim states have tried to find ways to deal with them.

In so doing, however, they have come across notable obstacles. The most important of these is that some proposed reforms seem to run contrary to Qur'anic text in the area of inheritance more than in almost any other area of law. For example, the fact that the Qur'an gives males the portion of two females makes it difficult to achieve a more gender equitable result. Some reformists have tried to address this by taking the position that the Qur'an was establishing a minimum distribution to females rather than a maximum, and in a society where women were customarily entitled to nothing. These reform efforts, however, have not usually succeeded in the long term. Hence, for example, though Iraq attempted in its 1959 Personal Status Code to achieve gender parity in inheritance, it had to abandon the initiative four years later given intense clerical opposition. Tunisia, by far the most progressive of the Arab states, is considering such a change now, but it has yet to take place.

At the same time, while Qur'anic text is an obstacle, it would be a mistake to call it a categorical one. 'Abd al-Karīm Qāsim, the Iraqi strongman who was the architect of the 1959 Code, expressed some frustration at the fact that clerical opponents to the equal inheritance rules seemed rather selective on which of the Qur'an's verses were nonderogable. Specifically, he pointed out the following in a 1960 newspaper interview:

> But some of my brothers, the men of religion, have come to me in protest against sections of the Personal Status Code—those sections, in fact, which we regard as representing forward leaps in putting in order the rights of the Iraqi family.
>
> For example, take the matter of inheritance. Truly God, be He praised and exalted, has revealed in the clear teaching of the Qur'an on this subject the verse: "Allah instructs you concerning your children: for the male, what is equal to the share of two females." . . .
>
> Yet God has revealed in the clear teaching of the Qur'an, and on the subject of the imposition of the fixed punishments, the following verse regarding matter of theft and the punishment of thieves: "[As for] the thief, the male and the female, amputate their hands in recompense for what they committed."

There is also another verse regarding another prescribed punishment: "The woman or man found guilty of illicit sexual intercourse—lash each one of them with a hundred lashes, and do not be taken by pity for them in the religion of Allah."

There is also a third verse in regard to wine: "O you who have believed, do not approach prayer while you are intoxicated."

Then there was a further development in this matter and the following verse appeared: "O you who have believed, indeed, intoxicants, gambling, [sacrificing on] stone altars [to other than Allah], and divining arrows are but defilement from the work of Satan, so avoid it that you may be successful." . . .

In so far as the salaries of civil servants are concerned, and our own salaries and even yours, you men of religion, both before and after the Revolution, these are derived from the proceeds of taxation, including the duty on wines. But has one of you refused to receive his salary?

There are, moreover, the fixed punishments prescribed for the thief and the fornicator, which have come in the form of commands such as 'Beat them' or 'Cut off their hands.' Yet has this fixed punishment been imposed on a single thief?

Qāsim's references are tendentious—the strict punishments to which he refers were understood by the classical jurists themselves to only apply in very rare circumstances, with impossibly high proof burdens. Nevertheless, the point is not inapt. A Penal Code such as Iraq's that does not even contemplate the possibility of lashing the unmarried for fornication under any circumstances, and indeed does not even criminalize it, seems as obvious derogation from Qur'anic text as gender equal inheritance rules would be.

Qur'anic text on its own, then, only goes so far by way of explanation. The rest requires consideration of sociological and historical circumstance. The Qur'an's scriptural punishments have not been applied at all by the modern Iraqi state, and have never been a feature of its postcolonial legal architecture. The same is true of most postcolonial Muslim states. By contrast, the classical inheritance rules remained the applicable rules of determination through colonialism, and that continuity undoubtedly created legitimacies of its own. When a society has derogated from Qur'anic text for long enough, the derogation begins to appear more natural than where Qur'anic text has continued to be the rule of decision across generations.

Nevertheless, there are significant enough differences between modern sociological realities (and consequent Muslim expectations) on the one hand, and the classical corpus on the other, to put pressure on some of the inheritance rules in contexts where the Qur'an is not so clear, and pressures are comparatively stronger. Those areas where there has been the most ferment are set forth below.

a. Inheritance of Daughters or Sisters

Perhaps the rule that has proven the most challenging to modern Muslim families is the one that seems to privilege distant male agnates at the expense of close family members. As noted at the start of this section, the idea of a paternal cousin receiving the same share of an estate as a daughter is not one with which many modern Muslims are comfortable. Similarly, many childless decedents are not comfortable with the idea of sisters sharing an inheritance portion with paternal cousins.

One immediate solution that potentially presents itself, explored in Chapter One in the context of marital dissolution initiated by wives, is the use of *talfīq,* or patching together rules from different Islamic schools of thought. With the death of the Sunni schools, modern states have been for the most part more willing to adopt the rules of any of the Sunni schools where it is convenient to do so, on the theory that each of them is equally legitimate and authoritative. The problem that arises in this particular context, however, is that none of the *Sunni* schools privilege the daughter or sister over the distant agnate. Rather, this is a purely Shi'i rule, undertaken on the uniquely Shi'i theory that nearer kin exclude more distant ones from inheriting.

In some states, such as Iraq, this presents no problem. Given its sizable populations of both Sunnis and Shi'a, Iraq's Personal Status Code is built on a practice of *talfīq* that encompasses the Shi'a as well as the four Sunni schools. Hence, sisters block off more distant agnates in Article 89(4) of Iraq's Personal Status Code.

More interesting is Article 91(2), added as an amendment to the Code in 1978. It reads as follows:

> The daughter or daughters in the absence of a son receive what remains of the estate after the two parents and the spouse receive their obligatory shares from it, and they receive all of the estate if none of these are present.

While this has some resemblance of the Shi'i rule, it is different in important ways. For the Shi'a, the daughter is a Class I heir and thus blocks off from inheritance any Class II heir, precisely as a sister, a Class II heir, does for the more distant heirs in Class III. However, a daughter is not somehow privileged as a Class I heir over other heirs in that class. Rather, she shares any residue alongside other Class I heirs, and most notably the parents of the decedent. Treating her as a son is treated, in the manner that Article 91(2) provides, privileges her over those heirs. That said, the distance of Article 91(2) from the Shi'i rule is not obvious to one unfamiliar with Islamic law, and explaining the disparity requires nuance. Accordingly, the provision on its own has received little notice or objection.

Outside of Iraq, and in particular in Sunni dominated countries, the adoption of the Shi'i rule is more problematic, given the significant theological divisions between the sects, and the rising sectarian tensions across the Muslim world. Hence, most Sunni states continue to privilege the agnate, despite at least some dissatisfaction voiced from time to time. As an exception to this trend, Indonesian courts have permitted the daughter to block off brothers and more distant agnates. Importantly, however, in so doing, they have not used Shi'ism as justification. Instead, they rely on their own interpretation of the Compilation of Islamic Law, a manual of Islamic law prepared by the Indonesian government in 1991 and distributed to the courts without legislative enactment. That Indonesian courts would feel more comfortable basing their reasoning on an unenacted compilation than Shi'i juristic rules is telling of the extent of the reluctance of the sects to borrow from each other in most nations of the Muslim world.

b. Inheritance Portion of the Wife

There is comparatively little controversy respecting inheritance portions of wives, which strikes some novice readers of Islamic law as odd. The idea of a wife receiving only one eighth of an estate is below expectations in vast portions of the Western world. It certainly creates the most obvious conflict with American law, where a spouse's "forced" share—that which the spouse is entitled to demand by law—exceeds 1/8 in almost all states in all circumstances. There are probably two mitigating factors to consider in this context, however, that diminish the importance of the issue in much of the Muslim world.

The first is the fact that women can, and frequently do, demand very high delayed dowers from their husbands at the time of marriage, as explained in

Chapter One. That delayed dower is primarily intended as a form of divorce insurance, as it is due in full if a husband exercises his right to repudiate the marriage. It is also due at the time of death if there has been no divorce. Because the delayed dower operates as a debt in the custody of the husband, it must be paid *before* inheritance portions are distributed. It is therefore possible for many wives to make adequate provision for themselves via these means rather than rely on an inheritance share.

Secondly, even if agnatic structures are no longer common in much of the Muslim world, tightly knit nuclear families tend to be the norm. Therefore, a widow with several sons might not object to inheritance portions running to those children, in light of broad and deep social expectations that the sons will then take care of their mother. Obviously such a practice is not universal, nor as broad in some states as it might be in others. Overall, however, it seems to mitigate any pressure toward recognition of larger spousal shares.

Further easing pressure on spouses is the fact that all of the schools of Islamic law recognize that adult children have the obligation to support their parents in times of need, and this principle has made its way into legislation in a fair number of Islamic states. Indeed, it has even been expanded in some cases to include stepchildren. Article 201 of the Kuwaiti Personal Status Law, No. 51 of 1984, as amended, provides a common formulation, as follows:

> If the ascendant is poor, whether a father or a mother, or a grandfather or a grandmother, from

the side of the father or the mother, and they have a child with means, male or female, [the latter] have the obligation of support. This includes food, drink, clothing, housing, medical treatment, domestic help if they need it, such as if the ascendant is sick, elderly, or something similar. Likewise support of the wife of the father who is not the mother [is an obligation on the children of the father], if she needs it. . . .

There are other ways that states work to increase the amount to which a wife is entitled to inherit. One relates to the assignation of property ownership at the time of the death of the husband. As Chapter One explained, Islamic law traditionally has no conception of joint marital property, as all property is owned by one spouse or the other. As such, a question could arise at death as to whether or not a particular household item was "owned" by the husband or the wife. In adjudicating such matters, Arab courts adopt patently patriarchal norms to assign those household items they deem to be for women's use to the wife, and those for men's use to the husband, irrespective of who happened to pay for them. A lawn mower, for example, is ordinarily deemed to belong to a husband, and a vanity to a wife. If the wife bought the lawnmower, or the husband the vanity, the presumption tends to be, absent overwhelming evidence to the contrary, that the purchase was a gift for the other spouse. On the basis of such gender driven distinctions and stereotypes, courts across the Arab world are able to ascribe property ownership to large numbers of household items.

Still, this leaves a fair number of items that might easily be ascribed to either party, where the question of who paid for the item, and for whose use it was, can be litigated. In such litigations, the courts tend to favor the wife, arguing, to take one example in a Jordanian court, that a high definition television belonged to her rather than her husband even where the husband paid for it because he purchased it at her request, and she watched much more television than her husband.

c. The Orphaned Grandchild

One of the most common legislative interventions into Islamic inheritance law in Muslim states involves the treatment of orphaned grandchildren. The reasons should probably be obvious. There is no better metaphor for the manner in which assumptions respecting agnatic connections seem ill fitted for a modern world than the classical rule excluding grandchildren from inheriting when there are living sons. Indeed, a grandparent in the modern world may be far more attentive to the needs of a grandchild whose parent predeceased the child than to direct children, who might already have means to support themselves.

Making matters worse is that not all schools of Islamic law obligate an uncle to support a nephew, nor is modern state legislation uniform on such a matter. For example, Article 200 of the Kuwaiti Personal Status Code adopts the Shafi`i position that only direct ascendants or descendants of a person are entitled to inherit from that person. This potentially leaves an orphaned grandchild in a rather perilous legal position.

Those Islamic states that have considered the disinheritance of orphaned grandchildren a significant enough problem to require redress have taken one of two approaches. The first, and the more controversial, is represented by Article 4 of Pakistan's Muslim Family Law Ordinance, which simply permits the children of a son or daughter to receive precisely the sum to which the son or daughter would be entitled if they had been alive. This is, in other words, an unambiguous *rejection* of Jabari's rule, set forth above, that those nearer to the decedent exclude those further away. That this reinterpretation does not contravene any clear Qur'anic verse renders it more politically palatable. Despite this, most states have shied away from this approach because of its rather open use of *'ijtihād* to reinterpret the received rules of the Sunni schools.

The other, more common approach is to establish what is referred to rather oxymoronically as an "obligatory bequest." The basis for this approach is the fact that the orphaned grandchild is not an heir entitled to inherit by law, and therefore may be the beneficiary of a will. Indeed, a grandparent with foresight might very well draft a will specifically to bequeath property to a grandchild. Where this is not done (which is frequent enough in most Islamic states), the laws of some Islamic states impose on a decedent a mandatory bequest pursuant to which the decedent grants to the orphaned grandchild the share to which the child's predeceased parent was entitled. This is not permitted to exceed one third of the estate, which is the maximum permitted to be willed under Islamic law. In some cases, such as Article 74 of Iraq's Personal Status Code and Article 76 of Law 71 of 1946 in Egypt, the right runs to a grandchild of a predeceased son or daughter. Some states, however, the right only extends to children of predeceased sons. The Selangor Wills Act, effective in Selangor, Malaysia, adopts this approach, seemingly under the theory that the daughter of a daughter is a uterine heir who would rarely inherit under any circumstances. The conclusion is curious, given that the point of the bequest is to put the grandchild in the position of her deceased parent, making the grandchild's status as agnate or uterine heir rather irrelevant.

The justification for the obligatory bequest is quite often Qur'an 2:176–80, which specifically refers to making bequests to kin as death draws near. There is some irony to this, because classical scholars regarded those verses as abrogated by the later inheritance verses that set forth the specific inheritance portions. While they rarely claim it, those lawmakers who invoke these verses are in fact practicing a form of *ijtihād* to reach this conclusion. After all, they are making use of Qur'anic verses deemed abrogated by the Sunni schools in order to impose a rather conceptually awkward legal fiction of a bequest that is obligatory. One wonders why they would not have instead simply invoked *ijtihād* to set aside Jabari's rule in this context, precisely as Pakistan's Muslim Family Law Ordinance does. That they were unwilling to reinterpret sacred verse away from the traditional rules in such an open and direct fashion, but instead preferred a more circuitous and logically tortured process to reach the same result, demonstrates the hold that the rules of the medieval jurists continue to have on the modern Muslim imagination, even on subjects on which the Qur'an is silent, to the frustration of countless reformers and progressives.

It might be noted that once deployed in the context of orphaned grandchildren, the concept of the obligatory bequest became rather easy to extend to others as well. Indonesia, for example, routinely extends inheritance rights via obligatory bequest to both non-Muslim children as well as adopted children of Muslim parents.

d. Wills

One final reform deserves brief mention, and this concerns the power of a decedent to bequeath part of an estate to those who are already heirs. As noted earlier, Shi'ism permits this, while Sunnism traditionally does not. As such, just as Iraqi lawmakers could adopt a Shi'i rule favoring daughters over more distant agnates, so they could adopt a Shi'i rule that permits bequests to any person, including heirs. Iraq did so in Article 1108 of its Civil Code.

Again, a similar approach is more difficult to apply in the Sunni states which do not recognize the legitimacy of Shi'ism. Nevertheless, Sunni dominated Egypt actually adopted the Shi'i rule to permit bequests to heirs in Article 37 of its Law on

Bequests, Number 71 of 1946. The fact that Qur'an 2:176 recommends bequests to near relatives may have offered lawmakers some much needed cover in order to justify their adoption of what is in actuality a Shi'i rule. The law was nonetheless challenged as un-Islamic and therefore unconstitutional, but the challenge failed. This is largely because of an arcane interpretation of the Egyptian Supreme Constitutional Court rendering all legislation enacted prior to 1980 immune from Islamic review. That interpretation is discussed in more detail in Chapter 7.

CHAPTER 4
THE *WAQF*

One final area of Islamic law containing elements of continuity from the classical era deserves exploration in this Nutshell, even if the extent of continuity is less pronounced than in the areas already explored. This is the law that pertains to the Islamic endowment known as the *waqf*.

It is difficult to gainsay the importance of the *waqf* in premodern Islamic societies. A great number of the major public service projects in the premodern period—including mosques, town squares, libraries, seminaries, cemeteries, hospitals, and bridges—were themselves *waqfs*, financed by *waqfs*, or both. During the Ottoman Empire, when the establishment of *waqfs* developed into a form of state policy, nearly one third of land was dedicated in *waqf*. There has been a tremendous decline in the prominence of the institution since that time, so much so that in a large number of Muslim countries, the administration of *waqfs* has been absorbed into the state bureaucracy, and their revenues have effectively become an ancillary part of the state budget. Still, in enough states, there are a sufficient numbers of properties that remain in *waqf*, and that are administered as traditional *waqfs* have long been administered, that the subject deserves discussion. It is, in the end, a legal field that has in some important if qualified way survived the colonial rupture.

The first part of this chapter will describe the rules of *waqf*, the second will explain the causes of its substantial decline, and the third will set forth those areas where the *waqf* remains most relevant in modern Muslim states.

A. THE CLASSICAL *WAQF*

Interestingly, *waqf* doctrine is nearly the polar opposite of inheritance law in terms of the extent of its reliance on revelatory source material. Where much of inheritance law comes directly from Qur'anic verse, the term "*waqf*" does not even appear in the Qur'an. Even the Sunna that relate to the subject provide only the very basic contours of what would evolve to be a very elaborate set of rules concerning charitable endowments. Hence, the most common (though by no means only) Prophetic report cited in Sunni accounts concerns the grant of a valuable piece of land to the second caliph 'Umar. 'Umar informed the Prophet Muhammad that he valued the property more than anything else and asked what he should do with it. The Prophet replied that he should "imprison the original property, and donate its fruits." Even this report does not use the term *waqf*, though at the very least it sets forth in very broad terms what the concept the *waqf* is. Much of the rest the jurists simply filled in through their own efforts, and connected back to plentiful and highly generalized source material in Qur'an and Sunna recommending charitable acts.

As the Prophetic report suggests, in a *waqf*, a grantor dedicates property by figuratively "imprisoning" it and appointing a trustee to administer it. The trustee then directs whatever proceeds it generates—the "fruits" of the *waqf*—to serve beneficiaries for some religious purpose. Those familiar with the common law trust will note its rather obvious similarities to *waqf*. This may not be incidental. Indeed, some noted scholars, including the late George Makdisi, have suggested that the origins of the common law trust may well lie in Islamic law.

That said, certain features of the *waqf* diverge in important ways from the law that pertains to trusts, at least as trusts operate in the modern world. Most importantly, rather than being subject to a rule *against* perpetuities, the *waqf* is itself perpetual. There are very limited exceptions to this, and even they apply only within some schools. Some jurists within the Maliki school as well as the Shi'a permit a *waqf* to expire if the beneficiaries no longer exist—for example, if the *waqf* was dedicated to a grantor's descendants, and the grantor's descendants all died without issue. The Hanafis do not even permit *waqfs* to end under such circumstances. Rather, they required as a condition of the validity of the *waqf* that there be designated a final, permanent beneficiary to the *waqf*, such as a mosque, if the originally intended beneficiaries are no longer in existence. This is because to the Hanafis, property "imprisoned" and dedicated to God could not possibly be returned to the ownership of a person.

Across schools and sects, a *waqf* is not only perpetual, but it is also irrevocable. The logic underlying irrevocability is the same as that which relates to perpetuity; namely, that the property has been dedicated to God, and cannot therefore be returned to the ownership of a person.

Jurists created ancillary rules to support these principles of perpetuity and irrevocability. The first of them relates to the potential of leasing the property under *waqf*. If the *waqf* is supposed to last forever because the property is "imprisoned", then the classical juristic concern with a lease of the *waqf* is that if the term runs too long, the *waqf* nature of the property might be forgotten. This classical era problem arises largely because classical jurists privileged personal testimony to prove that transactions such as contracts and *waqfs* had been concluded. With a longer lease, witnesses to the original *waqf* creation might die before it expires, thereby making it impossible to demonstrate that the property was endowed in the first place.

Given these issues, leases of property under *waqf* were not supposed to be for longer than one year. This hardly seemed feasible in many cases, however, as few lessees would be interested in investing much in property if their interest in it lasted for such a short time. Accordingly, the limitation was frequently avoided through the legal strategem of the *ḥikr,* where the property itself was not leased, but rather structures on it were. Thus, the land constituting a date farm that had been dedicated in *waqf* could not be leased for longer than a year. However, all of the trees on that land or subsequently to be planted on it could be leased for any length of time, or in perpetuity.

A separate question attends to the possibility of what is known as an "exchange" of *waqf* property. If, that is, the *waqf* is perpetual, is it possible to trade one piece of property for another under circumstances where the purpose of the *waqf* can no longer be served by the original property? An example might be a particular piece of property dedicated in *waqf* to be a library, in a location near where no person lives anymore. There might well be an advantage to selling the land to someone who might use it, and using the proceeds to buy another piece of land closer to a town, where another library can be built to whatever specifications the grantor had originally set. Rules differed among the schools, but in general jurists allowed this for properties other than mosques, which could never be exchanged. However, the jurists required that the trustee demonstrate to a court that certain stringent conditions had been met before an exchange could take place. These include that the property being exchanged be incapable of generating any revenue, and that the exchanged property resemble the original as closely as possible. There is evidence that at least at some points in the classical era, judges were more permissive in practice than the rules suggested they were supposed to be.

One final complication that arose as a result of the condition of perpetuity was reflected in debates about whether or not property other than land could be dedicated in *waqf*. The Hanbalis and Shafi'is regarded all moveable property as impermanent therefore not subject to *waqf*. The Malikis, the Hanafis, and the Shi'a took the more liberal position that any property could be dedicated in *waqf* so long as custom permitted it. However, this was explicitly subject to the principle that the property endowed would be of the sort that would be expected to last forever. A herd of male camels would be an example of something that could not be subject to *waqf*, as opposed to a herd of female camels. The theory is that the inability of males to reproduce necessitates the end of the male herd within a time certain, rendering it ineligible for *waqf*.

Another, more interesting example of an impermanent *waqf* that was deemed *per se* void across all of the schools for a period of centuries was the cash *waqf*. There is some nuance required to understand its deemed impermanence in the minds of the jurists, even those given to permitting *waqf* over property other than land. After all, it could be argued that if a *waqf* consisted purely of gold coins, then in theory it could last forever because the coins could be used to provide interest free loans to needy Muslims. These types of loans are known in Islamic parlance as *qarḍ ḥasan*. The Qur'an and Sunna describe them as a quintessential form of laudable charitable giving. The problem, however, was that jurists recognized that gold coins, unlike a herd of female camels, would decrease in value over time with inflation and currency devaluations. Also unlike female camels, which only require male camels to increase their number, there is no obvious way to increase the amount of the capital in the *waqf* without either (i) lending out some of the coins at interest, which is prohibited for the reasons explored in the next chapter, or (ii) investing it, which carries with it a risk of loss.

Accordingly, none of the schools permitted the cash *waqf*. However, as an excellent example of how *taqlīd*, or putative "imitation" of earlier juristic authorities, was used and manipulated by later jurists in flexible and creative ways, this Hanafi rule changed in the Ottoman era. At that time, later Hanafi jurists writing on the cash *waqf* were aware of its vast economic potential and therefore revisited the texts of the early Hanafis to find ways to explore its permissibility. When doing so, these later jurists referenced the first part of the rule of their juristic school as pronounced by the early jurists—that anything that was endowable in *waqf* by custom could be endowed—and simply omitted all mention of the second, namely, that the first rule was subject to the property being permanent, and cash was not permanent. Through such selective quotation, they took the position that Abu Hanifa permitted the cash *waqf*. Consequently, the practice of creating such *waqfs* proliferated throughout the mid to late Ottoman era.

Aside from rules that related in one way or another to the permanence and irrevocability of the *waqf*, a separate set of questions involved who could administer the *waqf*. The grantor was generally permitted to act as the *waqf's* trustee, and distribute its revenue to the beneficiaries according to the terms of the *waqf*. The grantor could also name a different person to be a trustee, or designate who should administer the *waqf* after the grantor's death. For example, the grantor could create a *waqf* whose revenue was dedicated to the Shi'i seminaries in Najaf, Iraq, and render herself the trustee, and then her eldest child as trustee after her, and then the eldest child of the next generation after that, and so forth, in theory into perpetuity.

Jurists presumed that trustees given the authority to distribute potentially vast amounts of revenue held in *waqf* would be subject to the supervision of judges, and for most of Islamic history, they were. In later classical times, this supervisory function was assumed by more specialized state bureaucracies. This trend continued into modernity, where most states that continue to have *waqfs* have a ministry that exercises supervisory authority. Generally speaking, these state officials approve the exchange of *waqf* properties, or any major improvements to it. They also appoint trustees to administer the *waqf* if the grantor has not done so, or if the grantor's appointment can no longer be followed—for example, if the grantor had designated his issue to serve as trustee, and all of his children had died without issue. Their primary supervisory task, however, is to ensure that the trustee was actually using the property to maximize its benefit for the beneficiaries and was not abusing it for purposes of self-enrichment.

As for the beneficiaries of the *waqf,* the grantor was largely free to designate them in any manner the grantor wished. In some cases, such as a mosque in the middle of a town center, the beneficiaries were obviously the general public. In other cases, specification might be necessary. If the proceeds of a date farm were to be sold and the revenues distributed to those who wished to perform the pilgrimage to Mecca, then a question could well arise as to whom among the Muslims had first right to these funds. The grantor would very commonly in such circumstances identify the intended beneficiaries, such as those in a nearby town. Other common beneficiaries of *waqfs* that generated revenue included seminaries, libraries, and, of course, the poor.

Given the above, the use of the *waqf* as state policy in the Ottoman era to provide public services seems quite natural. The state itself could not dedicate property in *waqf*, because only individuals were permitted to do so. However, high Ottoman officials could be encouraged to dedicate properties. These sorts of charitable endowments, and the public services brought about thereby, could engender goodwill on the part of local populations, and in particular populations living far from the Ottoman capital of Istanbul.

Finally, no discussion on *waqf* is complete without mention of the controversial issue of the family *waqf*. Though its permissibility was debated early in Islamic history, and indeed became a matter of dispute between two of Abu Hanifa's closest disciples, ultimately classical jurists across the schools settled on the view, well supported within the Sunna and the Qur'an, that to provide for one's relatives was a charitable act and that therefore dedicating property to that purpose was permissible. Accordingly, dedicating the proceeds of a date farm to one's issue was a form of *waqf* that was not only acceptable, but in fact common.

The next subsection will show some of the problems associated with "imprisoning" vast amounts of agricultural land for family, in particular in societies where there was a maldistribution of such lands to begin with. For now, it suffices to note that in the context of the family *waqf*, the relative flexibility of the *waqf's* rules respecting beneficiary designation do not harmonize well with the rigidity of classical Islam's inheritance scheme, the subject of the previous chapter. That is, the rules of the *waqf* permit the grantor to direct the distribution of proceeds from properties under *waqf* to whatever charitable purpose the grantor prefers, and in whatever proportion. This includes family members in the case of a family *waqf*. Inheritance law does not permit the favoring of one set of relatives over another in such a manner.

An example might better illustrate the problem. Suppose a wealthy grantor near the end of his life were to dedicate in *waqf* the vast majority of his landholdings in *waqf*, with the beneficiaries of the *waqf* being his sons and his male agnatic descendants. Obviously, in so doing, the grantor has almost entirely disinherited his wife and daughters, in a manner that runs directly contrary to Qur'anic verse mandating to them inheritance shares.

Though aware of this, with limited exception jurists seemed relatively untroubled by it, with the important caveat that the *waqf* had to be created during the lifetime of the grantor. If it was created via bequest at death, then, like all bequests, it would be limited to 1/3 of the grantor's estate. Moreover, if a bequest, the *waqf* proceeds could not go to heirs in the case of Sunni *waqfs* because of the prohibition of bequests to heirs.

Obviously this creates some limitation, because it means a grantor wishing to avoid inheritance rules requiring distributions to females will have to tie up his properties in *waqf* while healthy, and thereby lose the ability to sell, mortgage, or otherwise alienate such properties. For the Shi'a and the Malikis, the fact that the grantor could not be a beneficiary in the *waqf* created establishes another important limitation, at least for grantors of more limited means who might well need to live on the property they own. Nevertheless, these are not insurmountable problems for many grantors and, accordingly, it was possible to use the *waqf* to avoid the inheritance rules in many instances. This problem was not limited to antiquity but has proven acute enough to result in legislation to address it in some modern states, in particular as concerns the deployment of the *waqf* to disinherit daughters.

B. THE DECLINE OF THE *WAQF*

As might be clear from the previous subsection, even in classical times, control over the *waqf* was shared between jurist and state. Classical era executive authorities were obviously deeply invested in how vast tracts of lands within their dominion were being used, and given that they had supervisory power over trustees, their role was not insignificant. Similarly, jurists took a very pronounced interest in the *waqf,* because they were not only the rulemakers in the field, as they were in every field of Islamic law, but they were also beneficiaries of the *waqfs*. Major and minor seminaries of all sorts were funded through *waqfs* established by the wealthy.

As a result, within the classical era, these two considerable institutional forces achieved a sort of balance that led to the broad use of the *waqf* as a primary means to distribute public services, in a manner that genuinely seemed to facilitate both urban development and economic growth. As the classical period came to a close, however, and as the power of the state began to rise and the juristic academies began to lose considerable power (as described in the Introduction), it was perhaps inevitable that the *waqf* would not be able to withstand modernity in the same form as it always had. The jurists were no longer in a position to offer a form of counterbalance to the state.

In addition, by the nineteenth century, the *waqf* was no longer viewed as an economically dynamic instrument that helped provide public service. Rather, it had devolved into a rigid and inefficient one, which tied up lands to serve purposes that were largely obsolete. As such, many lands under *waqf* lay fallow or unused almost in their entirety, and others seemed dramatically misused.

In response to all of this, as early as the middle of the nineteenth century, efforts began in earnest to challenge classical *waqf* doctrine. Most notably, the reformist Muhammad Ali Pasha in Egypt initiated efforts at that time to abolish the *waqf*. He proved more successful than might have seemed possible given the deep roots of the institution. He was able to prevent grantors from establishing *waqfs* on land that was not actually owned outright by the grantor, but rather the state, over which the grantor merely had a right of usufruct. Much land in the Middle East falls into this category. He proved less able to limit *waqfs* dedicated on land owned by the grantor, despite many efforts, given their broad juristic support. As such, they continued to proliferate.

By the end of the nineteenth century, efforts to curtail *waqfs* began with renewed vigor and more success. Falling under particular scrutiny were the family *waqfs*, for several reasons. First, they tied up substantial amounts of agricultural land for the supposedly "charitable" purpose of providing for wealthy and landed families. This hardly seemed to accord with modern understandings of charity, and indeed seemed to be a perversion of what early Muslim jurists must have intended. Making matters worse was the fact that grantors were often corrupt, burdening *waqf* land with secured debt, and then seeking to escape from that debt by claiming the land had already been dedicated to God.

By way of example, in a late nineteenth century case arising out of India, a grantor dedicated land in *waqf*, named himself both trustee and beneficiary, designated his sons as beneficiaries after him, and then undertook to mortgage, alienate, or otherwise burden some of the properties soon after he had made the endowment. The sons brought a claim to remove the encumbrances on the title under the theory that they were not permissible when the property was dedicated in *waqf*. The Calcutta High Court rejected the claim and denied the validity of the original *waqf* because the grantor had never intended to actually dedicate a *waqf*. Instead, the Court found the entire affair to be an illegal stratagem by the family wherein the father would borrow money he never intended to repay by using the land as security, and then have his sons sue to eliminate that security on the grounds that the land was already dedicated to God. In justifying the conclusion, the Court made the following remarks:

> We cannot believe that the authors of Mahomedan law intended that, under cover of a pretended dedication to Almighty God, owners of property should be enabled to secure it for their own use, protect it for ever from their own and their descendants' creditors, and repudiate alienations in respect of which they have received full consideration. Abul Fata Mahomed Ishak And Ors. v. Rasamaya Dhur Chowdhuri And Ors., (1891) 18 Cal. 399 (India).

With examples, like this, it is not difficult to see why the *waqf* became associated with corruption rather than beneficence. Similar sentiments respecting family *waqfs* could be found across much of the Islamic world in court opinions, legislative records, and even bar association debates.

Abul Fata involved a *waqf* created to evade creditors. A separate problem that arose was that much land dedicated as family *waqf* was not in productive use. The reason was that with each passing generation, the number of beneficiaries proliferated, as a result of which each person's respective share of the revenue decreased. Given sufficient time, the expected return of any given beneficiary is reduced to such a paltry sum that no beneficiary has very much interest at all in developing the property in a useful fashion. To provide an example, the author of this Nutshell is a beneficiary of a date farm *waqf* established by his great grandmother well over a century ago in Iraq. The latest annual distribution received from the *waqf* given the large number of beneficiaries in existence is $52 (donated immediately to charity). Needless to say, the amount of care and consideration the author dedicates to the upkeep of property that earns him $52 in revenue annually is not great.

The result for many *waqfs* was resort to long term leases of the structures, trees, or other items on the property. These sorts of leases lended themselves to corruption, as trustees misused or misappropriated funds of which beneficiaries were unaware or with which they were unconcerned given their highly diluted interests.

Meaningful legislative action to deal with this problem finally began to take place toward the middle of the twentieth century. In 1949, for example, Egypt banned the creation of family *waqfs* and limited the duration of existing ones to no more than two generations. In so doing, it relied on justifications that reflected the concerns described above. The Explanatory Memorandum to the 1949 Law specifically reads as follows:

> Family *waqfs* and *waqfs* that are shared between a charitable side and a family side constitute in our social and economic life today a very dangerous problem that the state must take effective legal solutions to address, in order to end their deleterious effects and ward off their harm, in a manner that accords with the public interest and the interest of the deserving *waqfs*. What is established and demonstrated by actual observance is that these *waqfs* have for the most part trespassed beyond the bounds of the intended functions for which they were established and grown distant from the realization of the purpose of their founding. This is because in the passing of eras and the succession of years they have been afflicted with decay, and have a large number of beneficiaries who receive a very small amount of its revenue. [Family *waqf*] management has become a source of misuse and misappropriation. Thus, disputes have arisen among beneficiaries and trustees, and from the discussions, considerable property resources are lost, which could have been invested in a much better fashion. These tragedies accumulate day by day.... What is agreed is that the only means to end this situation is to prohibit the establishment of family and shared *waqfs* and to dissolve the existing *waqfs* of this type. Legislative Edict No. 76 of May 16, 1949, on the Abolition of the

Family and Mixed *Waqf,* and the Dissolution of Family and Mixed *Waqfs* and Their Liquidation.

Egypt's efforts were not the first in the Arab world—Syria had preceded Egypt with a total ban on family *waqfs* in 1946, the year that the secular nationalist Ḥusnī al-Zaʿīm came to power in a coup. However, following Egypt, the process of undoing the family *waqfs* gained momentum across the Arab world, and ultimately the Muslim world. The parallel rise of Marxism and other leftist movements across the globe only accelerated matters. There was no easier target for leftists to train their sights on than large landholdings preserved as a matter of law within particular families on the theory that this is charity approved by God. The fall of the family *waqf* proved the general rule across the Muslim world, though there remain some noted exceptions noted below.

As concerns charitable *waqfs,* the record is more mixed. While Turkey could simply abolish *waqfs* in keeping with its own radical secularist philosophy, this is considerably harder to achieve in most Muslim states. The treatment of mosques in particular was one that would have to be handled with sensitivity. Accordingly, the general trend as concerns the charitable *waqfs* lay not with their dissolution, but rather the assumption of their administration, and the distribution of their revenue, in a manner that the state saw fit. Egypt is once again instructive. Articles 1 and 2 of Law 247 of 1953 read as follows:

(1) If a *waqf* does not designate the needy group which is to be its beneficiary, or it

designates it, and it is not present, or it exists, but there is a group more in need, it is permissible for the Minister of *Waqfs*, with the permission of the High Council of *Waqfs* and the Sharia Court, to spend the revenues in whole or in part on the group which [the Minister] designates without being restricted by the condition of the grantor.

(2) If the *waqf* is for a charitable purpose, then the trustee in accordance with this law is the Ministry of *Waqfs* unless the grantor conditions the trusteeship for himself or to one designated by name.

An exception is made for smaller *waqfs,* but the general import is obvious. First, the state will administer all *waqfs,* save those administered by a grantor or one designated by the grantor *by name,* meaning, necessarily, alive at the time of the *waqf* dedication. Moreover, the revenue arising from the *waqf* may be distributed by the state to whoever it feels is most in need. There is even suggestion in the Explanatory Memorandum that this could be a reallocation to the defense budget, as the Egyptian Army serves an important public purpose. The previous balance as between state and jurist that sustained the *waqf* in the classical era is destroyed entirely with these changes. Instead, once revered seminary institutions like the Azhar, which traditionally relied on *waqf* revenue dedicated to it to sustain itself, became dependent on state revenue and little more than an organ of the state, funded effectively from whatever revenues the state chose to direct to it.

Not all states are quite as explicit as Egypt in permitting the state to reallocate revenue from the charitable purpose designated by the grantor to another one entirely. However, with significant exception, most have assumed control over the administration and management of all, or nearly all, of the charitable *waqfs* through state ministries or other departments. In so doing, given the opacity of state budget making in most of the Muslim world, it may very well be that the distinction between such states and Egypt may not add up to much of a difference. In either case, the state effectively manages the *waqfs,* collects their revenue, and distributes that revenue, without very much, if any, transparency or oversight. The *waqf* in such states are little more than an ancillary operation for the state to manage, and an ancillary budget for it to use. In such places, no sensible person establishes a new *waqf*. This amounts to a donation to the state, which hardly seems appealing to any donor when there are plenty of other, modern institutions on which to rely to establish charitable foundations. The *waqf* has thus become throughout much of the Islamic world an antiquated relic and a source of nostalgia more than any sort of driver of economic growth or major provider of public services. Thus has this once venerable institution largely met a rather ignoble end.

C. THE RELEVANCE OF THE *WAQF* TODAY

Notwithstanding its rather precipitous decline, the *waqf* remains deserving of the (brief) attention devoted to it in this Nutshell for three reasons. The first of these is the residual relevance of the remnants of the once mighty institution across much of the Muslim world. Even if administered almost entirely by the state in an opaque fashion, with revenues controlled by it, the fact remains that a not insignificant amount of landed property in much of the Muslim world remains under *waqf* today, in theory managed largely according to classical rules. Knowing how that property came to be so classified, how it is supposed to be managed, and how its revenues should be distributed, is therefore not an irrelevancy, even if the extent to which classical practice is actually being adhered to is not currently known.

Separately, and perhaps more importantly, there are the holdouts. Not every *waqf* has been completely subsumed by a state bureaucracy, nor has every state gone the ways of Egypt and Syria in effectively expropriating all *waqf* lands in the manner previously described. Perhaps the best examples of *waqfs* operating in a more traditional fashion that insulates them to some extent from overweening state control lie in those states with longstanding, sizable Muslim *minorities*. It is, after all, far easier for a Muslim state to seize control of land theoretically "imprisoned" for an Islamic charitable purpose by claiming that it will administer that land to its proper Islamic end than it would be for a non-

Muslim state to do the same. Hence, India has vast land under *waqf,* administered by trustees and then in turn supervised both by local governments as well as the central government in Delhi. Some of the same problems that caused the decline of *waqfs* elsewhere—trustee corruption, underutilization of real property resources, disassociation of the property from the public service it was intended to provide—are frequently reported in India as a result. The *waqf* also plays an important role in Israel, in particular as concerns the famed Al Aqsa Mosque and associated properties, which is administered by a *waqf* that is independent of the state and that frequently clashes with it on proper administration of the holy sites.

Separately, some Muslim societies have resisted rather strongly the trend toward state control over *waqf* revenues and administration. The most interesting cases in this regard are the Shi'i dominated states of Iraq and Iran, where *waqf* rulemaking, administration, and revenue distribution remains under the control of jurists. This is perhaps less surprising in Iran, given the political theory of juristic rule on which its current regime is based. Iraq, however, is considerably different. It is an Arab state, historically ruled by secular Sunni regimes notwithstanding its majority Shi'a population, and on a legal level profoundly influenced by the example of Egypt. Hence, the famed Egyptian legal scholar Abd al-Razzaq al-Sanhuri, who had drafted the Egyptian Civil Code (which included in it is original form important provisions limiting long term leases of the *waqf*), also drafted the Iraqi Civil

Code and served as Dean of Iraq's premier law school at the University of Baghdad. Moreover, reflecting the influence of Egypt, from the time of Iraq's monarchy through the end of the Ba'ath regime in 2003, successive Iraqi governments had put in place measures to limit the influence of the *waqf*.

At the same time, these measures were incremental relative to Egypt. Hence, where Egypt abolished family *waqfs* in 1952, Iraq in 1955 enacted an edict (since repealed as concerns Shi'i *waqfs*) that *permitted* the dissolution of the family *waqf* if a beneficiary or an heir of a beneficiary demanded it. Similarly, while Egypt put virtually all charitable *waqfs* under state control in 1952, Iraq's legislation concerning *waqf* administration only gradually extended state authority over the *waqfs*, and even its limited measures were in a few cases narrowed by the courts.

Nevertheless, the process of gradual assumption of state control of *waqfs* was moving inexorably in Iraq in the direction that it had in other Arab states like Egypt and Syria—until 2003. With the removal of the secular and largely Sunni Ba`ath regime from power, Iraq's juristic authorities and their political allies moved quickly to hand effective control of the *waqfs* back to the jurists. The only viable way to actually achieve that, as late as 2003, was through permitting the jurists to effectively run the state machinery that dealt with *waqf*. That is, rather than somehow attempting the nearly impossible task of reestablishing a premodern jurist-state balance in a modern state, jurists instead obtained legislative measures that granted them guardianship over the state bodies responsible for supervising and overseeing *waqfs*.

The jurists acted quickly to achieve this. In fact, the first measures were taken even before Iraqi sovereignty had been restored following the U.S. invasion. Thus, while Iraq had remained in theory under U.S. occupation, a group of largely expatriate Iraqis handpicked by the U.S. led Coalition Provisional Authority to advise it on governance matters, known as the Iraq Governing Council, enacted a resolution to disband the Ministry of *Waqfs*, replacing it with two bureaus, one for the Sunnis and one for the Shi'a. The resolutions also named the heads of each respective bureau, who in the case of the Shi'i bureau was an individual close to the juristic authorities. Two 2012 laws then lay out the structure of each of the Sunni and Shi'i *Waqf* Bureaus. The Shi'i *Waqf* Bureau Law clarifies that the head of the Shi'i *Waqf* Bureau is appointed by the Council of Ministers (i.e. the executive branch) and approved not by the legislature, as a Minister would be, but rather by Najaf's Highest Jurist. The religious scholars on the Board of Directors of the Bureau are then selected by the head of the Bureau, and the Board is responsible for supervising *waqf* trustees and approving exchanges of *waqf* property. The state body, in other words, is run by appointees and designees of Najaf's Highest Jurist, a person with no affiliation to the state.

Two articles of the 2012 law best exemplify the extent of juristic control, and jurist-state entanglement, in the area of Shi'i *waqfs*. These are Articles 14 and 15, which read, respectively, as follows:

Article 14. The administration of *waqfs*, and the regulation of their affairs, among them the appointment of the trustee, and his dismissal, shall be conducted in accordance with the widespread opinion of the Imami Shi'i jurists. In the event that there is no widespread [opinion], then the opinion of the Highest Jurist shall be taken, and this means the jurist with the most Shi'i followers in Iraq among the jurists of Najaf.

Article 15. The Bureau does not administer the religious schools, and other *waqfs* tied to the Shi'i seminaries. Nor shall it interfere except with the permission of the Highest Jurist.

In other words, Najaf's Highest Jurist makes the rules that pertain to the Shi'i *waqfs*, approves the appointment of the chief administrator of the *waqf* bureau overseeing them, and exercises indirect supervisory control over the distribution of *waqf* revenue.

There is some irony to this, given that the high jurists in the seminaries of Najaf, Iraq have explicitly disclaimed any role for juristic authorities in the administration of the state, in stark contradistinction to their counterparts in Qom, Iran. *Waqf* provides the limitation on this supposedly apolitical commitment, for perhaps obvious reasons. *Waqf* law is not only traditionally Islamic, as personal status law is, but there are also important economic consequences arising from its administration. The Shi'i seminaries are not as economically dependent on *waqf* as their Sunni counterparts such as the Azhar traditionally were, because the primary Shi'i seminary support comes from a tithe paid by the believers. Nevertheless, the seminaries receive sizable revenues from *waqf*, and they have long felt that the state has misappropriated those revenues and failed to give them their due. The jurists no doubt felt they had no choice but to seize control to protect their interests from the state encroachment that occurred in states such as Syria and Egypt.

The problem with all of this entanglement with the state, perhaps unanticipated by the drafters, is that the legislative formulations result in the state having considerable influence over all areas of traditionally exclusive juristic control. After all, according to Article 15, the state can insert itself directly into the affairs of the seminaries, so long as Najaf's Highest Jurist allows it. Given that the definition of "Najaf's Highest Jurist"—as the person with the highest number of followers in Iraq—is not one that is easy to ascertain, or even directly measure, this gives the state considerably more legal license to interfere in the seminaries than Saddam Husaynn could ever claim in his decades of extralegal oppression of Shi'i jurists. At the time of the enactment of the 2012 law, this was probably not perceived to be a problem, because of broad acknowledgment that the Highest Jurist was Grand Ayatollah Sistani. However, power struggles, often prolonged, ensue on the passing of a Highest Jurist, and Grand Ayatollah Sistani is advanced in years. Permitting the state to intervene into Najaf affairs with the approval of the Highest Jurist therefore provides a window of opportunity for the state in the future to play a role in determining the Highest Jurist, and in tipping the balance in favor of one figure over another by intervening in seminary affairs at the approval of their favored candidate. Given the historic juristic suspicion of state power, the failure to anticipate that this might happen is rather surprising.

Finally, it might be noted that there is much discussion in the Muslim world of the reinvigoration of the *waqf*, largely through its near entire reinvention. From Kuwait and Saudi Arabia to Malaysia, a variety of different foundations have arisen that claim to be *waqfs* revitalized in a form that renders them useful and indeed innovative in the modern world. An example of such a *waqf* is the King Abdulaziz Endowment Project, which owns vast properties near Mecca's Great Mosque, and whose revenues are supposed to support the Great Mosque. Included within it is a complex of seven skyscraper hotels and a five story shopping mall. Another example would be Malaysia's Waqaf An-Nur Corporation Berhad, which sold shares to the general public to purchase and develop real properties, with the proceeds to go to regional infrastructure projects.

In developing these structures, there is much reliance on modern company law. This includes (i) the establishment of an independent corporate entity with separate personality that itself holds a variety of different assets, some of which are liquid, (ii) the divisions of interests in that entity into tradeable shares, and (iii) the governance of that entity by a shareholder elected Board of Directors. Given all of these features, which were certainly not part of the traditional *waqf,* it is legitimate to ask whether or not the term *"waqf"* is more designed as a tool of marketing than as a demarcation of the historic Islamic institution. Certainly, it is hard to see how the *waqf* so reconstituted is meaningfully different from other sorts of public service corporations that do not owe their origins to Islamic law. This theme of precisely what is Islamic about Islamically reinvented vehicles, and whether they are instead a mimicry of their conventional counterparts with only superficial, rhetorical changes to differentiate them, is an important debate in Islamic finance, the subject to which we turn in the next chapter.

CHAPTER 5
ISLAMIC FINANCE

A. INTRODUCTION

With this Chapter, the Nutshell moves away from legal fields where Islamic law has exhibited broad continuity with the classical tradition into those that have been transformed entirely following the rupture of modernity described in Chapter One. Where classical Islamic law is relevant in these fields, it is in a reconstituted and reinvented form.

There is significant license afforded to interpreters undertaking the process of reconstitution and reinvention. It requires deciding what from the past needs to be adhered to, what may safely be discarded, and how to go about achieving compliance. In making these choices, the biases and assumptions that underlie the entire project—and the parallel expectations of the Muslim public respecting what Islamic law requires—are more transparent than they are in legal fields where conformity to premodern rules is more rigid. Nowhere is this truer than in the case of Islamic finance.

It is important in this context to emphasize how recent of a practice Islamic finance really is. While the first Islamic banks came into existence in the 1960's, Islamic finance did not mature into anything that could legitimately be called an industry until about two decades later. As Chapter One made clear, by that time, the caliphate had long disappeared, and most modern Islamic states had already emerged from a system of colonial rule that had entirely transformed their legal and political systems. Most relevant for purposes of this chapter, the financial and commercial sectors in virtually every Muslim society had undergone massive change. The operative laws in those areas were not Islamic in origin, but rather transplants from non-Muslim states in the developed world, and usually Continental Europe. What this means is that when the modern practice of Islamic finance came into being, it did so within a milieu of commercial and financial institutions that were thoroughly conventional, and resembled those of Western Europe more than medieval Islam. The professionals working in those sectors—as bankers, lawyers, directors, shareholders and managers—were schooled in modern, conventional methods but not those of the classical jurists, which they were not equipped even to understand, let alone practice. Therefore, the decision to reconstitute Islamic finance was in essence a modern one, and it was implemented among modern professionals accustomed to modern modalities of thinking, modern expectations of what commerce and finance were, and modern understandings of how they were supposed to operate.

The first question that might be asked is why Islamic *finance* came into being at all, given all of this. After all, many other areas of classical Islamic law that were displaced in modernity's rupture— Islamic contract, Islamic tort, Islamic bankruptcy, and Islamic property law (beyond *waqf,* the subject of Chapter Four) to name a few—never managed to reappear. What, specifically, is it about finance that has generated such interest as to merit the establishment of an entire industry?

There is one obvious potential doctrinal answer to this, which is that in the context of finance, there is source text in the Qur'an that condemns rather stridently the practice of *ribā,* which is often equated with money interest. Examples of verses include the following, taken from the second chapter of the Qur'an:

(275) Those who consume *ribā* cannot stand [on the Day of Resurrection] except as one stands who is being beaten by Satan into insanity. That is because they say, "Trade is [just] like *ribā.*" But Allah has permitted trade and has forbidden *ribā.* So whoever has received an admonition from his Lord and desists may have what is past, and his affair rests with Allah. But whoever returns—those are the companions of the Fire; they will abide eternally therein.

(276) Allah destroys *ribā* and gives increase for charities. And Allah does not like every sinning disbeliever.

(277) Indeed, those who believe and do righteous deeds and establish prayer and give zakah will have their reward with their Lord, and there will be no fear concerning them, nor will they grieve.

(278) O you who have believed, fear Allah and give up what remains [due to you] of *ribā*, if you should be believers.

(279) And if you do not, then be informed of a war [against you] from Allah and His Messenger. But if you repent, you may have your principal—[thus] you do no wrong, nor are you wronged.

(280) And if someone is in hardship, then [let there be] postponement until [a time of] ease. But if you give [from your right as] charity, then it is better for you, if you only knew.

While certainly Islamic contract and tort have source text as well, there is nothing nearly as unequivocal and vehement as the verses that appear above. This explanation—that finance remains relevant because the Qur'an makes it so—is therefore plausible, but incomplete. The main reason is that the equating of *ribā* with money interest is in fact more a modern interpretation than it is a classical one. To be clear, it is certainly a *reasonable* reading of both source text and classical doctrine, but not a *necessary* one. The Qur'an does not define *ribā* at all, beyond describing it, as per above, as rapacious and the opposite of charity.

There is Sunna that provides more clarity, including a report on a statement of the Prophet Muhammad that reads as follows:

Gold for gold,

silver for silver,

wheat for wheat,

barley for barley,

dates for dates,

salt for salt,

like for like, hand to hand, and whoever increases it or demands more is engaged in *ribā*,

both the one who takes it, and the one gives it.

The *ribā* ban under this Prophetic report focuses on the trades of particular commodities—specifically, gold, silver, dates, wheat, barley and salt—for delay, or with gain. In other words, one could not "sell" 10 dinars of gold, or 100 dirhams of silver (the major forms of currency at the time) for 15 dinars of gold, or 150 dinars of silver, to be paid back in a year's time.

This report, and others like it from the Sunna, led the classical jurists to delineate with casuistic precision which categories of goods could be traded, and which could not. Some classical schools focused on bans of items measurable by weight or volume (the Hanafis and the Shi'a), others concerned themselves with precious metals and foodstuffs (the Shafi'is and the Malikis). The detailed results of their disquisitions are lengthy, and hardly require excessive recounting here. It suffices to note that none of the classical jurists could possibly have conceived of free floating currency as an item that could be traded at all, because it did not exist. The idea of paper money not backed by gold as having some sort of intrinsic value, and then limiting the extent to which that commodity could be traded for "gain" (meaning in the end nothing more than a different piece of paper with a higher number printed on it) would be completely unfathomable to a classical jurist.

The decision, then, to equate paper money with the gold and silver currencies of the past is a product of *'ijtihād*. Certainly, one could have imagined a different result, where a distinction was made between paper money and historic gold coins, so that only the latter could not be traded with gain. Under this narrower reading, the *ribā* ban is as obsolete as the ban on fortune telling through the tossing of arrows, which is contained elsewhere in the Qur'an.

If the source text therefore plays a role, but not a dispositive one, what else led to the rise and the subsequent spread of Islamic finance? The next few sections discuss this subject, and in so doing, reveal a certain tension within the industry that perpetually threatens to destabilize it.

B. THE PROFIT SHARING IDEAL

What is perhaps most interesting about the classical rules surrounding *ribā* is how little they have to do with actually achieving some distinct policy objective, as opposed to narrow compliance with a formal rule. One can read at length extensive juristic analysis of the *ribā* ban, all derived from Sunna, and not have any sense at all of what it is that is supposed to be achieved by banning the trades of particular items, but not others. Whether or not, for example, cooked meats fall within the ban, as opposed to raw meat, or whether bread falls within the ban, if wheat does, are approached using analogical reasoning that tightly focusses on the text of the Prophetic reports almost exclusively.

The most obvious example of this formality lies within the Shafi'i school. The Shafi'is did not even prohibit the transparent artifice known as *'ina*, wherein one person would sell an item clearly not covered by the bans reflected in the Sunna (say, for example, an office desk) for its market value, and then immediately buy it back, with a promise to pay an inflated price in a year's time. Clearly, substantively, what transpires in such an exchange is that one party receives money (the first sale price) in exchange for a promise to receive more money later (the second sale price), which is the essence of money interest. Yet the fact that there was an asset being sold and resold took the matter beyond the confines of *ribā* according to the Shafi'is. Other schools rejected transparency that was this obvious, but managed artifices of their own. The Malikis, for example, indicated that the ban on gold and silver was meant to apply to all precious metals, but not common ones. This meant that the copper *fils*, which was a less valuable form of currency, could be traded for gain, with delay. Thus, one could not trade 100 *dinars* of gold for 150 *dinars* in a year's time, but could trade 1000 *fils* of copper for 1500 *fils* in a year's time.

There were some exceptional classical jurists who looked deeper so that they could lay out a coherent policy that underlay the *ribā* ban. For example, the Maliki jurist Ibn Rushd, or Averroës, was critical of his own school's conclusions on the *fils* and preferred a Hanafi rule that banned all items traded by volume or currency, because it would prevent such obvious artifice as trades of copper currencies. Ibn Taymiyya, who has proven remarkably influential in the area of Islamic finance, has likewise often attempted to justify some of the central prohibitions of Islamic finance in policy terms, as we shall see. Nevertheless, it is fair to say that for the most part, the jurists seemed to focus less on what a *ribā* ban was supposed to do, and more on how to create categories of prohibitions in order to better define it. This tendency created some rather obvious tension with the stridency reflected in the Qur'an on *ribā*—it is unclear why extracting a promise from a debtor to pay gold back in a year somehow demonstrates greed and signifies war against God and His Prophet, but extracting a promise to pay copper back does not. Nevertheless, the intense classical focus on taxonomy was a plausible, if narrow, way to understand the Sunna.

The narrow and formalistic approach of the classical jurists certainly was not shared by the founders of what came to be known as Islamic finance in the middle of the twentieth century. In perfect converse with their classical forebears, the founders were as dramatically unconcerned with the classical juristic categories and their technical arcana as the classical jurists had been respecting the achievement of substantive societal ends. Instead, their only real concerns were societal ends. Reflecting a broad and popular dissatisfaction with global forms of economic organization during the height of the Cold War, the earliest of these theorists (among them Sayyid Qutb of Egypt, Maulana Maududi of Pakistan, and Baqir al-Sadr in Iraq) defined Islam as a third way between rapacious capitalism and authoritarian communism. They called for revolution of both the political and economic sort to bring the system into being.

Central to their vision was a ban on the taking of interest, which they tied directly back to the Qur'an's strident treatment of *ribā*, nearly entirely ignoring the Sunna on which the classical jurists had been obsessed.

In the telling of the economic revolutionaries, Islam forbade interest because it was inherently exploitative. It permits people with capital to increase it at no risk or cost to themselves, merely by demanding more money later. At the same time, the debtor, who is the person actually producing goods or providing services, is forever destined to work harder to pay back more to the idle rich. This is an evil, in their view, that Islam was revealed to stop. The parallels to Marxism, with its division as between the bourgeoisie as the owners of the means of production, and the proletariat, as the working class who actually produce, is unmistakable.

Yet if the revolutionaries were inspired by Marxism, they clearly took positions that proved more capitalist in the end, including the respect for private property, the enforcement of contracts, and for a belief in the value of individual enterprise. What they demanded was that these be achieved through profit and risk sharing mechanisms, such as partnerships, rather than lending. In some cases, the partnerships would be easy to imagine, as they would involve two entrepreneurs working together on a shared project, with profits and losses divided between them. However, this does not resemble, nor does it seem to replace, traditional financing. After all, entrepreneurs may often need partners, but they just as often need money from stakeholders with little to no experience in the business of the entrepreneur. In these situations, what proponents of Islamic finance chose to rely upon was a classical form of silent partnership known as the *muḍāraba*. In this arrangement, a financing partner would supply the capital, a working partner would provide the labor, and they would share profits and losses between them according to a ratio determined by them. Hence, for example, if Zaid wished to open a restaurant, and Rebecca had the capital to support it, they would enter into a partnership wherein Rebecca would invest a certain amount in the restaurant, Zaid would actually manage the restaurant, and any money made would be divided between them according to whatever ratio they saw fit. Importantly, losses would be borne in the same ratio.

In theory, this silent partnership was superior to interest taking because a financier could not possibly appropriate profits to itself even when the venture was losing money, and demand that the debtor take the entire risk for the venture. Instead, the financier would earn money and succeed in its individual enterprise *only if* the debtor also succeeded. This would induce the two partners to work together in a spirit of brotherhood and sharing, and it would also be more efficient, in that it would lead financiers to support only those ventures that were likely to succeed.

The obvious gap that this solution left was that it required financiers and working partners to find each other, which does not seem particularly plausible in the modern environment. Indeed, one of the central purposes of a bank is to offer this sort of intermediation between depositors and borrowers. To take the simplest example, it seems fanciful, to say the least, that a group of individual borrowers would ever find a way to pool their capital to fund a home purchase for a borrower in the absence of an institution such as a bank.

Modern Islamic finance and economics theorists therefore refined the classical silent partnership to suit their modern ends, so that it would resemble a bank more closely. However, in so doing, they effectively transmogrified it, thereby rendering it unrecognizable to classical jurists.

The form they imagined was *two* silent partnerships tiered together as per below.

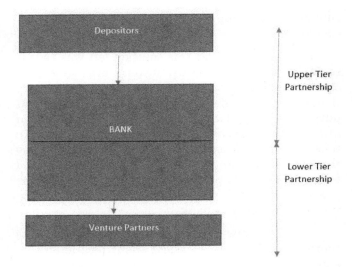

As the above diagram shows, the depositors are engaged in a silent partnership with the bank, wherein the depositors supply money, and the bank, as working partner, engages in the task of finding appropriate investment opportunities. When the bank finds such an opportunity, it invests in a silent partnership of its own, wherein the silent partner is the bank, and the working partner is engaged in whatever work it is that earns profit. Profits then are shared by the bank and that working partner in an agreed upon percentage. Thus, where the entrepreneur makes money, the entrepreneur shares it with the bank, and the bank shares it with its depositors, in a manner that diverges from interest taking, where some parties earn their return, and others are left to bear much more risk.

SEC. B THE PROFIT SHARING IDEAL

It is difficult to overstate the extent to which the two tiered silent partnership, and with it the broader idea of profit and risk sharing, have captivated the modern Muslim imagination. While Islamic finance has moved far from its revolutionary roots, the vision of profit sharing that proved central to its founding continue to resonate with the Muslim public today. Hence, more casual media accounts tend to describe Islamic finance as being distinguishable from conventional finance because of its reliance on profit sharing. This characterization is largely inaccurate, as we shall see. However, it is fair to say that profit and risk sharing are what Islamic finance aspires for itself, or at least what influential theorists working within it aspire it to become, even if it falls far short of these ideals.

The reason it falls short is that it is very difficult to make profit sharing work in the context of banking. The problem is not the structure per se—private equity funds operate on bases that are not entirely different than a two tiered silent partnership—but rather that the structure does not replace or replicate a bank. Any effort to do so largely results in failure for several reasons.

First, just as profits cycle up through the partnership to depositors, losses do as well, in the same proportion. While a private equity investor might accept a loss, given the expectation of high returns, a depositor in a bank almost never does.

Making matters worse is that a bank, as opposed to a private equity fund, is supposed to manage liquidity mismatches, in that its loans, or investments in the case of the ideal Islamic bank, pay off in the longer term, while the depositors that fund those loans, or investments, as the case may be, require immediate access to their money. This leaves a bank in perpetual danger of having too many depositors withdraw their money at once due to a lack of confidence. This then causes a cascading effect known as a bank run. In a bank run, all, or nearly all, depositors seek to withdraw their money, and even a healthy bank cannot satisfy them all due to the illiquidity of its assets. It cannot, after all, demand all of its borrowers to pay back their loans at once.

While a bank run is possible even in profitable banks due to false rumors, the risk is exacerbated in a bank where there are more significant risks of loss, as a two tier partnership would be. Losses would naturally make depositors even more likely to withdraw their money. Government insurance is supposed to address this problem, but it is hard to see how the government could insure a bank against losses when it describes itself as not interest taking, but profit and loss sharing.

Beyond losses and bank runs, one other major problem is apparent. The level of monitoring expected of a two tier partnership is much higher than that which attends to a conventional bank. A conventional bank merely expects a payment of a certain amount on a certain date in a manner that reflects a prevailing interest rate. A partnership, by contrast, must monitor the accounts of the venture in which it invests much more closely, so as to ensure that it is in fact disclosing its profits properly.

Monitoring imposes costs, which the bank would have to pass on to its clients and customers through noncompetitive interest rates. This is not sustainable in the longer term.

For these and other reasons, Islamic banks have not actually been built on profit and loss sharing. While in theory the depositors in such institutions are often silent partners vis a vis the institution, in practice this is more of a convenient fiction than a reality. The Islamic bank's assets are in vehicles that resemble in all substantive respects interest bearing loans (forms to the contrary notwithstanding), making the bank no more prone to losses than any conventional bank.

In other words, what replaced the ideal of profit and risk sharing was the practice of mimicry of conventional financial institutions. It is this mimicry that currently serves as the edifice of Islamic finance. The essence of the practice is to identify conventional transactions and then find ways to replicate them in economic and legal substance as closely as possible while still purporting to maintain some narrow compliance with Islamic law. This has been remarkably successful from an economic point of view. Islamic finance has grown very rapidly, to over US$2 trillion in assets, with such major institutions as Citibank, HSBC, and AIG having specialized units dedicated to Islamic finance. Yet, as noted above, the Muslim public continues to have aspirations and expectations for Islamic finance to provide some greater social good, precisely as its founders and earliest proponents claims. This creates a tension, existential in scope, that underlies much of Islamic finance and that helps to explain its evolving doctrine.

Having set out the profit sharing ideal above, and described in brief the concept of mimicry in the industry, let us turn now to the forms used in Islamic finance to achieve this mimicry.

C. THE ARTIFICES AND THEIR RISKS

The previous section makes reference to one form of artifice that can be used to mimic an interest based transaction, the sale and immediate buyback permitted by the Shafi'i school. As used in modern Islamic finance, the arrangement, also referred to by the jurisdictions that permit it as *bay` bil-thaman 'ajil,* or sale for delayed payment, involves three separate transactions, entered into simultaneously. To illustrate them, I will use the common example of a real estate developer seeking financing to develop property that the developer owns. In the first transaction, the developer sells the property to a bank or consortium of banks for its immediate cash value. In the second transaction, structured to take place an infinitesimal amount of time after the initial one, the bank sells the property back to the developer for a higher sum, which is not paid immediately, but in monthly installments over the course of years. In the final transaction, the bank takes a security interest in the property upon its sale back to the developer, to ensure it is paid.

It is not difficult to structure the payments made by the developer to the bank on a monthly basis over the period of years to mimic exactly what they would be in a conventional, fixed rate, interest-based transaction. This is achieved through setting the sale and repurchase price at the proper amounts. Hence, for example, a loan of $100,000 at 5% interest requires monthly payments of $1060.66 over ten years, for a total of $127,279.20. In a sale and buyback, the property owner sells the property to the bank for $100,000, paid immediately, and then buys it back for $127,279.20, to be paid in monthly installments of $1060.66 over ten years. Economically, the results seem identical at first glance, even if one transaction required a fictitious double sale that the other did not.

Most jurisdictions have tended to abjure the sale and buyback, with the exception of Malaysia, which has always used Shafi'i rules. In particular, it is not part of Islamic finance practice in the Gulf Cooperation Council ("GCC"), where the significant majority of Islamic finance transactions by volume take place, nor is it commonly used in Islamic finance transactions in London, Frankfurt, or the New York. Accordingly, it is not often discussed in manuals of Islamic finance.

Much more globally common, and broadly accepted, is the cost plus financing method known as the *murābaḥa,* which resembles the sale and buyback in many ways. In a cost plus financing transaction, as opposed to a sale and buyback, the bank does not purchase the property from the original owner. Instead, it buys property from a third party, pays for it in full, and then enters into a second transaction wherein it sells the same property to its eventual owner at a higher price. As in a sale and buyback, the new owner commits to pay the bank for the property over a period of years in monthly installments, and the bank takes a security interest in the property to ensure that it is paid. As with the sale and buyback, it is not difficult to set the original sale price, the final sale price, and the monthly installment amount to mimic an interest rate.

In theory, the cost plus financing method is more salient to Islamic finance because the bank seems to be engaged in doing work for which it is being compensated. It is locating the property to be sold to the ultimate owner, and it is serving as an intermediary of sorts as between the purchaser and seller. Moreover, it is undertaking the risk of ownership for a period of time as the property moves from its original seller to the ultimate buyer. All of this would justify its taking a higher price on sale than that for which it purchased the property. A retailer, after all, routinely sells items to consumers at higher prices than the price at which it purchased them from a wholesaler. Nobody would contend that the price difference arising therefrom was somehow unjustified, much less akin to interest on a loan. Distinctions such as these populate many primers on Islamic finance, and are a point of some emphasis.

In practice, however, the distinctions as between interest based financings and cost plus transactions can be collapsed rather significantly by limiting the bank's risk and actual effort to only that borne by a conventional financial institution. Illustrative is the rather well known case of *Islamic Investment Company of the Gulf (Bahamas) Ltd. v. Symphony Gems N.V. & Others,* 2001 Folio 1226 (Queen's Bench). In the case, the bank offered to the purchaser a revolving purchase and sale facility wherein the purchaser would locate gems it wished to purchase, deliver an "offer" to the bank respecting the gems, and the bank would then "buy" them up to a maximum commitment of $15 million in the aggregate, and $7.5 million per transaction. Under the terms of the agreement, the bank would then immediately sell them to the purchaser, with payment to be made in installments that reflected the prevailing interest rate. The bank transferred any warranties that it had in the gems from the original seller to the purchaser, and the purchaser disclaimed any warranties to the bank. Indeed, the bank was never expected to take physical possession of the gems it supposedly bought at all—they would be transferred from the seller, whom the purchaser identified, to the purchaser, with the bank's only role as intermediary by virtue of its purchase and sale facility. Clearly, the only thing the bank is actually doing is providing financing—paying for the gems procured from the third party immediately, and then selling them on to the party who ultimately seeks to have them.

What gave rise to litigation in *Symphony Gems* was the fact that the seller, Precious HK, never actually delivered the diamonds that it was supposed to deliver under the agreement, leading the purchaser not to pay the bank back for the gems it never received. The bank then sued for recovery of the purchase price. In a bona fide sale, the purchaser's argument seems rather sound. To quote the Court:

> It is said [by defendant's counsel] that the defendant[ ] ha[s] a defence to the claim because it is a claim to recover the sale price and, he says, if not goods have been delivered how can the sale price have become payable?

The Court nevertheless held for the bank, stating that the contract "provides that the instalments are payable whether or not the seller is in breach of any of its obligations under the relevant purchase agreement, which must include a failure to deliver. Payment is not conditional upon the happening of any event." The Court then made the following important observation.

> Once the basic shape of the agreement is understood and regard had to its express terms, it quickly becomes apparent that the central plank of [the] defence is unsustainable. That is of course because this is no orthodox contract of sale.

In other words, the bank was not in fact finding gems, taking on the risk of holding them, and then selling them on to the purchaser, in the manner of a retailer, such that its contract with the purchaser was an actual contract of sale. In such a case, of course a retailer who did not deliver goods could not collect payment on them. In the cost plus financing at issue, however, the purchaser identified the goods it wanted to buy, took possession of them directly from the original seller, not the bank, and received any warranties associated therewith from the seller, rather than the bank. The purchaser's claims were then exclusively against the seller, with the bank's sole obligation to provide the money for the purchase, in exchange for a promise to receive a higher amount of money later. The Court thus recognized the series of transactions as being equivalent to a financing rather than a sale, in substance and spirit if not in form. In a financing transaction, the failure of a seller to deliver the good is not the responsibility of the bank financing payment for that good. This justified the Court's ultimate holding in favor of the bank.

The fictions inherent in the *Symphony Gems* transaction can be taken one step further with one final additional sale. Imagine, that is, that the purchaser of the gems did not need them, but instead sought money for some other purpose. It could then sell the gems back to their original seller for their full cash value. In that case, the purchaser would have money on hand, and an obligation to pay more money back to the bank in the future. The result of such an arrangement, known as *tawarruq,* or liquidation, is almost indistinguishable from a loan. While controversial, the *tawarruq* is commonly deployed by many financial institutions. In fact, some institutions offer *tawarruq* credit cards that involve three separate and simultaneous transactions at the end of each month where the consumer has an outstanding an unpaid balance. First, the bank purchases an amount of palm oil or platinum from a third party, in an amount equivalent to the value of the outstanding balance. Second, the bank sells that palm oil or platinum to the consumer, with the consumer agreeing to pay the bank in the future at the amount of the original sale price, plus 18% per annum for the palm oil or platinum. Third, the consumer sells the palm oil or platinum back into the market at its original value, thereby clearing the balance on the consumer's credit card, in exchange for its future payment obligation.

It is difficult to overstate the importance of the cost plus financing methods described above to the rise of Islamic finance. At one point in its history, well over 80% of Islamic financial transactions were a variation of one sort or another on cost plus financing. While Islamic finance has diversified beyond such heavy reliance on any single tool, in particular with the rise of Islamic capital markets, described below, cost plus financing remains a staple of the industry, and a fundamentally important one at that.

Yet in relying so heavily on mimicry and artifice, Islamic finance exposes itself to notable risks. These arise out of the fact that popular interest in it is not attributable to some sort of formal desire to adhere to some aspect of historic Islamic doctrine—as, say, dietary rules might be. Rather, there genesis is dissatisfaction with global economic norms and a firm belief that Islam provided some sort of alternative means of economic organization that was more just. Put more concretely, the halal food industry does not need to justify that its products are somehow healthier than ordinary meats, it being sufficient to merely describe the meat as compliant with Islamic law. However, Islamic finance is under pressure to explain how it brings substantive benefits that are lacking in conventional alternatives because this is precisely what the Muslim public expects. In its current form, this is nearly impossible to do.

Making matters worse is the fact that in some cases, inadvertently, outcomes in Islamic finance are altogether worse for distressed borrowers than they would be in conventional finance. Imagine, for example, the earlier example provided of a sale or buyback of a property which the owner sells to the bank for $100,000, and then purchases back for $127,279.20, to be paid over ten years. The result is similar to a conventional 5% fixed interest loan only if the buyer does not default. If the buyer defaults, then the result will differ dramatically. In a conventional finance transaction, the bank may foreclose on the property. However, the only amount it can claim from the borrower (beyond fees associated with foreclosure and due bills unpaid) is the outstanding principal on the loan, which is $100,000 less any principal already paid. A bank would not be able to claim interest payments that had not accrued. By contrast, if there is a default by a property owner in a sale and buyback, or the highly popular cost plus arrangement, then in theory the borrower owes the entire sale price it agreed to pay, or $127,279.20. A buyer who fails to pay a sale price, after all, does not owe a lesser amount if they cannot make their monthly payments.

The Kuala Lumpur High Court commented on this problem in the noted case of *Arab-Malaysian Finance*

Bhd. v. Taman Ihsan Jaya Sdn. Bhd. et. al. (Kuala Lumpur High Court 2008) 5 Malayan L.J. 631. Referencing an earlier decision that prompted it to set aside a sale and buyback transaction on the grounds that the sale was not bona fide, the court made the following observations:

> [I]t is self-evident that if a conventional loan must be avoided because of the prohibition of "*ribā*" or interest, surely the alternative must result in a consequence that is less burdensome than a default on the conventional loan with prohibited interest. But it is equally evident in this case that the result of what is presented as the application of the Qur'anic principle is that the defendant became liable, upon default at any time, to an amount that is 2.2 times the facility he obtained. It could hardly have been intended by the terse words in the [Qur'an] that an Islamic financing facility should result in consequences far more onerous than the conventional loan with "*ribā*" that is prohibited and unequivocally condemned.

> One might pause and observe that the harshness of usury is hardest upon those who default, and much less so, if at all, upon those fortunate enough to be able to service the loan successfully. The Qur'an could hardly have intended that its followers, faithfully and trustingly seeking an Islamic compliant facility, should be delivered to those who offer what appear to be perfectly Islamic compliant facilities, but upon a default, had an

interpretation applied that imposes a far more onerous liability than the conventional loan with interest. It is difficult to conceive that the religion of Islam intended to discourage its followers from the conventional loan with interest, condemn lenders for such loans, and deliver its followers into the hands of banks and financiers who under sale agreements with deferred payments, exact upon default payments far exceeding the liability upon default of a conventional loan with interest. One cannot say that the religion of Islam is so much more concerned with form than substance as would sustain the bank's interpretation of "selling price."

After these disquisitions, the Court set aside the transaction and denied the Bank the interest profits it sought.

The specific problem of default (and, conversely, voluntary prepayment) has largely been addressed through the rather creative use of *'ibrā'*, or voluntary forgiveness. The concept arises from the fact that a lender can always forgive a loan, and indeed to do so is a commendable act in Islamic law. Islamic finance has taken advantage of this to contractually obligate such "forgiveness" in an amount that corresponds exactly to the amount of interest not yet accrued when principal is prepaid, either because of foreclosure or because the borrower wishes to pay in advance. However contentious the reasoning, the solution has been broadly applied.

The broader problem of expectations reflected in the Court's opinion, however, remains. If Islamic finance is built on mimicry, it will not lead to the "less burdensome" result on buyers that the Court describes, as it is not designed to do that. It is designed, instead, to imitate the conventional result. The persistent fear among architects of Islamic finance deals is that more courts will do as the *Taman Ihsan Jaya* court did, and refuse to enforce a mimicry based transaction as it was designed to be enforced precisely because it is not "truly" Islamic. This sort of "sharia risk" bears significant costs, because it limits the willingness of parties to enter into Islamic finance transactions if they are not certain they will be able to enforce them according to their terms.

That said, there are ways that this risk can be minimized. In the specific case of Malaysia, where *Taman Ihsan Jaya* was decided, the internal judicial system was able to manage it. The Malaysian Court of Appeals decided in the noted case of *Lim Kok Hoe* that the lower courts should not decide on the Islamicity of particular transactions, but rather leave this to the determination of the Central Bank of Malaysia.

Elsewhere, the most commonly used technique to ensure that transactions are enforced according to their terms are choice of law and forum clauses that seek a hospitable forum interpreting the law in a hospitable fashion. *Symphony Gems,* quoted above, is a good example of this phenomenon. The Court in that case had little difficulty dispensing with any arguments that somehow the transaction did not meet Islamic law requirements. It simply pointed out that the transaction was governed by English law, and so its permissibility under Islamic law was irrelevant. To further limit the risk of nonenforceability, parties frequently add "sharia defense waiver" clauses, wherein each party waives its right at adjudication to claim that the agreement is not valid or enforceable because of any putative conflict with sharia.

The purpose of such mechanisms is to render a so-called "sharia review board" of established scholars, either formed ad hoc or as part of an existing financial institution, the only real authority for determining whether or not a transaction is in fact Islamically compliant. They do this on an ex ante basis. Virtually any financial transaction of any size within Islamic finance conditions its consummation on the obtaining of an opinion from a sharia review board that the transaction is Islamically compliant. The hope is that with the sharia review board's blessing, given in advance, all questions of Islamicity are finally and fully resolved and parties can be assured that the transaction will be enforced on its terms.

That said, risks always remain. One of the most common is reflected in the case of *Investment Dar Company KSCC v. Blom Developments Bank SAL,* [2009] EWHC 3545 (Ch). The case involved a highly questionable "agency" contract with a series of complex provisions, the sum total of which guaranteed the plaintiff investor a 5% return on investment irrespective of how much money the defendant agent, a Kuwaiti investment company, managed to make or lose with the money invested. This seems to be the very definition of an interest bearing arrangement. In seeking summary judgment, the plaintiff investor pointed out that the transaction was governed by English law, and there was a choice of forum clause for English courts. Thus, the plaintiff claimed, the court did not need to concern itself with Islamic law rules, exactly as was the case with *Symphony Gems*.

Notably, the court disagreed, and denied summary judgment on the grounds that the investment company's memorandum of association prohibited the company from engaging in activity that violated Islamic law. This meant that there was a triable issue of fact as to whether or not the transaction was *ultra vires,* which it might well be if it violated Islamic law. This is precisely the realization of the type of unenforceability risk that Islamic finance seeks to assiduously avoid in its deal structuring.

D. THE SPECULATION BAN AND THE LEASE CONTRACT

1. GENERAL

One type of contract that classical jurists recognized across the schools is the lease, or hire, contract, known as the *'ijāra*. Encompassed within this contract would be the hiring of an employee for a set monthly fee, or the renting of a good or real property for a set fee. In some ways, the lease/hire provides a more promising means to mimic an interest rate than the asset sales described above. This is because the risk profile of a lease resembles in some important ways that of an interest bearing transaction. After all, a landlord renting property to a venture, or an employee agreeing to work for a venture, receives a set monthly payment, just as a lender does, and the amount of that payment is unrelated to the success of the underlying venture. For this reason, lease financing is not uncommon in conventional industries with high cost assets. Aircraft, for example, are very frequently lease financed. The airline leases the aircraft for a number of years that comprise most of its economically useful life. At the end of the period, the airline has the right to purchase the plane at a nominal cost. Were Islamic finance to do the same thing on any number of assets, it could mimic interest rates rather easily, and indeed permit them to vary, simply by changing the lease rate from time to time based on a prevailing interest rate.

Indeed, Islamic finance does use the lease form to achieve mimicry. However, in doing so, it must grapple with the second major prohibition that is inherent in Islamic finance. This is known as *gharar,* or excessive speculation. While the term *gharar* is not directly used in the Qur'an, Islamic finance proponents often liken it to the Qur'anic prohibition against *maysar,* or gambling. Verse 5:90 of the Qur'an reads as follows:

> O you who have believed, indeed, intoxicants, gambling, [sacrificing on] stone altars [to other

than Allah], and divining arrows are but defilement from the work of Satan, so avoid it that you may be successful.

There is no necessary reason this relates to *commercial* speculation—indeed the other prohibited acts described in the verse seem more like frivolities that take one way from the serious worship of God rather than commercial activity, which could be thought of as a form of perfectly legitimate work. That said, the Sunna are less equivocal about the types of speculation that qualify as *gharar*. In particular, various reports indicate that the Prophet forbade the sale of fish in the open sea, the runaway slave, the unborn calf, milk not yet pulled from the udder, and the semen of stallions. The idea seems rather straightforward—there is no direct value associated with these items. Their only value is derivative, and depends entirely on fortuity. Semen that impregnates a mare is valuable, and semen that does not is useless, precisely as an unborn calf that lives is valuable and one that is still born is of no use, at least prior to the contemporary age. Accordingly, given the highly speculative nature of the good, its sale is prohibited. The highly influential Hanbali jurist Ibn Taymiyya elaborates:

> *Gharar* is an unknown outcome.... [T]he slave if he runs away, or the horse or the camel if it has fled. The owner if he sells, sells with a risk, so the buyer purchases at a lower price. If he obtains [the horse or camel], then the seller says, "you have beaten me at a bet, and taken my property for a low price." If he does not obtain it,

then the buyer says, "you have beaten me in a bet, and taken from me price without a countervalue." This is the corruption of gambling, and the creation of enmity and hatred which comes from the devouring of property falsely, which is itself a form of oppression. So in the sale of *gharar* there is oppression, enmity and hatred. Of the types of *gharar* that the Prophet peace and blessings upon him prohibited were the sale of that carried in the womb, and the sale of sperm and that which is sheltered, such as the sale of milk [sheltered] in the udder, the sale of dates before ripe, and similar things.

The obvious problem, of which the classical jurists were quite aware, is that once a legal system decides that *excessive* risk is too akin to gambling to be acceptable, and internalizes that outcome as just, then it must decide what type of risk is too excessive to be contemplated. After all, every transaction carries some risk. Even the sale of a present, living, and healthy camel is not free of risk, because the animal might well die minutes after its purchase. And yet, Qur'an 2:275 makes clear that trades are generally permissible.

The line drawing problem is not unlike the obsessions over causation that attend to modern tort law, where it is not enough that one person's negligence was a "but for" cause of another's injury, but rather, the cause must be "proximate" as well. As with causation, the lines on excessive risk are not particularly easy to draw, and seem in close cases to be rather arbitrary. Classical jurists did their best with this, categorizing *gharar* as either major, minor, or, among some jurists, moderate. The final category always proved the most nettlesome.

The failure to recognize the subtleties of this line drawing exercise has caused some non-Muslim courts to go wildly astray in their attempts to apply the *gharar* doctrine. Perhaps the worst example of this lies in the case of *National Group for Communications and Computers Ltd. v. Lucent Technologies,* 331 F. Supp. 2d 290 (2004), where a US federal court decided that a company could not be valued on the basis of the share price of equivalent companies because share price included an expectation of future value, and future value was *gharar.* The court admitted that this reading meant that the *gharar* doctrine prevented anyone from being able to enforce a contract to buy or sell stock in Saudi Arabia. However, the court reasoned, it was not within its province or duty to comment on the wisdom or practicality of *gharar.* Wisdom or practicality aside, one wonders why the court did not consider whether or not its conclusion could possibly have been correct given that Saudi Arabia enjoys active capital markets trading, has had a Capital Markets Law since 2003, and has created a Capital Markets Authority that regulates the practice.

Needless to say, the court is quite wrong. One can sell a stock and enforce the sale notwithstanding the rules of *gharar,* just as one can sell a camel and enforce that sale. Both the stock price and the camel's price reflect future value, but this is not in and of itself sufficient to call the sale *gharar*, unless all sales of all goods are uniformly prohibited, and, as noted several times above, the Qur'an permits trades. In the end, what happened was that a court with no exposure to the *gharar* prohibition and not acculturated to the underlying norms it presupposes, found the idea of *gharar* retrograde, confounding, and virtually impossible to apply sensibly, even in the case of the sale of a discrete item. Presumably, the same court would have found the equally arbitrary rules respecting proximate cause quite rational and capable of predictable adjudication. This demonstrates more than anything the limits of legal comprehension across vastly different systems.

To limit the problem of line drawing, jurists across school and sect created bright line rules in some circumstances. From the perspective of modern financiers seeking to mimic an interest rate, these rules have proven difficult. The most important rule is that the lease contract is cancellable at will. Otherwise, given fluctuating prices for goods and services, it could very well be that years into the future, a party is paying a lease rate far above or below market value. A second rule is that the lessee is normally responsible for upkeep. Finally, one cannot sell an item where both payment and delivery are supposed to occur at some distant date, as occurs in lease financing at the end of the lease term, because of uncertainties in future value.

This combination of rules would seem to make the lease contract an entirely impossible one in modernity, at least as a means to achieve financing.

However, Islamic finance has found ways around these restrictions. The easiest workaround relates to the rule that the lessee is supposed to be responsible for maintaining the property. To avoid this problem, the parties can simply execute a separate lease/hire contract, or an agency contract, wherein the lessor agrees to take on this responsibility for a fee.

The greater problems relate to the lease being cancellable and the prohibition against the sale at end of the lease term for a price set at the start of the lease term. The best way to describe the means by which these problems are avoided is through creative semantics more than formal restructuring. Specifically, separate from the lease finance documents, the lessee executes what is described as a *wa`ad,* or "promise", to purchase the property at the amount of the outstanding lease payments if it fails to make a payment. That "promise" effectively means that if the lessee "elects" to cancel the lease, as is its right under Islamic law, the result is an acceleration of all outstanding lease payments, which is not dissimilar to what occurs with respect to a default on a conventional lease. Similarly, the lessor makes a "promise" to sell the property to the lessee for a nominal sum in the future, again separate from the lease finance. There is some cleverness in deploying the Arabic term *wa`ad,* with its premodern pedigree, and attempting to achieve some at least documentary separation as between the lease finance and these separate undertakings. Nevertheless, it is rather difficult to see how the overall transaction is not a rather direct flouting of the rules of *gharar,* in particular in those many circumstances where these mutual "promises" are legally enforceable as part of the overall transactions.

In any event, with these sorts of mechanics in place, the use of lease financing becomes much easier to achieve, and indeed rather common in the Islamic finance industry. Hence, for example, rather than using cost plus financing to sell a home, one can engage in what is known as a diminishing partnership. Basically, the home purchaser and the bank together purchase the home through what is known in corporate law as a "special purpose vehicle" (SPV), meaning a legal person such as a company whose sole asset is the home. The purchaser's interest in the SPV at closing is based on the amount of the down payment relative to the entire home, and the bank owns the balance of the SPV. The home purchaser is then obligated to make lease payments on a monthly basis into the SPV. These payments flow to the two owners of the SPV (the bank and the home purchaser) in proportional amounts to the ownership interests. The amount that is supposed to go back to the home purchaser is then used to purchase a small share each month of the bank's interest in the SPV. Over time, the owner's interest in the SPV rises as that of the bank falls, thereby mimicking a conventional mortgage finance. By pegging a lease rate to a reliable indicator, such as the London Interbank Offering Rate, or LIBOR, the transaction can mimic a variable interest rate as well.

Perhaps most revealing in demonstrating the extent to which lease contracts of this sort are in essence a financing arrangement is Interpretive Letter #806 of the Office of the Comptroller of the Currency ("OCC"), issued in 1997, granting the United Bank of Kuwait permission to engage in Islamic lease financing for the retail purchase of homes. The basis for the permission was that the lease financing was "functionally equivalent to a financing transaction in which the [Bank] occupies the position of a secured lender." The letter elaborates as follows:

> The transaction conveys the benefits and burdens of ownership to the Lessee. Once the Lessee enters into the sales contract, but before UBK funds the remainder of the purchase price, UBK and the Lessee negotiate the terms and conditions of the Agreements. Under the Net Lease, the Lessee will make periodic payments, maintain the property, pay charges, costs, and incur expenses attributable to the property that the owner would otherwise pay. UBK will ensure that the Lessee is capable of complying with the terms and conditions of the Net Lease. The Branch will review the creditworthiness of each Lessee to ensure that the Lessee can make minimum monthly lease payments. UBK will use the same formula that it uses to set traditional mortgage payments to determine the amount of monthly lease payments. The amount of the monthly lease payments will cover principal and interest and will be sufficient to amortize the entire purchase price by the end of the lease term. The Lessee will acquire title to the property at the end of the lease term or

earlier if the Lessee pays the remainder of the purchase price. And, as is the case in a conventional mortgage transaction, the Lessee will not have to take any additional action to acquire title after the lease expires. Thus, UBK's Net Lease proposal, in substance, has the characteristics of a financing transaction.

Descriptions of Islamic finance transactions reflected in such material help to reveal the promises of the practice as well as the core, existential peril with which it is faced. On the one hand, framing the transactions in the manner as the 1997 OCC Letter did renders it much easier for Islamic banking to function in a modern, conventional economy with heavily regulated financial institutions. On the other hand, the framing makes it very hard to convince anyone that Islamic finance brings with it the substantive benefit over conventional counterparts that is expected among broad sections of the Muslim public.

2. INSURANCE

There is another type of contract that has become entangled in the speculation prohibition worth discussing. This is the contract for insurance. At one level, this might come as some surprise, given that insurance is not in reality a form of speculation. That is, no policyholder is paying premiums as some sort of "bet" that they will pay off in greater sums in the future. It would be the most unusual holder of a term life insurance policy who would celebrate upon learning that she had contracted a fatal disease and would not live past the expiration date of her policy, thus entitling her to an insurance payout far in excess of any premiums she has paid. The purpose of the policy, rather, is to limit risk. Some early Islamic finance proponents made precisely this argument, likening an insurance contract to the hiring of a guard to protect property. Just as one must pay the guard, whether or not someone actually comes to steal the property, one must pay the premiums, whether or not the event being insured against occurs.

The primary problem with this sort of analysis, from the view of the Islamic finance industry, is that it looks at the transaction from one side only—that of the policy holder. The insurance company, by contrast, is very much engaged in some form of speculation on the expected dates of death of its clientele in order to turn a profit. Defenders of insurance attempted to distinguish this from the ban against the sale of fish in the sea, because there is some reliability to actuarial tables respecting dates of death given sufficient numbers, whereas the sale of a fish in the open sea is more clearly a gamble. The position has its weaknesses, among them that some of the commercial transactions prohibited by the Prophet—such as the ban on the sale of the sperm of a stallion—seem to encompass types of risk that are potentially no less predictable year of death. It would probably more accurate to say that premodern societies never conceived of the idea of quantifying risk, and that therefore the distinction modernists seek to interpose as between gambling and the predictable risk has no easy premodern reference point on which to rely.

In any event, Islamic finance settled on the position relatively early in its development that insurance was a forbidden form of speculation. In its place, it developed an institution known as *takāful,* or solidarity. The institution seeks to take advantage of the fact that within the Maliki school (though not the other schools), there was no ban on speculation for gift contracts. In other words, one could give away a runaway horse, but not sell it, on the theory that enmity does not arise from that which is given freely and without expectation of countervalue.

Thus, in a *takāful*, rather than buying insurance from a provider, the insured collectively provide for themselves by making "donations" into a fund, from which any one of them may withdraw proceeds when certain qualifying conditions occur. The payments to the insured themselves would thus be donative and thereby immune from speculation. Naturally, someone would have to organize the venture, and that manager would be entitled to compensation either through receiving a percentage of excess revenue collected or a set fee. This is not in and of itself fatal—charities have paid employees, after all.

One important distinction exists, at least in theory, as between the *takāful* and the insurance company. This is that the *takāful* would not be responsible for making any payments to any policyholder in need to the extent that the premiums already collected did not provide sufficient funds to do so. No charity, after all, is obligated to serve the needy beyond the amount that the resources provided by its donors would enable it to. Asking the charity's founders to supply their own funds to help those in need if the donations were insufficient is a proposition that is absurd on its face.

Of course, no *takāful* could possibly survive if its clientele could not be assured that they would be compensated for insured losses when they occurred, irrespective of whether there were sufficient funds collected from the other policy holders to make this possible. The most common way to address this is through the use of yet more charity based fiction; namely, by requiring the *takāful* manager to supply "benevolent loans" to the extent necessary to satisfy the insurance obligations. These loans are generally nonrecourse as concerns the policy holders (meaning they cannot be recovered from the personal assets of the policy holders) and can only be paid back from future profits that the *takāful* manager might generate in managing the insurance company. With this change, the distinction between the solidarity company and the conventional insurance company collapses into one that is based almost entirely on semantics.

3. ISLAMIC CAPITAL MARKETS

Finally, this chapter could not be complete without a discussion of the explosion of Islamic finance activity that has taken place in the capital markets. In some ways, the Islamic capital markets would have been a more natural place for the industry to have started, given that interest taking is less central to the idea of capital markets trading than retail banking. Yet, of course, as already thoroughly discussed, the initial purpose of the entire Islamic economics enterprise was not to explore areas of congruence with conventional commerce, but rather to identify loci of confrontation and resistance, as a means to establish an independent economic paradigm. Once the revolutionary ideals began to fade, however, and the practice of mimicry developed sufficient momentum in earnest, it was only a matter of time before the industry would move more aggressively into those areas of commercial activity to which mimicry was more congenially suited; to wit, the Islamic capital markets.

This section explores the entry into that sector sequentially, on the basis of the areas where Islamic capital markets have been the most developed, to those where significant doctrinal barriers to entry remain. We begin, therefore, with the standard equity markets, where interest and speculation seem to play almost no role at all.

a. The Dow Jones *Fatwa*

There is no obvious problem with the purchase and sale of equity, i.e. stock, from an Islamic finance perspective. After all, one is trading an ownership interest in a company on the basis of its perceived value. There is no guaranteed return in such an investment to create the problem of interest, and the risks associated therewith are no more speculative than the risks associated with any business enterprise. Buying someone else's business, or a part of it, seems no more controversial than buying their automobile.

The problem lies in the ubiquity of interest in conventional commerce. Suppose, for example, that one were to take an ownership interest in a new enterprise involving the sale of fast food burritos where only fresh and high quality ingredients are used. Such a company makes most of its money off of retail sales, obviously, and it might even eschew the sale of alcohol given the nature of its business. However, it is hard to believe that it has no debt of any kind on its books. Surely it borrows money from time to time to support new initiatives. If investment in the company is forbidden by virtue of such debt, which is paid back with interest, then it would effectively be impossible for a pious Muslim investor to invest in this company, or indeed any conventional company.

To address this issue, leaders in the Islamic finance industry issued what is known as the Dow Jones *fatwa*. Citing the seemingly completely unrelated Prophetic prohibition against a decedent bequeathing more than one third of the decedent's estate by will, described in Chapter Three, the Dow Jones *fatwa* effectively bans investment in any company whose (i) debt, (ii) accounts receivable, or (iii) cash and marketable securities, divided by its market capitalization, exceed 1/3. Thus, to take our earlier example, a burrito company may have some debt, but it is probably not 1/3 of its entire market capitalization. Similarly, its accounts receivable are surely small and nowhere near 1/3 of its market capitalization. Most of its revenue does not come from clients who promise future payments, as with a bank, but from customers, who provide present cash for food. Finally, while the company might own some stock and surely has some cash on hand, the amount of such cash and stock almost surely does not near 1/3 of its market capitalization. None of these would be true for a bank, or any other venture that relied heavily on debt or credit to fund itself.

The *fatwa* does not apply to businesses whose core operations are themselves un-Islamic, including pornography companies, weapons sellers and manufacturers, alcohol and tobacco companies, and companies that sell pork products. Investment in such businesses is instead absolutely forbidden. There are difficult line drawing exercises—almost no company, for example, sells *exclusively* pork products. The *fatwa* tries to address such matters, in detail that lies beyond the scope of this Nutshell.

Finally, where the *fatwa* does apply, it requires that a shareholder donate to charity any proceeds received that can be attributed to the receipt of any interest payments. In practice, this is nearly impossible to do in most cases. Few actually attempt this with any rigor. Instead, they make regular charitable donations (as conventional institutions do) and hope that it is enough.

There are further elaborations that need not be recounted here. It suffices only to note that the Dow Jones *fatwa* has proven remarkably influential since it was first introduced in 1998. It has permitted a massive influx of Islamic investment into equity markets around the globe and indeed led to a massive rise of Islamic investment vehicles and mutual funds active in exchanges all over the world.

Again, given the general conduciveness of Islamic finance to the idea of profit and risk sharing, this growth in the equity markets is of little surprise. Harder to deal with is the second major sector within the area of capital markets, the bond market. We turn to it next.

b. Ṣukūk

The problem with a bond, from an Islamic finance perspective, is that it entitles its holder to a fixed return. This falls squarely within the core interest prohibition around which Islamic finance is centered. In their customary efforts at mimicry, Islamic finance practitioners attempted—clumsily at first— to create instruments known as the *ṣukūk*. It was defined as an ownership interest in a venture rather than a debt interest. However, the *ṣukūk*, unlike stock, had a "target rate" of return associated with them, which might be fixed, or variable and based on a market interest rate, such as LIBOR. Any amounts that the venture earned for the *ṣukūk* holder above the target rate belonged to the issuer of the *ṣukūk*, as a reward for its activities.

So far, there was little problem, except that sane investors were unlikely to place their money in an instrument that capped their gains, but not their losses. Accordingly, the early *ṣukūk* indicated that to the extent that the venture failed to make the profits reflected in the target rate, it would use money that it had paid to itself in earlier years as reward for exceeding the target rate. This, also, was not deemed problematic. What was problematic, however, was the fact that the early *ṣukūk* also provided that if the issuer had exhausted its reward supply, and still not achieved the target rate, then it would be required to issue zero interest non-recourse "beneficent" loans to the *ṣukūk* holders, which could only be paid back from future payments made to the issuer. This proved too much for the scholars upon whose support the industry depends, chief among them Taqi Usmani, who in 2008 declared such an interest free loan to be an obvious sham, and an attempt to circumvent the ban on guaranteed returns that Islam requires. The result was a catastrophic drop in the global value of *ṣukūk,* though how much of this was due to Usmani's *fatwa* and how much to the overall financial crisis that occurred around the same time is difficult to know.

Since the Usmani *fatwa*, the *ṣukūk* industry has recovered, not by avoiding mimicry but rather by demonstrating far more sophistication in trying to achieve it. One can, for example, develop rather artificial early profits that are then placed into a reserve account that is held for the account of the issuer. To the extent that the issuer then fails to meet future target rates, this fund can be used rather liberally to make up the difference. If the large artificial fund is depleted, then the venture is almost surely in some rather serious trouble. To deal with that case, the parties can insert insolvency provisions to ensure that the *ṣukūk* holders bear the same loss as any ordinary bondholder would bear.

This can prove burdensome, and thus in many cases, it is easier to develop *ṣukūk* on a lease model that avoids fluctuations in return rates. For example, a rental car company seeking to issue *ṣukūk* for a new affiliate in Jordan might very well simply create a special purpose vehicle ("SPV") which the *ṣukūk* holders own through their investment in the SPV. The SPV could use its cash from the holders to purchase automobiles in Jordan and lease them to the rental car company at a fixed rate. The lease payments would be the sole revenue of the SPV, and this amount would not fluctuate based on the profits of the underlying rental car enterprise, as they would be based not on that enterprise, but on lease payments the enterprise was making to the SPV for the automobiles.

c. Derivatives

Finally, we come to the area of capital markets activity where Islamic finance doctrine has proven the thorniest. These are the derivative markets, among them options, which give the holder the right to buy stock in the future at a given price, and futures, which give the holder the right to purchase particular goods at a set future price. The problems, obviously, relate to the *gharar* ban. After all, if the Prophet prohibited the sale of milk in the udders, then how could it be lawful to contract to purchase 1 ton of oranges six months into the future, when such oranges do not currently exist? Derivatives seem to be types of trades that fall squarely within what the Prophet was trying to prohibit. This perhaps explains why there is no such Islamic finance market in derivatives and why most scholars tend to regard the creation of one as doctrinally challenging, to say the least.

That said, there have been efforts to legitimize the derivatives markets. Chief among the them is the notable reformist scholar Mohammad Hashim Kamali. Kamali has argued that there is a difference between the sale of a specific object which one does not currently possess or whose existence is uncertain, such as a runaway horse, or milk in a particular sheep's udder, and objects which are reasonably certain to exist in the future, such as a horse or a set quantity of sheep's milk. The sale of the former is fraught with risk that is akin to a gamble, the theory runs, while the sale of the latter is not. Indeed, Kamali argues, there is ample example of the Prophet permitting the advance sale of commodities, through the practice of *salam,* and jurists in some schools have long permitted the practice of manufacture for hire with payment made in advance. In neither case is the object of sale in the possession of the seller, nor even in existence necessarily.

By and large, Kamali's arguments have not managed to change the general outlook of the industry toward derivatives trading. Most jurists tend to read the classical permissibility of advance sales and manufacturing for hire more narrowly than Kamali does. That said, Kamali's arguments have gained some favor, and certainly one would imagine they may gain more in future years, if the industry finds itself under pressure to expand its capital markets practice. Whether or not this will lead to an explosion in derivatives trading that mirrors the one that took place in the equity markets through the Dow Jones *fatwa* is of course impossible to know.

What can be said with reasonable confidence, however, is that whether or not that happens, the tensions inherent in the practice of Islamic finance, between revolutionary ideals rooted in a rejection of the twin capitalist and communist hegemons on the one hand, and practical realities rooted very much in mimicry of conventional techniques on the other, will continue for the foreseeable future.

CHAPTER 6
ISLAMIC CRIMINAL LAW

A. INTRODUCTION

In turning to the subject of criminal law, this Chapter continues the discussion of areas of Islamic law largely displaced in modernity. Islamic criminal law resembles Islamic finance in a notable number of ways. As with Islamic finance, Islamic criminal law ceased being relevant in the lives of the vast majority of Muslims around a century ago. This means that generations of law students, law professors, lawyers, and judges in most Muslim countries have had little exposure to it, and only a rudimentary understanding of its underlying principles. Moreover, as with Islamic finance, Islamic criminal law has enjoyed something of a resurgence in recent times, within the context of legal systems that are otherwise transplanted from systems of European origin. In order to achieve this, as with Islamic finance, Islamic criminal law has had to evolve, and in some cases transform nearly entirely.

Nevertheless, there are differences between Islamic finance and Islamic criminal law. The primary one is that there is more doctrinal coherence associated with Islamic criminal law. Though there was no such category as "criminal law" in classical juristic accounts, there certainly were several independent, internally stable areas of law that could each be described as falling within the ambit of what is referred to in modern parlance as criminal law. An effort to take them in part and insert them into a modern criminal system is different from what arose in Islamic finance, which was to assemble an entire structure of financing that bore very little resemblance to anything from the classical era. The analogy might be the difference between, on the one hand, finding a way to incorporate a colonial era wood burning stove into a modern home, and, on the other, inventing the very concept of an in-home kitchen where before all cooking was done out of doors.

Given the broad resemblance of the constituent elements of modern Islamic criminal law to their classical antecedents, it is easier to introduce this Chapter through the structures of the classical law. That is, we can look first at the doctrines of classical Islamic law that might fairly be described as criminal, and, from there, seek to comprehend the manner in which parts of those doctrines have been introduced into modern states. This will enable us to assess where the classical law remains relevant, and why certain pieces, but not others, have been imported. It will also help reveal how the classical law has changed, in some cases quite significantly, to meet the demands and expectations of modern Muslim societies.

We will begin with the most well known category of Islamic criminal law, and the one that is the subject of most popular attention. This is the category that encompasses the relatively discrete class of crimes known as the Scriptural Crimes.

B. CLASSICAL ISLAMIC CRIMINAL LAW

1. THE SCRIPTURAL CRIMES

The Scriptural Crimes, or the *ḥudūd* (which literally translates as "limits"), refer to those crimes that at least in theory are delineated in the Qur'an or the Sunna as meriting specific earthly punishments. This is in contradistinction to various forms of conduct described in revelatory material, in some cases stridently, as sinful, but to which the revelatory material reveals no earthly punishment. Examples of the latter include the sin of gambling, or commercial gains associated with *ribā*, both of which are explored in the previous Chapter. Whether an Islamic state criminalizes such activity or not, there is broad consensus that they are not Scriptural Crimes. This is important, because classification of a crime as scriptural has significant consequences. To commit a Scriptural Crime is to transgress the limits that God has set for Muslims in their conduct, for which God demands a specific penalty. Accordingly, punishment is generally mandatory, severe, and, with certain exceptions noted below, human beings have no discretion to modify or mitigate the punishments. Hence, to carry out the punishments set for the Scriptural Crimes is a manner of demonstrating societal obedience to God, as perhaps best revealed by the Sunna that to impose such a punishment brings more nourishment to the earth than forty nights of rain.

While this is broadly understood, it is less understood, among lay Muslims and casual, journalistic commentators alike, how rare application of the Scriptural Crimes was expected to be, under the conceptions of the classical jurists themselves. In fact, this is perhaps the most important point to make about the Islamic Scriptural Crimes. Despite the supposed obligation to carry out the punishments where applicable, the fact is that the elements of the crime, and the evidentiary rules, are laid out in a manner that renders them so obviously burdensome that it is difficult to imagine how they could possibly ever be implemented without the consent of the perpetrator. Nowhere is this truer than with respect to the primary Scriptural Crime, the one that the classical jurists invariably discuss first and the standard against which the succeeding Scriptural Crimes are measured. This is the crime known as *zina,* or fornication.

The relatively narrow definition of fornication does not differ greatly among the jurists. By way of example, and in terms that are characteristically blunt for classical jurists, the medieval Shi'i scholar known as the Second Martyr defines the crime as "the insertion of a person of his penis into the prohibited genitals of a woman, without a [marriage] contract, nor ownership, nor doubt. It is realized upon the disappearance of the glans, in the front [i.e., the vagina] or the rear [i.e. the anus]." Thus, licit sex, which in the medieval era encompassed both marital sex and sex as between a master and his female slaves, does not fall within the fornication prohibition. Nor does illicit sex where there was some level of doubt as to the nature of the relationship between the man and the woman involved. Hence, if a marriage is concluded that does not meet the marriage conditions of a given Islamic school, such as the Hanafi requirement of two male Muslim witnesses, but the couple *thought* they were married based on their own conceptions of what a marriage contract required, then the they have not committed the crime of *zina*.

Even more importantly, sexual activity that falls short of vaginal or anal penetration by a penis does not constitute *zina*. This by itself creates a rather obvious problem of proof, given what witnesses are likely to be able to attest to. The evidentiary problem is further compounded by the fact that a variety of verses in the 24th Chapter of the Qur'an require the testimony of four morally upright witnesses to the specific act of penetration, and punish those testifying with 80 lashes each if less than four come forward to offer testimony. This four witness requirement is taken so literally across the sects and schools that, with the exception of only one school, the Maliki, even pregnancy of an unmarried woman is deemed insufficient proof of fornication. For the Malikis, pregnancy leads to an inference of fornication where there is no evidence that the pregnant woman resisted the intercourse. The Malikis soften this by presuming a maximum gestational period of five years, meaning that a pregnant woman married within the previous five years would not only be innocent of fornication, but would also be able to establish the child's lineage through her ex-husband.

As should be clear, it is not realistically possible to prove *zina* in all but the most unusual of circumstances. Indeed, most of the reports contained in foundational materials relating to punishing *zina* involve those who seem to have freely confessed to the crime, seemingly as a means to expiate for the sin. A confession usually requires the alleged perpetrator to admit to the fornication four times, to equal the number of witnesses required to implement the penalty without a confession. The perpetrator is free to retract the confession at any time, at which point the punishment cannot be imposed.

For those determined guilty, by confession or otherwise, the punishment is death by stoning if they fall within the class of individuals known as *muḥṣan*. For everyone else, it is one hundred lashes. The sects differ on who fits within the category of *muḥṣan*. For the Sunni schools, the *muḥṣan* is anyone who is a nonvirgin. For the Shi'a, the category of *muḥṣan* is limited to those with access to lawful sex, meaning the person is married (or is a man with female slaves), and the person's spouse (or slaves) are accessible. The one exception among the Shi'a is to those who are in a temporary marriage. For reasons that are unclear, they are not deemed *muḥṣan*.

The disparate punishments given to the *muḥṣan* and the non-*muḥṣan* is curious, in that it seems to contradict Qur'an 24:2, which indicates that those who fornicate, whether men or women, should be lashed with a hundred lashes, with no mention of stoning at all. The consensus view among the classical jurists, however, was that there is Sunna which imposes the punishment of stoning on the *muḥṣan*, and that therefore the Qur'anic verse applying a punishment of one hundred lashes must be limited to those who are not *muḥṣan*. This classical interpretive move, which has come under criticism by those advancing modernist understandings of Islamic law, demonstrates the manner in which traditional jurists tended to use Sunna not only to supplement Qur'anic text, but to limit its application as well.

The natural question that follows these disquisitions on fornication as between a man and a woman is how illicit same sex relations are treated. None of the four Sunni schools regard lesbian relations as a Scriptural Crime, as the absence of a penis takes the activity outside of the realm of *zina*. The Shi'a have a separate Scriptural Crime for lesbianism, which generally carries a punishment of one hundred lashes, with some jurists imposing stoning on married women.

For male-male sexual relations, there is more variety among the schools and sects. The Shi'a and the Malikis are the most severe, creating a separate Scriptural Crime for anal intercourse between males and imposing extremely severe punishments that include burning the perpetrator alive, throwing him from a tall building, or stoning him. The Hanbalis and the Shafi'is analogize anal sex between men to fornication, and impose the same punishments on them as they do on fornicators.

Most interesting are the Hanafi jurists, who do not deem it permissible to exceed the strict definitional limits of the Scriptural Crimes through analogy, even if they use analogy freely in other areas of law. Moreover, quite notably, in contradistinction to the Malikis and the Shi'a, the Hanafis do not believe that there is any source text in the Qur'an or Sunna that speaks of homosexuality as a punishable sin. Nevertheless, some early Hanafis decided that the term "fornication" was broad enough in its lexical sense to include anal penetration of one man by another. Others did not. This means that at least one prominent group of Muslim jurists in the medieval era did not believe that homosexuality was a practice that necessitated any sort of earthly punishment. The point is important enough to dwell on, and easy enough to overlook in light of the fact that in today's world, severe repression of homosexuals occurs disproportionately in Islamic countries.

While all classical schools and sects agreed on the basic contours of *zina*, there was less consensus on what the remaining Scriptural Crimes were. Thus, for example, Shi'i jurists established a Scriptural Crime for lesbianism, while none of the Sunni schools did. Some jurists included sorcery or witchcraft as a Scriptural Crime as well, but this was far from universal. Despite these differences, there was broad agreement on a certain subset of Scriptural Crimes, discussed below.

First, there was the crime known as *qadhf*. In modern Arab legal systems, this term refers to any type of defamation or slander, but in the classical context, it referred to an accusation of *zina* where there were not the requisite number of morally upright witnesses to corroborate that the crime had taken place. If convicted, the slanderer is administered 80 lashes.

Secondly, on the basis of Qur'anic verse, jurists universally agreed that *theft* was a Scriptural Crime. To qualify, the amount stolen needed to exceed a certain minimum value, the property had to be under guard, it had to be taken surreptitiously rather than openly or by force of arms, and it could not have been entrusted to or partially owned by the person taking it. Two morally upright make Muslim witnesses must be able to testify to all of these matters. Their failure to do so, or any discrepancy of any sort in their testimony, would take the matter beyond the narrow limits of the Scriptural Crime. If proven, which was rare for the reasons set forth above, the punishment was amputation of the right hand, followed by the left foot for a second offense.

Third is *banditry*, which comes from the following two verses of the Qur'an:

> Indeed, the penalty for those who wage war against Allah and His Messenger and strive upon earth [to cause] corruption is none but that they be killed or crucified or that their hands and feet be cut off from opposite sides or that they be exiled from the land. That is for them a disgrace in this world; and for them in the Hereafter is a great punishment.
>
> Except for those who return [repenting] before you apprehend them. And know that Allah is Forgiving and Merciful. [Qur'an 5:33–34].

In classical conception, banditry involved open use of arms on land or sea, in the city or a remote region, in order to frighten people in a manner that foments disorder and mischief. While theft or killing often accompanied such acts of banditry, they were not necessary elements of it, and indeed the idea of "waging war" against God and the Prophet suggest that banditry may in some cases have connotations of violent political uprising as well. The caliph was generally authorized to decide which of the harsh punishments for banditry laid out in the Qur'anic passage set forth in the quoted passage above should be implemented in any given case.

Drinking alcohol was another broadly agreed upon Scriptural Crime, with the punishment generally agreed to be 80 lashes. Given their reluctance to apply analogical reasoning in the context of the Scriptural Crimes, the Hanafis applied the punishment only to wines (i.e. alcohol arising from fermented fruits), or to drunkenness, both of which are specifically prohibited by Qur'anic verse. The other Sunni schools extended the crime to cover all intoxicants. The Shi'a took the same position as the majority of the Sunni schools, not on the basis of analogy, which they reject as an interpretive tool, but rather on the authority of statements from the Sixth Imam, who did not differentiate among intoxicants in defining the Scriptural Crime.

Finally, the general but not universal view among the jurists was that *apostasy* constituted a Spiritual Crime with a required punishment of death for men, on the basis of Sunna that those who change their religion should be killed. Unlike the other Scriptural Crimes, the definition of apostasy tended to be broad, and include any sort of intentional denial of the absolute certainties of Islam. This would include a denial of the existence of angels, for example, or a denial of the prohibition against drinking. This rather draconian doctrine was softened by the fact that among the Sunni schools, a person always had the opportunity to repent their apostasy and return to the faith. Thus, a casual utterance or one made in anger could easily be retracted without the speaker being subjected to mandatory death. The Shi'a only granted this opportunity for repentance to those who had converted to Islam and were seeking to convert back to their original faith. Those born into Islam who denied its certainties were supposed to be killed without the possibility of repentance.

As for women, three of the Sunni schools deemed their punishment to be death as well. By contrast, the Hanafis and the Shi'a punished women by repeated beatings until and unless they repented and returned to the faith. Moreover, these punishments were discretionary rather than scriptural, meaning there was no absolute obligation to carry them out.

Related to apostasy was the *cursing of the Prophet*. There was a universal view among Muslims that this was a Scriptural Crime, though the schools differed as to its treatment. The Hanafis considered it to be apostasy. One consequence of this is that under Hanafi rules there is no Scriptural Crime associated with insulting the Prophet for non-Muslims. The other Sunni schools and the Shi'a regarded the cursing of the Prophet to be its own Scriptural Crime, carrying a mandatory sentence of death for Muslim and non-Muslim alike, without the possibility of repentance. This creates the rather odd result, not unnoticed among some classical jurists, that one who insults the Prophet Muhammad is killed without the possibility of repentance while one who insults God Himself can repent and return to the faith.

2. THE DISCRETIONARY CRIMES

It should be relatively obvious that, in addition to being exceedingly difficult to prove in most cases, the Scriptural Crimes are also rather narrow in their scope. This latter point may cause some initial confusion. It seems rather difficult to understand why a person who lies under oath about fornication should be lashed 80 times, but one who lies about theft should suffer no punishment at all. Similarly, it appears to make no sense at all to have a set of rules whereby a person who embezzles money entrusted to him or her is not punished, yet someone who steals guarded items not entrusted to them has a hand amputated. Such rules hardly seem to be of the sort that will create a stable public order.

In this regard, it is important to reemphasize the point that the Scriptural Crimes are not intended to lay the foundations of a system of criminal justice that leads to a well ordered society. Rather, they are intended to identify particular, limited crimes for which God demands retribution, based on textual support from Qur'an and Sunna. The relationship to the public interest, to the extent it exists at all, is therefore purely incidental.

To fill in the obvious gaps the Scriptural Crimes create, for the precise purpose of establishing a well ordered society infused with an Islamic ethos, medieval jurists created an entire body of law known as the Discretionary Crimes, or the *ta`zīrāt,* that were largely left for a judge to apply. Hence, if a person were to steal an item, and there was a very minor discrepancy in testimony as between two witnesses relating to the act of theft, the judge would almost surely decide that there was insufficient evidence to apply the Scriptural Crime of theft. Yet if the judge believed that a theft took place, the judge could use discretionary power to impose a punishment for the theft. Similar, and quite common, was the imposition of punishments for sexual activity that either did not rise to the level of fornication ("thighing" was a common one discussed in juristic accounts), or where there was insufficient proof of fornication, because the required number of witnesses were lacking.

Discretionary Crimes did not arise exclusively in a gap created by a narrow definition of a Scriptural Crime. Fraud in the marketplace—for example, using false weights or measures—was also a common discretionary crime, and its relationship to any Scriptural Crime is tenuous at best. The purpose of the category in the end is not to close loopholes, but rather to establish a fair and just society that punishes wrongdoing. In defining what conduct constituted Discretionary Crimes, judges were therefore largely unconstrained by any formal rules. While various jurists would offer opinions on particular types of conduct they considered to be deserving of sanction, the general understanding was that judges were guided, and not limited, by these various disquisitions, which were necessarily impartial and not consistent with one another. A judge would hear a case, and make an independent determination as to whether or not the conduct alleged merited sanction.

Judges were also unconstrained in setting the punishments. The main limitation was that they could not impose a punishment beyond what would be imposed for an associated Scriptural Crime, if there was one. By far the most common punishment judges imposed was lashing. Reprimands, fines, prison sentences, and even capital punishment were also possible.

Finally, it was not only judges who could determine the content of criminal activity outside of the scope of the Scriptural Crimes. Executive authorities could exercise their own powers to declare particular activity punishable, and courts would then impose punishments for violations of that activity as well.

While they are neither the focus of most scholarly or popular attention, in fact it is the Discretionary Crimes that serve as the bulwark of the Islamic criminal system. They are intended to preserve public order and morality, and they impose genuine retribution against those understood to violate public norms. In this way, they contributed much more to the actual implementation of criminal justice than the Scriptural Crimes did.

C. ISLAMIC CRIMINAL LAW IN MODERNITY

This section explores the influence of the classical doctrine on modern criminal law and practice in Muslim states. It begins with the area where the classical imprint is the most obvious; namely, in the codification of the Scriptural Crimes. After this, the Section turns to the more limited impact of the classical discretionary crimes on modern criminal law.

1. THE SCRIPTURAL CRIMES IN MODERN COURTS

This section explores the most well-known example of the codification of the Scriptural Crimes is the enactment of the Hudood Ordinances by General Zia al-Haq in Pakistan in 1979, shortly after Zia orchestrated a coup and sought Islamic legitimacy for his authoritarian rule. Other efforts toward partial or full codification of the Scriptural Crimes exist as well, including (but not limited to) states as varied as post-revolutionary Iran, the Sudan, the Maldives, Malaysia, the province of Aceh, Indonesia and several of the northern states of the Nigerian Federation. The extent of the codification, and the substantive components involved in it, differ from place to place. Nevertheless, two general observations are worth noting, as noted below.

a. Scriptural Crime as Instrument of Repression

One immediate and obvious observation of the implementation of Islamic criminal law in modernity is the rather dramatic extent to which it has been used as a means to repress women, religious minorities, and other disfavored groups. Hence, for example, in nearly every place where fornication has been criminalized, the accused have overwhelmingly been women, for a crime that by definition requires the involvement of at least one man.

One reason for this particular result, albeit probably the least important, relates to the substantive Islamic law itself. The high evidentiary burden of fornication makes it difficult to prove that a man committed fornication, but not a woman who becomes pregnant. While under the rules of most of the schools of Islamic law, pregnancy on its own is insufficient proof of the Scriptural Crime of fornication, this is not true in the Maliki school. In the states that adopt the Maliki rules, among them the Muslim majority northern states of Nigeria, this does lead to clear disproportionality. As an example, in a high profile case that took place in the Katsina state of Nigeria, the defendant Amina Lawal was found guilty of fornication and sentenced to stoning by a lower court on the basis of the fact that she had confessed to the sexual encounter, and indeed had become pregnant from it. The man alleged to have had intercourse with her was freed, after denying involvement, because there were not four witnesses to prove his presence. The sentence was upheld on appeal, even after Lawal sought to retract her confession. It was not until the court of final appeal—the Sharia Court of Appeals of Katsina—that the conviction was reversed. The Court made the rather basic point, of which the lower courts were seemingly unaware, that Islamic law permitted a defendant to retract a confession to a Scriptural Crime at any time. Moreover, the defendant had been married within the previous five years. As noted above, under the rules of the Maliki school, the maximum gestation period for a child is presumed to be five years. Thus fornication cannot be proved without doubt for any pregnant woman married within five years of the birth of a child. Decision of the Sharia Court of Appeals, Katsina State (Nigeria), *decided* September 25, 2003.

It is worth noting, however, that even in states where Maliki rules do not apply, it is women who are overwhelmingly the accused in *zina* prosecutions. This may well arise because of the dramatically lower tolerance in most Islamic societies toward sexual permissiveness on the part of females relative to males. Indeed, in some cases, there is legislation that runs contrary to Islamic law that is obviously intended to advance the aim of using fornication laws to target women. In Pakistan, for example, the laws against *qadhf* exempt from their purview an accusation of fornication made "in good faith" to a person who has "lawful authority" over the person accused. This obviously refers to husbands and fathers, who are free to make false accusations of fornication of their wives and daughters, respectively, so long as they meet a rather low threshold of "good faith." This exemption, which is granted to men alone and pertains almost exclusively to women, does not exist in classical texts.

The bias against women as concerns *zina* extends beyond this peculiar legislative exemption to the broader application of the Scriptural Crime by the courts, where Islamic law has been contorted in rather perverse ways to facilitate rape and punish rape victims. The high profile case of *Zafran Bibi v. The State,* decided by the Federal Shariat Court of Pakistan in 2002, is illustrative of the problem. Zafran Bibi was a village woman whose husband, Niamat Khan, had been in prison for a period of years. On March 26, 2001, accompanied by her father in law, she filed a police report indicating that 11 or 12 days prior to the report, a man by the name of Akmal Khan had raped her. Upon a medical examination, it was discovered that she was seven weeks pregnant, rather than 11 days. She was accordingly arrested along with Akmal Khan to face trial.

When she was interrogated by the police in connection with the arrest, she claimed that she was illiterate, that she did not know the contents of the report she had earlier filed, and that in fact it was her own brother in law, and not Akmal Khan, who had raped her. Her father in law, she insisted, had prepared the earlier report (presumably in an attempt to deflect blame from his own son for the rape), and she had not had anything to do with it. The husband moreover testified that he had enjoyed lawful sexual relations with his wife while in prison and acknowledged the child as his. There was, to say the least, sufficient doubt, as that term is used by classical jurists, to render the Scriptural Crime of fornication inapplicable.

Nevertheless, Akmal Khan was freed, but Zafran Bibi was sentenced to death by stoning for committing the Scriptural Crime of fornication. The evidence to support the Scriptural Crime was not the rape itself—Pakistan is governed by Hanafi rules, which require four witnesses—but only that the defendant had "confessed" to fornication by claiming rape.

The Federal Shariat Court reversed the conviction, pointing out in the process that a report of rape is not a confession to fornication, but rather an assertion of forced fornication on the part of another person. In any event, the Court indicated, there was no basis to conclude that the defendant had committed fornication, given that her husband confirmed paternity of the child and given that the father in law had not sought any sort of reprisal against the defendant, as he certainly would have had he believed she had been adulterous. *Zafran Bibi v. The State,* Criminal Appeal No. 6P 2002, Federal Shariat Court of Pakistan, decided June 6, 2002.

After *Zafran Bibi,* the extremely troubling phenomenon of rape victims in Pakistan being imprisoned for years for a fornication to which they had "confessed" while their alleged rapists walked free became considerably rarer. It finally came to an end with the enactment of the Zina Ordinance Amendment of 2006, which narrowed the definition of fornication solely to the core Scriptural Crime, placed rape back into the ordinary Penal Code, and made clear that a complaint of rape could not be converted into one of fornication.

Beyond women, religious minorities are often victims of the application of the Scriptural Crimes as well, even in states that do not adopt Islamic criminal law. An example of this lies in Iraq in the case of the children of parents who convert to Islam. The General Panel of the Iraqi Court of Cassation decided a case in the year 2000 dealing with a girl of the Sabian faith who was ten years old when her father converted to Islam. The case arose because upon reaching the age of majority, the girl sought to return to her religion of origin, on the basis of an executive order which authorized this. The Court pointed to a subsequent executive order, which both rescinded the earlier one and further indicated that conversions would only be recognized if undertaken in accordance with Islamic law.

The problem is that as a matter of Islamic law, classical era jurists differed on the extent to which a child whose parents convert to Islam is deemed a Muslim. Shi'i jurists, for example, were primarily concerned with a child's status at birth or conception, not at the time that a parent converts. By contrast, some Hanafi jurists maintained that a young child whose parents converted to Islam was deemed a Muslim. The Court of Cassation seemingly was unaware of or did not care about these nuances and treated it as a matter of absolutely clear Islamic law that when a father had converted to Islam, his minor children converted with him involuntarily. As a result, the Court ruled, the litigant would not be recognized as a Sabian, but as a Muslim, meaning as a practical matter, among other things, that her identity card would reflect that she was Muslim and that she would be unable as a Muslim to marry a Sabian man. Case 318/General Panel/2000, Court of Cassation of Iraq, decided Feb. 14, 2000.

Notably, Iraqi courts have continued to apply this rule even after the regime change in 2003. This is despite a 2005 Constitution with robust religious freedom protections for religious minorities and despite the fact that the executive orders on which the earlier Court of Cassation decision relied were issued from none other than the totalitarian Saddam Hussein, whose impact on the law was elsewhere being steadily eradicated. Equally notably, the Iraqi courts apply this rule to boys who are as old as fifteen when one parent converts. Case 285/Personal Status Panel/2008, Court of Cassation of Iraq, decided December 31, 2008. This creates something of a cognitive dissonance, given that nearly all schools of Islamic law would deem a fifteen year old boy an adult, at least to the extent that he had reached puberty. Thus, the courts seem to apply *secular, Iraqi* law to determine the age of majority, and then apply their understanding of classical Islamic law to convert them forcibly into Islam.

Interestingly enough, the Court of Cassation in the more secular autonomous Kurdistan region reached a different result on this same question of forced child conversions. The case in Kurdistan involved a woman who had converted to Islam and her child, who had no interest in doing so. Some of its reasoning was based on the peculiar facts of the case. The woman was estranged from the rest of her family, and she had converted after she had lost contact with them. Under these sorts of circumstances, where the parent has lost contact with the child entirely, there is even classical authority to suggest that the child is not deemed Muslim.

The Court also cited the religious freedom protections of Iraq's constitution, and, interestingly enough, the provisions of the Qur'an itself, to take the position that nobody should be compelled to remain Muslim, even those who had themselves converted to Islam. General Panel, Court of Cassation of the Autonomous Kurdistan Region of Iraq, decided December 25, 2004.

The Kurdistan court approach is quite a progressive one within courts in the modern world. The specific verse cited by the court in its defense, and the one most cited by reformists, is 2:256, which begins "there is no compulsion in religion, so that truth may be manifest from error." Yet one searching for comparable Qur'anic verses would not have trouble finding them. Among them are the following:

> And say, "The truth is from your Lord, so whoever wills—let him believe; and whoever wills—let him disbelieve." [Qur'an 18:29.]

> And whether We show you part of what We promise them or take you in death, upon you is

only the [duty of] notification, and upon Us is the account. [Qur'an 13:40.]

For you is your religion, and for me is my religion. [Qur'an 109:6.]

The classical jurists did not understand these verses to mean that Muslims were free to leave the faith. They relied on other authority, and in particular Sunna, to reach an alternative conclusion. Modern reformists exercise *'ijtihād* to reinterpret revelatory texts. In so doing, they claim that whatever Sunnaic authority there existed to impose a death penalty on apostates applied exclusively to those who had left the faith and made war on it. What these reformist efforts and the Kurdistan decision demonstrate is that there is perpetual ferment and churn in how Muslims understand and approach their sacred texts.

Nevertheless, it is fair to say that the more common position of modern Muslim courts is that irrespective of how to treat children whose parents convert, conversion for those born Muslim away from Islam is not possible in light of the Scriptural Crime of apostasy. Hence, in Malaysia, individuals seeking to convert away from Islam have found it impossible to do so. The well known case of *Lina Joy,* involving a secular Muslim woman who wished to marry her Christian boyfriend and needed to convert to be able to do it, provides an excellent example. The Court of Appeals framed the question as one of administrative law, and indicated that the National Registration Division could not issue an identity card that changed Lina Joy's religion without an order from a sharia court that indicated that she had renounced the Islamic faith in accordance with the tenets of the faith. Yet the Court was of course aware that no sharia court would ever issue such a decision because it would be tantamount to convicting her of apostasy. In requiring that the appellant follow the rules of Islam to leave Islam, the court was effectively forcing her to remain a Muslim forever. *Lina Joy v. Muslim Religious Council for the Federal Territory of Putrajaya et al.*, Civil Appeal No. 1-2-2006, decided May 30, 2007.

One notable point to reemphasize is that neither *Lina Joy* nor the Iraqi cases are penal in nature. There is no actual effort to punish the putative Muslims who are seeking to leave the faith. Instead, their departure from the faith is not being recognized by civil courts for other purposes. This demonstrates both the deep seated biases within Muslim societies against apostasy, informed by the classical law, as well as the equally strong and somewhat contrary biases in favor of the modern principle of legality, explored further in the next section. That is, it would not occur to the Iraqi court to sentence to death a Christian adolescent forced into Islam who wishes to return to Christianity, simply because the act of converting away from Islam is not described as criminal in the Penal Code. Nevertheless, the Iraqi courts, and the Malaysian ones, quite clearly permit the historic criminalization of apostasy to inform their decisions in other areas, as the case law described above demonstrates.

Finally, beyond being used to target disfavored groups, the Scriptural Crimes have become a tool to stifle debate and dissent within Islamic circles. The case of Nasr Abu Zayd is quite instructive in this regard. Abu Zayd was a linguistics professor at Cairo University whose views respecting Islamic law were rather unorthodox. Among other things, Abu Zayd regarded the expressions in the Qur'an relating to angels, *jinns,* devils, and God's Throne as being subject to evolution, from a literal meaning among early Muslims to a more nuanced and metaphorical one that should be espoused in modern times. Abu Zayd further suggested that the Sunna should not be understood as an independent source of law, but rather as the Prophet's human understanding and indeed expression of what was in its essence divine inspiration.

These views did not win the favor of prominent Islamists associated with the Muslim Brotherhood, who filed a case against him in personal status court in 1993 seeking a divorce between him and his wife, despite the fact that neither of them desired such a dissolution. The theory was that Abu Zayd's denial of the literal meaning of the Qur'an was a denial of the certainty of Islam, and in that sense a form of apostasy. As Abu Zayd's Muslim wife could not be married to a non-Muslim under Islamic law (as described in Chapter Two), and as Egypt applies Islamic personal status law for its Muslim population, a divorce was necessary. Again, as with *Lina Joy* and the Iraqi conversion cases, nobody thought to bring criminal charges for the presumed apostasy because the Egyptian Penal Code has no provisions relating to apostasy.

The Personal Status Court of Appeals agreed with the claimants and ordered the divorce (Case No. 287 of Judicial Year 111, District 14, Personal Status Appeals Court of Cairo, Egypt). In so doing, the Court read apostasy broadly so as to suggest that virtually any interpretation of Islam that differed from the received consensus of the jurists of the classical era was itself a form of apostasy. This included not only the figurative understandings of angels and devils, but even problematic aspects of historic Islamic law doctrine that Nasr had challenged in connection with his more metaphorical understanding of divine revelation. These include the imposition of a special tax on religious minorities, and the traditional right of male masters to sexual enjoyment of their female slaves. The Egyptian Court of Cassation affirmed the judgment, which ultimately resulted in Nasr Abu Zayd fleeing Egypt with his wife for the Netherlands.

The Abu Zayd case arose in the 1990's, decades before the rise of the Islamic State of Iraq and Syria ("ISIS") and its overt claim to restore some of the more problematic rules of the premodern era relating to religious minority taxes and concubinage. It is hard to believe that today, an Egyptian court would have been as willing to insist that denial of the right of a man to have sex with female slaves was somehow apostasy. Nevertheless, decisions such as that of Nasr Abu Zayd certainly can be understood to have legitimized—unwittingly to be sure—the rise of ISIS. When civil courts in the heart of the Arab world claim that concubinage and religious taxes are so central to Islam that to deny them is to commit apostasy, it makes it rather difficult to claim subsequently that a radical insurgency is unIslamic for imposing taxes on religious minorities and instituting a system of sex slave trading.

This was far from the problem that the Egyptian courts found themselves facing in 1996 following the Abu Zayd case. Instead, they found themselves facing a plethora of lawsuits instituted by well funded and well organized Islamist groups against Egypt's leading intellectuals—among them feminists, secularists, and a Nobel laureate—demanding in each case a forcible divorce of the accused for something the accused had said or done that, the Islamist group in question claimed, constituted a form of apostasy. This would have been troublesome enough on its own, but the Abu Zayd saga had also led to much unwanted publicity, and the authorities were eager to put an end to the embarrassment the case had engendered. The result was the enactment of Law 3 of 1996, which required litigants seeking forced divorces of other people to register their complaints of alleged apostasy through the public prosecutor's office rather than the personal status courts. This enabled a public prosecutor to serve as a gatekeeper of sorts, and seems to have been remarkably effective in ending the practice of forcing happily married couples into divorces they did not seek.

It is notable that the solution that the Egyptian lawmakers adopted to avoid a repetition of the Abu

Zayd problem was procedural in nature. This seems in keeping with broader trends. Given the thorough incorporation of Western-style court systems into most states in the Islamic world, there has been little alternative but to adopt secular procedural rules to accompany those systems. Moreover, such procedural secularization has met with little resistance. Indeed, even Abu Zayd's initial defense to his supposed apostasy began with a procedural argument; namely, that the claimants lacked standing to raise the suit for divorce, when none of them were parties to the marriage nor even related to the married parties themselves. Though the claim was rejected, it helps to demonstrate the manner in which litigants, courts, and legislatures alike often try to use modern procedure to avoid the application of Islamic law.

Finally, beyond women, religious minorities, and reformists, political dissidents have also been subjected to persecution through the codification of the Spiritual Crimes. The most common way to do this is through the use of the Spiritual Crime of banditry to repress those expressing dissent against an authoritarian regime. As noted above, the general conception of banditry involved the open use of arms, often in daylight, in a fashion that was intended to frighten people and sow corruption. Nevertheless, the Arabic term for banditry, *ḥirāba,* relates to the waging of war, and indeed the Qur'anic verse from which the Spiritual Crime is derived refers to making war against God and His Messenger. Therefore, to challenge an existing Islamic regime through the open use of arms can be thought of as a form of "banditry" as well. Demonstrators, of course, rarely carry weapons, but there may be enough violent malcontents within any given demonstration to make an allegation of banditry possible. If not, then a pliant court in an authoritarian state might be persuaded to find on thin evidence a supposed conspiracy to overthrow a state by force of arms.

Using such techniques, Iran, among other states, makes notorious use of "banditry" as a basis to pursue those it deems suspicious or threatening to it. Victims include journalists, demonstrators, and even researchers accused of spying for Israel or Western powers.

b. Uneven Implementation of the Punishments for Scriptural Crimes

Beyond the observations above, it is important to note that the application of the Scriptural Crime punishments across those jurisdictions that have them is highly uneven. For example, state courts almost never order a stoning, a crucifixion, or cross amputation. These punishments are generally not difficult to avoid under classical rules, either because of a high evidentiary bar (in the case of stoning) or because they require the use of a ruler's discretion to implement them (in the case of crucifixion or cross amputation).

The record respecting implementation of the punishment of amputations for theft is more mixed. On one end lies Pakistan, whose bar and bench are common law educated and are frequent participants in demonstrations demanding the rule of law and the separation of powers. These elites overwhelmingly opposed the enactment of the Hudood Ordinances by General Zia and his junta, and have been rather notorious in seeking to limit their effect. As a result, conviction rates for Scriptural Crimes are lower in Pakistan than they are elsewhere, and reversals on appeal and acquittal are astonishingly high. Over 80% of defendants were at least partially successful on appeal before the Federal Shariat Court between 1980 and 1984, according to one study. As a result, the most severe punishments, very much including amputation, are almost always avoided.

By contrast, during the Islamist rule of Omar Hasan Bashir, Sudanese courts seemed far more willing to order amputations, even when the punishment did not seem to necessarily apply. Hence, for example, amputations were recorded for embezzlement, and yet embezzlement certainly does not meet the elements of the Scriptural Crime of theft, because the item was partially entrusted to the person doing the embezzling.

Broadly in the middle are courts in countries like Saudi Arabia and Iran, where it is quite clear that the preference of the courts is to reject claims by the prosecution for a Scriptural Crime conviction for theft, on the grounds that one of the elements of the crime was missing. Following this, the court then feels free to impose its own discretionary penalty for whatever wrongdoing occurred, which usually takes the form of lashing, imprisonment, or both, depending on the circumstances. It is only on very rare occasion that a court will order an amputation.

2. LEGALITY AND THE TRANSFORMATION OF THE ISLAMIC CRIMINAL SYSTEM

a. Discretionary Crimes Reinvented

One very significant difficulty inherent in a modern state adopting classical Islamic criminal law is the internalization of the principle of *legality*. This refers to the idea that a person cannot be convicted of a crime, nor can the person be subjected to punishment, in the absence of public legislation defining the activity in question as criminal, and punishable. In particular as to discretionary crimes, this is not something that a court in the classical period would have even contemplated as a possibility.

Yet it is difficult to overstate the universalization of the legality principle among legal practitioners of all sorts across the entire modern Islamic world. Indeed, the Latin maxim that encapsulates the principle—*nullum crimen, nulla poena sine lege*—has its own Arabic versions which reads *la jarīma wa la aqūba illā bil naṣṣ*. This phrase finds itself in nearly every constitution across the Arab world.

As a result, overwhelmingly, in criminal court decision in countries as varied as Morocco, Egypt, the Maldives, and Malaysia, to name but a few, the court will not issue a conviction unless it can locate a specific law that *both* criminalizes the activity in which the accused was allegedly engaged *and also* imposes a punishment, or a range of punishments, associated with that crime.

Indeed, the idea of legality so deeply pervades that even Saudi Arabia, which usually demonstrates the greatest degree of continuity with the premodern past, includes a modified version of the legality principle in its own Basic Law. Article 38 of the Basic Law states that there is no crime, nor punishment, except as set forth in a sharia text, *or* in a legislative text. This seems to imply that a judge would not have discretion to impose a punishment for an act unless it is prohibited in sort of uncontroverted text—in other words, unless the act constituted a Scriptural Crime. In practice, Saudi criminal courts operate more closely to their classical forebears, and apply discretionary crimes and punishments widely, without reference to legislative or revelatory texts. Hence, for example, in a 2006 case, the general court in Da'er sentenced a woman to 30 days' imprisonment and 70 lashes for forcefully shearing the hair of her ex husband's 12 year old daughter. The court described this as the realization of a "public right," with the "private right" of compensation covered through a payment to the girl's father. Decision May 30, 2006, Da'er General Court, *Mudawwana al-aḥkām al-qaḍā'iyya* 3:364. On appeal, the Court of Cassation in Mecca remanded the case and asked the lower court to reconsider it. The lower court then reduced both the jail sentence and lashings in half. Decision July 29, 2006, Court of Cassation, *Mudawwana al-aḥkām al-qaḍā'iyya* 3:367. If there was a legal text or sharia provision that specifically criminalized hair shearing, it was not mentioned by either of the courts.

Iranian law is similar to that of Saudi Arabia in theory. Article 167 of the Iranian Constitution obligates a judge to deliver judgment on the basis of "authoritative Islamic sources and authentic fatwas" where there is no specifically applicable legislation. Article 220 of the Iranian Penal Code then specifically indicates that Article 167 of the Constitution authorizes criminal punishment for any Scriptural Crime, whether or not codified. On this basis, Iranian courts have issued death sentences for apostasy, even though it is not described as a crime in the Penal Code itself. Unlike Saudi Arabia, however, Iranian courts do not seem to invent their own discretionary crimes for which they impose punishment. Thus, legality principles have pervaded modern Islamic societies to such an extent that even after an Islamic Revolution, the state feels the need to enact provisions like Articles 220 of the Penal Code and Article 167 of the Constitution to justify the imposition of penalties that would have been obvious and unproblematic to any premodern court, with or without an executive edict.

In any event, once a society makes the rather large imaginative leap required to impose a principle of legality on classical Islamic criminal law, the discretionary crimes become rather easy to assimilate into a modern criminal code. In effect, the legality leap transforms these crimes so that they become the subject of legislation through a uniform penal code rather than the product of individualized, unbridled judicial determination. With this change, virtually any penal code can be deemed "Islamic", in that it is the exercise of "discretionary" authority to declare particular activities punishable on the basis of public interest and public order.

The extent to which this is true is reflected in the fact that following the Islamic Revolution in Iran in 1979, the ruling authorities enacted a series of laws meant to codify Islamic criminal law. One of these was a 1983 law that claimed to be the implementation of Islamic discretionary crimes. The law, however, was virtually identical to the Iranian Penal Code prior to the Islamic Revolution, except that it introduced the punishment of lashing for some number of offenses where it had not been present in the past. That 1983 law was rewritten in 1996 and then introduced as Book Five of a comprehensive Iranian Penal Code. Its content remains quite similar to that which one finds in modern penal codes generally, with some limited exceptions, among them, for example, a prohibition on the taking of interest in Article 595 that carries a prison sentence, a fine, and potentially up to 74 lashes. Yet such provisions are exceptions that prove the rule of broad conformity to modern trends.

The one significant variation that appears across the Iranian Code is the presence of lashings as a potential punishment. Purely by way of example, Article 602 of Book Five of the Penal Code reads as follows:

> Article 602—Any civil servant that on the basis of their duties has been entitled to employ some people and charges the government's account more than the number he has actually employed, or if he includes his personal servants

among the civil servants and pays their salary from the government's account, he shall be sentenced to 74 lashes and restitution of the amount he has charged the government's account.

It is neither a surprise that a modern jurisdiction has a law to prevent embezzlement of this sort, nor is the requirement of restitution of the embezzled amount particularly surprising. It is only the mandatory lashing that renders the provision unusual as a comparative matter. Indeed, this may be the reason that the lashing has been inserted into the provision. It is not necessary, as the punishment for a discretionary crime does not need to involve lashing. However, the fact that lashing is historically associated with Islamic law, and that the Iranian regime relies heavily on its maintaining Islamic law to preserve itself, might help explain its insistence on including lashing as a potential punishment in so many crimes.

b. Discretionary Sexual Crimes

Notwithstanding the above observations, there are areas of law where lawmakers have used their discretionary authority to Islamize their criminal codes by drawing more heavily from the classical corpus than merely assigning a punishing of lashing to an ordinary crime. Classical doctrine remains particularly relevant in two areas of law—the policing of sex on the one hand, and blasphemy on the other. Each is discussed in turn.

Given the difficulty of proving fornication, and given the extreme severity of the punishment for married fornicators, the law on fornication serves as an imperfect instrument to police sexual mores, as many states that claim Islamic legitimacy seek to do with some fervor. To address this, these jurisdictions have enacted laws that criminalize expressions of intimacy and affection between unmarried couples that fall well short of fornication. The most common of these are the criminalization of what is known as *khulwa,* or "seclusion" of an unmarried man and woman together, on the basis of the well-known Prophetic report that when a man and a woman are in seclusion together, the devil becomes the third among them.

Seclusion is not a Scriptural Crime because neither the Qur'an nor the Sunna mandate a punishment for it. However, it is a sin, and one closely enough associated with fornication as to be easy to justify criminalizing as an exercise in discretion. The tie to fornication, however, can at times be so explicit as to be limiting. Hence, for example, Law 6 of 2014 in the province of Aceh, Indonesia defines seclusion to be "an act of two persons of the opposite sex who are not prohibited because of kinship from marrying but are not married to each other being together in a non-public or secluded place leading toward the commission of fornication (*zina*)." Interestingly, at least some courts in Aceh have read this as requiring a form of seclusion wherein it was plausible that sexual intercourse actually took place. For example, in a 2010 case decided by the Islamic Court for Kutacane, a married woman met a man who had bought her a blouse, and the two of them swiftly disappeared into the woods beside the road. Unbeknownst to either of them, the woman's husband was following them, and, after having questioned the relative who drove his wife to the secret meeting place, he pursued the couple to the location where they had disappeared. Upon hearing the husband, the man emerged swiftly to speak with him, fully clothed, and the wife came out several minutes later. Both denied wrongdoing. The Court found that they were not, and could not have been, guilty of the crime of seclusion, because they were not secluded long enough to have made fornication possible. The couple was at best guilty of *attempted* seclusion, the court indicated, and there is no law prohibiting that. Case 27/2010, Islamic Court of Kutacane (Indonesia), dated December 10, 2010. The case is striking, not only in the effort the court undertook to avoid punishment, but also in its highly legalistic, civilian reasoning to reach that conclusion. A classical era court would not have found any legal impediment to declaring the activity in which the two accused were engaged as un-Islamic and corrupting, and sentenced them to what it deemed to be an appropriate punishment. This court, by contrast, read the statute, identified elements, and, because it found one element lacking, it set the couple free. This reflects common practice among modern judiciaries, but is hard to reconcile with the methods of classical Islamic law.

Other statutes relating to sexual activity are drafted more broadly than Aceh's is. Several Malaysian states, for example, define as criminal a seclusion of a man and a woman "under circumstances which may give rise to suspicion that [the offending couple] were engaged in immoral acts." Even a few minutes of seclusion would seemingly be sufficient under this definition. Iran's laws are even broader. For example, Article 637 of Iran's Penal Code prohibits "indecent acts other than fornication, such as kissing or sleeping next to one another," and Article 638 prohibits the commission of sinful acts in public places. The former carries a sentence of up to 99 lashes and the latter a sentence of up to 74 lashes. Notably, Article 638 also provides that women who appear in public without a headscarf are subject to up to two months' imprisonment and a modest fine.

There are other laws relating to perceived immodest behavior in various Muslim countries, though it would be something of a mistake to overstate them. In significant parts of the Muslim world, the closely knit nature of societies has led to a remarkable absence of state law as concerns immoral sexual conduct and behavior. The broad expectation in those jurisdictions is not that sexual activity outside of marriage is permissible, but rather that it is best policed by other forms of traditional authority—tribes, village elders, clerics, and patriarchs of extended families—rather than by the state. Hence, for example, Iraq and Egypt have no laws prohibiting fornication or seclusion at all. Rather, they criminalize only adultery (in the case of men, only if the adultery is undertaken in the marital home), and only if the spouse of the offender makes the claim. The penalties for adultery range from a maximum of six months (for men in Egypt) to two years (for women in Egypt, and men and women in Iraq). The unmarried may do as they wish from a state legal perspective.

To be clear, these states are certainly not permissive in terms of their sexual mores. Women in particular face severe reprisals for associations with men that fall far short of (perfectly legal) sexual intercourse. Yet these reprisals, which (depending on social class, education levels, and nature of deemed offense) range from social ostracization to death, will not be undertaken by the state. Indeed, the traditional authorities would object rather vociferously to any sort of interference by the state in what they would deem to be their own internal affairs, whether that interference be in the form of the state attempting to impose its own punishments for the deemed immoral behavior, or the state preventing or limiting whatever reprisal the traditional authorities see fit to impose. From the point of view of no small number of nonstate authorities, that state should not concern itself with these matters, and this explains the absence of extensive morals laws in large numbers of Muslim states.

The same expectation of state withdrawal is not true respecting the other area of discretionary criminal law in which there has been an explosion of interest in modern times. This concerns blasphemy, discussed next.

c. Blasphemy as Discretionary Criminal Law

The closest analogy in the juristic texts to a modern blasphemy prohibition is the classical era prohibition against insulting the Prophet, which jurists in most schools deemed a Scriptural Crime. Indeed, it is rather obvious that negative depictions of the Prophet Muhammad, whether undertaken in a French satirical magazine, on a YouTube video, or as part of a purported art exhibit organized by America's most notorious Islamophobe, stoke the sensitivities of large numbers of ordinary Muslims and incite a radical fringe to violence.

Perhaps unsurprisingly, therefore, there is modern legislation that specifically addresses itself to the protection of the personage of the Prophet Muhammad. Articles 262 and 263 of the Iranian Penal Code, for example, declare it a Scriptural Crime meriting capital punishment to curse the Prophet Muhammad. Interestingly, the Code draws a distinction between a "curse", which calls upon God to punish the Prophet in some way and is a capital crime, and a more general "insult", which is a broader discretionary crime for which the punishment is 74 lashes. This very fine distinction, not well supported in historic Shi'i texts, enables authorities in a broad spectrum of cases to reduce the punishment from death to lashing.

Iran is something of an exception in codifying the act of cursing the Prophet as a Spiritual Crime. Pakistan treats this as a discretionary crime, and criminalizes it in § 295 C of the Penal Code. The penalty may be death or life imprisonment, as well as potentially a fine.

Moreover, Pakistan's blasphemy prohibitions extend well beyond the relatively narrow issue of insulting the Prophet. It is also a crime to insult the Prophet's wives, family members, or companions under§ 298 A of the Penal Code (with the penalty ranging from one to three years, as well as a fine), or to defile the Qur'an under § 295 B (with the penalty being life in prison).

It would be a mistake to imagine laws of this sort as actually being used to punish Qur'an burning, or the publication of cartoons depicting the Prophet Muhammad in an unflattering light. The thought of committing such an act so overtly would never occur to any sane individual in most Muslim societies, given the negative repercussions, often extralegal, that would be sure to follow. Rather, even more than the laws concerning apostasy, blasphemy law is a means to reinforce strict notions of orthodoxy, not only within Islam, but also among other religions as well. There are two ways this is achieved.

The first is through the opaque judicial process that attends to such proceedings. It is not at all uncommon to read of a death sentence being issued and in some cases even affirmed on appeal (whether or not ultimately implemented) in states such as Iran, Saudi Arabia, Bangladesh, Afghanistan, and Pakistan, for an insult to the Prophet, or other blasphemy, without any specification at all as to what, precisely, the offender said that could be regarded as an insult or what evidence there was for it. This rather shocking lack of transparency for a capital case is often less the focus of media attention, given that most of the critics of these cases do not think that any statement insulting the Prophet merits criminal sanction at all, whether or not clearly insulting and whether or not proven. Nevertheless, the process deserves some attention, because it gives courts wide berth to chill all sorts of speech that actually falls well short of an insult to the Prophet. Moreover, the opacity enables the rise of frivolous claims that seem to arise out of a debt dispute, a personal vendetta, or animus against a despised minority. Hence, Shi'a or Christians in Pakistan, or Sunnis in Iran, seem to be disproportionately implicated in a fair number of blasphemy charges, for reasons that seem highly suspect.

The second way in which the laws enforce orthodoxy is that they are often drafted in a manner that is much more vague than the somewhat more clearly defined acts of insulting holy personages or defiling the Qur'an. In some cases, in fact, they are not artifacts of Islamic law, or even expressly about protecting Islam. Rather, they represent a more ecumenical prohibition imposed by colonial powers that was designed to limit interreligious strife. Section 295 A of the Bangladesh Penal Code is an example of this. It reads as follows:

> Whoever, with deliberate and malicious intention of outraging the religious feelings of any class of the citizens of Bangladesh, by words, either spoken or written, or by visible representations insults or attempts to insult the

religion or the religious beliefs of that class, shall be punished with imprisonment of either description for a term which may extend to two years, or with fine, or with both.

Egypt's comparable provision of its Penal Code, Section 98(f), post-dates the colonial era but was also enacted to limit interreligious disputes that often turned to violence. It reads as follows:

Whoever exploits religion through extreme ideas by word of mouth, in writing or in any other manner, with the intent of giving rise to discord, humiliation or contempt of one of the heavenly religions or the sects belonging to them, or harming national unity, shall be punished with imprisonment from six months to five years, or pay a fine of at least 500 Egyptian pounds.

As a final example, there is Indonesia, which is generally regarded as tolerant and syncretic in its approach to faith. Article 156a of its Penal Code reads as follows:

Any person who intentionally and in public expresses feelings or engages in conduct:

(a) that is essentially hostile to, missuses, or desecrates one of the religions adhered to in Indonesia; or

(b) has the purpose of dissuading another person from adhering to a religion based on the One and Only God,

is punishable by imprisonment for a term of no more than five years.

As is clear from the text of the provisions, the purpose of this sort of legislation appears to be to prevent someone from inflaming a religious group by depicting its holy figure in an unflattering light (or, in the case of Indonesia, causing discord or violence by aggressively seeking to convert people away from their existing faith). Nevertheless, it is relatively obvious how Islamist organizations, and indeed non-Muslim religious institutions, can use them to stifle any sort of dissent by characterizing such dissent as an "insult" to the religion, or an attempt to "humiliate" the faith. As a result, various seemingly legitimate expressions of opinion that hardly seem insulting or humiliating—including questioning of the authenticity of all Prophetic statements traditionally regarded as reliable, decrying the mass slaughter of sheep at the Muslim pilgrimage, and even jokes involving the generic use of the name "Muhammad"—have been prosecuted as crimes, with prison sentences ensuing.

Finally, and largely in keeping with the foregoing, the blasphemy laws are used not only to prosecute the panoply of outspoken reformists, secularists, comedians, and pranksters who might be the most willing to probe the outer limits of what might safely be said of received tradition. They are also used, and indeed in many cases designed, to persecute religious groups whose views are deemed heretical. The most notorious example of this comes from Pakistan, and its seemingly maniacal quest to suppress the spread of a Muslim minority known as the Ahmadiyya. In general, the faith of the Ahmahadiyya is consistent with that of Sunni Islam, with one major deviation.

It adds to Sunnism a belief that a late 19th century individual, Mirza Ghulam Ahmad, is the promised Mahdi. In some sense, the deviation is not substantively different from that of Shi'ism, which Pakistan at least officially tolerates as a *de jure* matter. However, to the Pakistani authorities, there appears to be a significant difference between believing in a Mahdi who last appeared on earth more than a millennium ago, as the Shi'a do, and one who appeared only about a century ago, as the Ahmadis do. To those intent on preserving orthodoxy and tradition, the latter is far more threatening and far more deviant. Analogies to the hostility among some Christian groups to the description of Mormonism as a form of Christianity might well be made.

In any event, in connection with its own blasphemy laws, Pakistan enacted two provisions that directly address the Ahmadis. The first, which appears in § 298B of the Penal Code, makes it a crime for an Ahmadi to refer to his or her place of worship as a *masjid* (Arabic for mosque), the Ahmadi call to prayer as the Muslim *'Adhān,* or any person as Caliph or Commander of the Faithful other than the historic caliphs themselves. Under the second provision, § 298C, Ahmadis who refer to themselves as Muslims or invite others to their faith have committed a crime that merits a maximum prison sentence of three years, along with a potential fine.

Other states have likewise tailored their rules prohibiting desecration of religion specifically to target religious minorities. Indonesia has a curious

Presidential Decree (No. 1/1965), Article 1 of which specifically prohibits individuals from "intentionally and in public voicing, advocating, or encouraging public support for an interpretation of one of the religions adhered to in Indonesia, or engaging in religious activities that resemble the practices of such religion, where such interpretation deviates from the basic teachings of that religion." The Decree was broadly understood to have been drafted to counter the influence of indigenous mystical groups.

In the end, it seems relatively clear that blasphemy laws enacted throughout the Muslim world render open and earnest discussions about Islam difficult to have. This is, to say the least, rather unfortunate, and results in the stultification of religious interpretation in all too many Muslim countries.

D. THE LAW OF RETALIATION AND ISLAMIC CRIMINAL LAW

There is one final aspect of classical law that is customarily described by modern commentators as criminal. This is the law of retaliation. Classical jurists often classified it as the *Kitāb al-Jināyāt,* which would be translated in modern Arabic as the "Book of Felonies." In fact, however, while this area of law provides for the potential imposition of sanctions for homicides and physical assaults, it probably belongs more within the realm of private law than public. Certainly, it is not the means by which homicide and assault are normally punished, even in states that retain elements of this law. Accordingly, it is given brief treatment here.

The law of retaliation enabled the victim of an intentional physical assault to exact a retributive injury on the perpetrator of the assault. Hence, for example, if a person broke a tooth of a victim, the victim could demand the same injury be exacted on the perpetrator. If the assault was an intentional homicide, then the victim's family could demand that the perpetrator be put to death. Alternatively, the victim, or the victim's family, could accept the blood price instead of retaliation. The standard blood price for the life of a free Muslim man was set at 100 camels, with a woman's blood price set at 50 camels. The blood price for non-Muslims varied between equivalency with Muslims in the case of the Hanbalis to the very low price of 800 dirhams in the case of the Shi'a, which is roughly 3% of the blood price of a Muslim. For body parts, the blood price was reduced by the number of comparable body parts the injured person had. Hence, for example, the hand of a free Muslim man is set at 50 camels, because a person has two hands, while the nose is set at 100 camels, because a person has only one nose.

There are a large number of cases where retaliation is not possible. Most importantly, it is not available for unintentional injuries, even when they result from recklessness. It is also not available if, in trying to carry it out, it would lead to a more serious injury. In other words, a person who paralyzed another by throwing the victim off of a mountain is not then himself paralyzed, given the practical difficulty of being able to inflict such a punishment. Finally, for most schools, the blood price of the victim must be at least as great as that of the perpetrator. A man cannot be killed for killing a woman, for example, because the woman's blood price is half that of the man. (The exception to this are the Shi'a, who permit the family of a female victim to demand retaliation if a man kills her, but then require the victim's family to pay the perpetrator's family the difference in blood price as between the victim and the perpetrator.)

As should be clear, the punitive aspects of the law of retaliation are only relevant when demanded by a victim, or a victim's family, and they may be dispensed with by the victim, or the victim's family. Accordingly, they fall more comfortably in the area of tort than of crime. Moreover, courts in most states that recognize the law of retaliation, including Pakistan, Iran, and Saudi Arabia, show notable reticence in actually imposing it. Rather, they impose a discretionary penalty for homicides and assaults that resembles comparative criminal provisions respecting homicide elsewhere in the world. Accordingly, while the classical rules receive no shortage of attention, the actual impact of the retaliation rules throughout the Muslim world on the administration of justice tends to be muted.

CHAPTER 7
ISLAMIC CONSTITUTIONALISM

A. INTRODUCTION

As the previous sections have made clear, while modern Muslim states use the classical corpus of Islamic law as an important part of their legal infrastructure, they have not sought to make it the backbone of their respective legal systems. Indeed, in some rather significant areas of law, such as tort and contract, the classical corpus is largely obsolete and therefore ignored. Moreover, the modern regulatory state exercises control over broad, newer legal fields, such as corporate and securities, tax, and immigration, to name only a few, where the classical corpus provides limited guidance to modern legislators.

As a result, no modern state that has advanced beyond the most rudimentary stages of development is likely to be able to define itself as Islamic through a commitment to refer to classical Islamic law to resolve all, or even most, legal questions. In this quite important sense, the modern state is quite distinguishable from the political systems that operated during the classical period.

This presents something of a problem. On the one hand, most Muslim majority states seek to characterize themselves as Islamic, in conformity with broad public demand. Yet these states cannot demonstrate their Islamic character through a commitment to administer themselves according to classical juristic law, and there is no other obvious method they can deploy to establish their Islamicity.

The burgeoning field of Islamic constitutionalism is meant to provide an answer of sorts to this core quandary. Islamic constitutionalism relies on the modern presumption that the state defines itself largely through its constitution, and therefore any principles that establish the state's Islamic character must be set out there. It also relies on a series of classical era principles that are translated, and some might argue transmogrified, in order to render them applicable in the modern constitutional state. These principles are inserted into the constitution, and are expected to then be applied by modern state institutions so as to ensure that the state is in fact as Islamic as it claims to be. The theory is contestable, though no more so than the modern theories underlying the practice of modern Islamic finance. Unlike Islamic finance, however, Islamic constitutionalism has yet to establish itself as a legal field that is capable of functioning effectively. Its start has been anything but auspicious.

The first part of the chapter describes the classical era principles from which Islamic constitutionalism purports to derive, and the second sets out the constitutional commitments that make up Islamic constitutionalism. It further explores the practical application of these principles in modern Islamic courts.

B. THE ROOTS OF ISLAMIC CONSTITUTIONALISM

The previous two chapters showed how the fields of Islamic finance and Islamic criminal law are in a sense modern inventions. That is, in these areas of law, rules derived in the classical era are used to create a new legal doctrine that is responsive to modern conditions but would appear quite foreign to the classical jurists who derived the original rules. Islamic constitutionalism takes this approach one step further. It draws a series of principles not from mature areas of classical law (as could be said of Islamic criminal law, or even Islamic commerce) but rather from scattered and skeletal classical era public law concepts. These principles are then collected, rendered into a cohesive whole, and inserted into a modern, Westphalian constitutional state, with its division of powers as between executive, legislative and judicial powers that no classical era jurist would recognize. As might be obvious, and as is explored below, the fit is somewhat awkward.

The core classical doctrine upon which modern Islamic constitutionalism depends is predominantly a Sunni one, known as *siyāsa shar`īyya*, which translates most completely, albeit awkwardly, as "religiously permissible policy/lawmaking."

The concepts underlying *siyāsa shar`īyya* derive from the fact that even in the earliest classical periods, not every law was jurist derived Islamic law, and not every court rendered its decisions according to the rules of the classical era jurists. For example, during the reign of the Abbasid caliphate, there arose a court system that operated independently of the general courts known as the *mażālim* courts. The courts were not strictly bound by Islamic law as derived by the jurists, and certainly not by the detailed procedural rules of the general courts. However, there was some sort of broad expectation that they would adhere to the general Islamic ethos in rendering their verdicts.

In addition, and more importantly for these purposes, rulers throughout the classical period issued edicts from time to time that served as a form of law. These edicts did not purport to reformulate or define Islamic law so much as supplement it to address problems of the time. To demonstrate the temporal nature of these edicts, as opposed to the permanence of jurist derived Islamic law, a caliph's edict lasted no longer than his own life. The idea was that caliphal decrees could not be expected to bind a future ruler, in contradistinction to the jurist derived Law of God, which was absolutely binding upon every caliph. It was not until the twilight of the classical period, and specifically, the last few centuries of Ottoman rule, when caliph issued decrees began to resemble modern lawmaking practices more closely, so that edicts lasted beyond the lifetime of the sultan issuing them and in many cases purported to be an interpretation or reformulation of Islamic law.

Separately, and in addition, jurists regarded it as axiomatic that in a true Islamic state, a ruler would be bound by, and seek to implement, Islamic law as the jurists defined it. Statements can thus be found within classical texts that a ruler who attempts to derogate from Islamic law is implicitly suggesting that Islamic law is imperfect, and that the ruler has some capacity to fix it. This in itself would be a form of blasphemy. Hence, jurists accepted that caliphs could issue edicts, and *mażālim* courts could render decisions. In so doing, they did not need to rely on juristic rules. However, implicit in their disquisition was an assumption that there were limitations on these edicts and decisions, in that they could not somehow stray from Islamic law as the jurists defined it.

The problem is that the jurists never quite developed these disparate, skeletal ideas into a complete political theory that would set forth tests, and outline actual processes and institutional mechanisms, to ensure that authorities comply with Islamic law. In other words, the jurists never explained on what basis a ruler's edicts might be invalid, and what institution would check the ruler to invalidate the rule.

The difficulty of creating a workable political theory around these embryonic ideas is compounded by the fact that the institutional structure of the modern state has no natural classical era antecedents. Even the core, fundamental juristic idea that the caliph must implement Islamic law requires some translation to be meaningful in the modern constitutional order. There is, after all, no caliph in a modern state, but only a series of different institutions with powers that are intended to balance each other. What specific functions, therefore, is each branch of government supposed to undertake to ensure that the state retains its Islamic character? There is virtually nothing in classical texts that could help provide a useful answer to this question.

The challenges are therefore immediate and obvious. Nevertheless, the desire across so many modern Muslim populations, including many of its political and social elites, that the state be Islamic in character has been quite intense. Accordingly, states have attempted to internalize institutional commitments in their respective constitutions on the basis of these ideas, and implement processes and mechanisms to realize these commitments, in order to ensure the Islamic character of the state. The balance of this Chapter describes what types of commitments states have made to ensure the state's compliance with Islamic law, and describes the manner in which these commitments have been implemented across various Muslim states.

C. ISLAMIC CONSTITUTIONAL COMMITMENTS

There are three provisions relating to Islam that reappear with sufficient frequency in constitutions in Islamic states that they are worthy of recounting here. The first of these, which is nearly universal, establishes Islam as the official religion of the state. The second, which is common, states that Islamic law is a source (or *the* source, as the case may be) of state law. The third, which exists in a minority of Muslim states but is becoming increasingly popular, establishes that any law issued by the state that conflicts with fundamental precepts of Islamic law is invalid. Each of these is discussed in turn below.

1. ISLAM AS RELIGION OF THE STATE

Overwhelmingly, constitutions across the Muslim world, from relatively secular Tunisia to jurist-ruled Iran, indicate that Islam is the official religion of the state. As with nearly everything pertaining to Islamic law in modern states, there are exceptions, most significant among them Turkey, where the Ottoman Empire was once situated, and Indonesia, the most populous Muslim majority state.

What is not clear, however, is what legal effect the establishment of Islam as state religion is supposed to have. The provision is not frequently invoked in courts in Islamic states, and certainly no doctrine has built up respecting the obligations of the various branches of governments that arise by virtue of the state having an official religion. Legislators of an Islamist bent do from time to time refer to the state as Islamic as justification to advance various policies, whether that be amendment of a family law code to render the state more Islamic, establishment of women only public transportation services, or the institutionalization of greater religious education in public schools. Yet these exhortations have yet to coalesce into what might constitute a general understanding of the legislature's obligations in an Islamic state vis a vis Islamic law.

By far the most significant effect of the clauses establishing Islam as state religion lies in what they prevent rather than in what they obligate. That is, by rejecting the secular notion of disestablishment so unambiguously, Islam as state religion provisions foreclose any argument that state policies and practices have to be religiously neutral. The state, in other words, is clearly not violating any sort of constitutional principle by instituting religious education in public schools, funding the construction of mosques, opening legislative sessions with readings from the Qur'an, and taking other measures that make absolutely clear that Islam holds some sort of special status in the state relative to any other religion.

It should be noted in connection with this that the Islam as state religion clause is almost never understood to signify a prohibition against the presence of any religion within the state other than Islam. Thus, in many constitutions, constitutional provisions that specifically indicate that particular religious minorities enjoy freedom of workshop are often placed alongside the provisions that establish Islam as state religion. For example, Iraq's Article 2(1) indicates that Islam is the religion of the state, and then Article 2(2) "guarantees the full religious rights to freedom of religious belief and practice of all individuals such as Christians, Yazidis, and Mandean Sabeans." Article 3(1) of Malaysia's Constitution indicates that "Islam is the religion of the Federation; but other religions may be practiced in peace and harmony in any part of the Federation." Even Iran guarantees the right to worship to its Christian, Jewish, and Zoroastrian populations, though not, notably, its Baha'i citizens.

Thus, the near universal practice among Islamic states is to include a freedom to worship for at least some religious minorities in the state's constitution. (Saudi Arabia, which has no provision of the sort, provides the most notable exception.) That said, even with such provisions, Islam is privileged as the state religion, thereby rendering other faiths, even if protected, of inferior status. Islamic states thus rarely fund the construction of churches, subsidize religious education for non-Muslims, or omit religious education in public schools in deference to non-Muslim minorities. Instead, they more often tolerate private construction of churches and schools, and permit non-Muslim students and teachers to be absent during religious education sessions.

In the end, the clauses that set Islam as state religion parallel the broad and undefined sensibilities of the jurists of the classical era, who demanded that the state both implement, and comply with, Islamic law, without much specification as to what that meant or how it was to be achieved. In this sense, the clauses help to establish a certain Islamic ethos, and to set expectations respecting compliance therewith. However, they do not on their own impose very many specific obligations on the state.

2. ISLAMIC LAW AS A SOURCE OF STATE LAW

While provisions declaring the state to be Islamic are deemed fundamental to the identity of the state and thus generate little public controversy, the same is not true as concerns the two remaining major constitutional clauses intended to reflect Islamicity. The controversies are clearest in a provision that began to appear in various Islamic constitutions starting around the middle of the twentieth century, particularly in the Arab world, respecting the sources to which a legislature was to refer in order to craft modern law. One of these sources, according to the various formulations of the provision, was supposed to be Islamic law.

The precise wording of the source clause tends to differ from state to state, reflecting a balance among competing forces. In Iraq, for example, the relevant clause indicates that "Islam", rather than "Islamic law," is a source of law. This wording originated with Iraq's post-Ba'ath interim constitution. It was inserted there by the American occupying authority and its more secular Iraqi allies at the time, in the hope that it would somehow mean that laws would be inspired by broad Islamic principles, rather than taken from juristic rules.

Another common source of dispute concerns whether or not Islamic law is to serve as "the" source of state legislation (as in Egypt), "a" source of it (as in Iraq), or a "major source" of legislation (as in Syria and Kuwait). Finally, there are frequent debates over whether legislation must take as its source the more amorphous and aspirational term for Islamic law—sharia—or the rulings of the jurists, which, as more fully explained in Chapter One, are more commonly encompassed within the Arabic term *fiqh*.

Despite the heated nature of the debates, the actual effect of the clauses themselves on state practice is rather muted. The major reason for this is that, with one major exception to be discussed below, the clauses are not the subject of adjudication. In other words, there is no court or other body that reviews modern state legislation and makes some sort of determination as to whether there is sufficient Islamic content within it so as to comply with the requirement that state law treat Islamic law as a source of law. The constitutional directive is (often implicitly) left for the legislature itself to manage.

Legislatures in turn take considerable liberty in deciding upon the manner that they incorporate Islamic law into legal codes. In the context of personal status law, as we have seen in Chapters Two and Three, legislators overwhelmingly either draft a code that is largely codification of rules from the juristic tradition, or they direct courts to use the rules of one of the juristic schools as the basis for decisionmaking. In other circumstances, such as the famed Sanhuri Civil Code that dominates much of the Arab world, broad principles of Islamic law developed from generalized juristic trends across the Sunni schools are inserted into a modern code that also incorporates many provisions from more developed civilian jurisdictions, such as France, Germany, and the Netherlands. Finally, in specialized areas of law, from environmental protection to competition law, either because there is comparatively less for drafters to draw upon from the juristic tradition, or because legislators are not invested in the effort, or, most likely, both, Islamic law is all but ignored. Instead, legislators instead adopt a model from a more developed jurisdiction, and transplant it nearly entirely. The ultimate decision on where and how to use Islamic law does not seem to be affected in any way by the precise phrasing of the constitutional obligation to render Islamic law a source of state law.

There is one partial exception to the trends described above that deserves mention. This is the case of Egypt, where the Egyptian Supreme Constitutional Court interpreted a 1971 amendment to the Constitution changing Islamic law from being "a" chief source of Islamic law to "the" chief source of Islamic law to be justiciable, at least for legislation enacted after the date of the amendment. According to that Court, such a requirement obligates the legislature to ensure that any legislation that it enacts is consonant with, or at least not repugnant to, core principles and dictates of Islam. Decision 20/JY1, Supreme Constitutional Court of Egypt, decided May 4, 1985. This is discussed in the next section, which deals with the subject of repugnancy and Islamic law more generally.

3. REPUGNANCY CLAUSES

By far the provision that is most closely associated with the emerging concept of Islamic constitutionalism is the so-called repugnancy clause, pursuant to which a constitutional court or some similar body is empowered to strike down laws that are deemed repugnant to the "principles," "settled rulings," or "Injunctions" of Islam or Islamic law, as the case may be. The concept can be traced back to the start of the twentieth century, and in particular

Article 2 of Iran's 1906 Constitution. Under that article, the legislature selected five jurists from among twenty proposed to them from the juristic authorities to serve on a committee that could invalidate any legislation that was "at variance with the sacred rules of Islam, or the traditions of his Holiness [the prophet Muhammad]."

The specific term "repugnancy" in the specific context of Islamic law seems to owe its origins to the 1956 Pakistan Constitution, which refers in Article 203D to the invalidity of law "repugnant to the Injunctions of Islam, as laid down in the Holy Qur'an and Sunnah of the Prophet. . . ." There is an irony to the use of the term "repugnancy" in this context, in particular in South Asia. This is because it was used by the British in administering the subcontinent to mean nearly the opposite; namely, that indigenous law on the subcontinent would continue to apply under British administration so long as such law was not repugnant to the Crown. Here, repugnancy means that law not of Islamic origin is valid to the extent that it does not conflict with Islam. That at the dawn of colonialism the default was assumed to be indigenous law (unless repugnant to Western law) and that this has evolved to nonindigenous law most often transplanted from Western sources (unless repugnant to Islam) demonstrates to the extent to which Muslim jurisdictions have largely adopted Western legal frameworks to regulate their respective societies.

The Islamic justification for repugnancy originates in the classical juristic premise, explored above, that a ruler of an Islamic polity was bound to uphold and execute Islamic law as developed by the jurists and that any rules instituted by the ruler that are "repugnant" to Islamic law must therefore be invalid. If classical jurists lacked a mechanism through which such invalidity might be realized, the modern version of the theory goes, the modern constitutional state supplies that mechanism, through the process of judicial review. In this reimagination of the respective roles of the classical era actors, the legislature together with the executive take on the role of the classical era ruler, and the constitutional court, or some other quasi adjudicatory body, occupies the juristic role. The legislature and executive may enact and execute law, but may not do so to the extent that the law somehow contravenes, or is repugnant to, Islamic law. If it does enact such repugnant law, then the judiciary is institutionally equipped to invalidate the offending legislation in a way that classical jurists never were.

The analogy to classical era principles is rather awkward, in particular as concerns the analogy of the modern judge to a traditional jurist. After all, jurists were responsible primarily for "revealing" Islamic law, and the ruler was then responsible primarily for enforcing it. Whether and to what extent the ruler could supplement that law with additional edicts was largely secondary given how sporadic that practice was through most of Islamic history, and jurists had no power to review it in any event. By contrast, a modern constitutional tribunal does not have the capacity to make law in the manner that the jurists did, but only to review legislation enacted by another body. As a result, the idea that repugnancy will ensure the Islamicity of the state is at least somewhat curtailed. For example, a caliph who permitted the open and free distribution and consumption of alcohol within the House of Islam would surely be considered to be failing in his duty to uphold Islamic law given broad juristic consensus against alcohol consumption. Yet no court in a modern state could use the tool of repugnancy to invent a criminal prohibition of alcohol that the state had neglected to enact on its own. The one, limited tool the court has is to strike down legislation.

A related problem is that because the juristic assumptions respecting the ruler's obligations were expressed in broad terms, there is no real standard by which to decide whether or not a particular law departs so far from generalized principles of Islamic law as to be "repugnant" to it.

That said, classical era jurists were not entirely bereft of framing devices to which modern courts could turn when seeking to impose a repugnancy standard. Most notable is the frequent reference among modern courts to the so-called "purposes," or *maqāṣid*, of the sharia, which are generally understood to be the protection of mind, family, property, religion, and life. These are of classical provenance and most commonly associated with the jurists Abu Ḥāmid al-Ghazāli and Abu 'Iṣhāq al-Shāṭibī, who posited that every sharia rule has one of these purposes in mind. Hence, for example, rules such as the criminalization of alcohol consumption and apostasy (discussed in Chapter Six) serve to protect the mind and religion, respectively.

Though Ghazāli and Shāṭibī never envisioned that this classification would serve as a means to strike down caliphal edicts, courts try to make use of his *maqāṣid* in order to establish tests of Islamicity of law. In essence, a law that serves one of Islamic law's underlying purposes is valid, while one that fails to serve such purposes is invalid. The test is easier to describe in conception than it is to apply in practice, in particular because of the rather extreme versatility of the *maqāsid* themselves. It is hard to imagine any law enacted in any jurisdiction at any time that could not be justified as intended to protect of one of the *maqāsid*.

It should be noted in conclusion that in spite of all of the attention that they have received, the repugnancy clauses only exist in a handful of jurisdictions, most notable among them Pakistan, Iraq, and Afghanistan. In addition, Egypt's Supreme Constitutional Court has ruled that its constitution imposes a requirement that legislation conform to Islamic law. Hence, while the scholarly attention given to repugnancy clauses is not misplaced, it is important to contextualize the matter. The norm across the Muslim world remains one in which courts are not empowered to strike down law on the grounds of Islamicity.

4. IMPLEMENTATIONS OF REPUGNANCY

Unfortunately, constitutional courts hearing cases on repugnancy have yet to develop anything that might resemble a coherent framework to evaluate the Islamicity of legislation. The approaches seem alternatively scattershot, wildly inconsistent, politically influenced, and jurisprudentially clumsy attempts at policymaking through an Islamic justificatory lens. To the extent that repugnancy is supposed to help ensure the Islamicity of modern state legislation, it is apparent that it has some way to go before it can fulfill this ambition.

Specifically, there are four fundamental difficulties that courts have had in attempting to develop some sort of test by which to judge whether or not a particular law or state action violates core precepts of Islam or Islamic law, as the case may be. The first, and most profound, problem is that the courts seem in many cases to be unaware of, or at least unwilling to engage with, fundamental aspects of Islamic law, or Islamic political theory. Even the central concept of *siyāsa shar`īyya* proves elusive at times. A good example lies in a 1994 case in Egypt, where the Supreme Constitutional Court upheld a law that permitted a wife to make a child support claim against her husband for amounts owed prior to her instituting suit. In so doing, the Supreme Constitutional Court of Egypt recited, and rejected, the consensus Sunni Hanafi rule that indicates that a father is not responsible for amounts due his children until such time as suit is instituted for such amounts. The decision was salutary in result, but its reasoning decidedly unsound.

In its analysis, the Court offers its praises for the concept of *ijtihād,* or interpretation from original revelatory sources, as a means by which a legislature might change earlier juristic rules, to the extent that such rules are not "absolutely clear in authenticity and meaning." To quote the Court:

> ... *ijtihād* is designed for the matters in dispute, for which there is no possibility of the provisions being frozen, in a manner that denies the perfection of the sharia, and its flexibility. *Ijtihād* is nothing more than a mind's effort, aspiring to discover the applicable provisions of the sharia from the detailed evidence. And thus it cannot be imitation in devotion to those who came first, nor can it be invention of a lie attributed to God by rendering permissible, or prohibited, that which does not belong in the categories. It cannot be averse to coming down to the circumstances of people and seeking what is sound in their customs.... *Ijtihād* does not render sacrosanct the statements of any jurist as concerns any matter within it, nor does it transfer without its sources, its standards and its alternatives. Opinions arrived at by *ijtihād* do not have, on their own, a power of obligation that extends beyond those who issue them. As a consequence, they cannot be deemed an established and decided upon rule which cannot be challenged, as this would be a denial of consideration and discernment in the religion of God the Sublime, and a denial of the reality of a potential mistake in every *ijtihād*.... Thus it is understood that the *ijtihād* of those before are not a final source nor a sole basis to rely upon for practical rulings. To the contrary, the Guardian

of Affairs [i.e., the head of state] may pass laws in conflict with them, and organize the affairs of [God's] servants in a specific environment that is unique in its circumstances and situation, with any conflict [with previous jurists in disagreement] left to God and His Prophet. . . .

What the Court appears to be suggesting is that the legislature is permitted to derogate from the Hanafi rule and apply its own rule of *ijtihād* wherein a father is responsible for child support even for periods prior to a suit being filed for such support. This is both because there is no absolutely revelatory text on this matter and because, according to the Court in a separate passage, the settled rule among Hanafi jurists was based on an assumption respecting a lack of need on the part of the child who had not filed a claim. Such an assumption seems misplaced in modernity, where it is much harder for a minor child to file suit. Hence, "the change of times calls for derogation from this *ijtihād* based on the flexibility that the sharia contains in its detailed provisions, which respond to developments, aiming to bind them to the interests of the people, their renewed needs, and their changing customs to the extent they do not conflict with an absolutely clear ruling." Decision 29/JY11, Supreme Constitutional Court of Egypt, decided March 26, 1994.

The problem that the Court fails to grasp is that the case has little to with *ijtihād*. The right to practice *ijtihād* never belonged to rulers and "Guardians of Affairs" in Islamic history in the first place, but rather to jurists. Accordingly, the Court's discussions seem misguided. The fundamental question should have been whether the legislature was entitled as a form of policy making to enact a rule that obligated a form of child support that the jurists, by consensus, did not deem obligatory.

So analyzed, the case becomes considerably easier, and the florid descriptions respecting the flexibility accorded to *ijtihād* seem beside the point. The fact that the Hanafi jurists did not deem it necessary for a father to pay child support prior to the initiation of suit would not seem to prevent a legislature from imposing that obligation on a father as a matter of good policy. At most, this constitutes a wealth transfer that the medieval jurists did not think was necessary. The same might be said of any other form of wealth transfer from one private party to another mandated by modern legal rules but not by juristic ones. Egyptian law, for example, permits a party to recover damages for defamation and yet medieval juristic rules regarded physical harms rather than moral ones to be compensable. If the juristic rules are irrelevant in that context, because they simply refer to what Islam requires in the form of compensation for physical injury rather than what other forms of state mandated compensation might be available in different legal settings, then surely the juristic rules are equally irrelevant in this case. The court's discursion into the subject of *ijtihād* seems to reflect a rather profound lack of appreciation for the nuances of Islamic political theory.

For its part, the Iraqi Federal Supreme Court seems to suffer from deep problems respecting its awareness of, or willingness to engage in, Islamic law when evaluating legislation under that state's repugnancy clause. An excellent example lies in the first case that the Federal Supreme Court of Iraq decided that dealt with a challenge to legislation on the grounds of a putative violation of Islamic law. The case involved a claim by a litigant that a provision of the Iraqi Law of Evidence requiring that contracts be in writing was invalid because it violated Islamic law. In the briefest of opinions, the Court cited a verse of the Qur'an urging believers to record their debts in a writing, and, as a consequence, determined that the rule requiring a writing was supported by Islam's settled rulings. In so doing, the Court breezed past centuries of extensive and nuanced argument respecting preferences for oral witnesses over writings, which has been the subject of much scholarship over the past several decades. This is not to say that the Court's decision was unjustifiable, only that its cursory reasoning and analysis was problematic. Decision 60/2010, Federal Supreme Court of Iraq, decided December 21, 2010.

Elsewhere the Iraqi Federal Supreme Court fared little better when it evaluated the Islamicity of a Saddam era rule requiring that the deferred *mahr,* or dower—promised to a wife by a husband at marriage and paid at death or divorce—be valued in gold at the time of the marriage, even if it was promised in currency. This rule was instituted to address the hyperinflation that had significantly devalued the Iraqi dinar after the First Gulf War from approximately seven dinars to the U.S. dollar to 1500 dinars to the dollar. Without the rule, a wife who had been promised a deferred dower of 10,000 dinars in 1985 would have had her expectation of the amount she was entitled to receive on death or divorce reduced from approximately US$1400 (roughly half of the annual per capita GDP in 1985) to a figure closer to $6.

The husband in the case before the Court claimed that the gold substitution decree violated Islamic law because Islamic law permitted the couple to set the dower at whatever value and in whatever form they wished, and it was not for the state to change the form or the amount. The Court rejected the claim, indicating that deferred dower constituted a form of compensation to a wife for an injury that has befallen her, either through a divorce or her husband's death, and that Islam's settled rules mandate that there be compensation for harm as an overarching principle. Decision 45/2012, Federal Supreme Court of Iraq, decided September 19, 2012.

The ruling is rather perplexing. After all, the gold valuation rule does not in any way measure the amount due a wife on the basis of harm arising out of a divorce. Other provisions of Iraqi and Egyptian law do this. The most obvious are provisions discussed in Chapter Two that obligate a husband to pay support to his wife prospectively for a period of years if he divorces her in a fashion that a court deems capricious. The gold valuation rule, by contrast, purports to restore contractual balance, in that it ensures that the amount the wife receives on death or divorce corresponds to what she (or her family) reasonably expected, not what injury she suffered.

Indeed, even the maxim that the court sets forth, that every injury caused by another mandates compensation, is more reflective of civilian law than it is anything that might be found in a compendium on Islamic law. This might be why the court makes no reference to Islamic law at all beyond vague platitudes concerning the "highest justice" that the sharia seeks to realize.

In the end, what the court seems to have done was articulate a principle that it deemed obvious and just, attribute that principle to Islamic law for no reason other than that Islamic law seeks the highest form of justice, and then clumsily apply it in a rather specious fashion to a case that appeared before it. The result, to put the matter directly, is not particularly attractive as a model of Islamic constitutionalism.

Beyond the problem that modern state judges do not seem to know enough about Islamic law or Islamic political theory to apply any sort of theory of Islamic constitutionalism coherently, the profoundly ambiguous nature of Islam's higher end purposes renders it difficult to develop any sort of coherence even if a court was predisposed to do this.

Egypt here is again instructive. In a 1995 case, the Court heard a case dealing with one of its many antiquated leasing laws, and specifically Article 29 of Law 49 of 1977. The law limits very strictly the amount that a landlord may charge a tenant for rent to a price that is artificially quite low. Article 29 further permits tenants to pass on their leases to their spouses' parents, children, siblings, grandparents, grandchildren, uncles, aunts, nephews, or nieces under the same terms for an indefinite period. The result, according to the Court, was "an attack on ownership through a denial of some of its elements. It cannot be classified as regulation [of ownership], but rather the entire destruction of it through overuse and exploitation, attaching to the landlord alone the overt and exorbitant harm."

The Court claimed that this violated the Islamic repugnancy clause, and in so doing characterized the core and immutable Islamic law principle of property ownership as follows:

> The original principle is that all property belongs to God the Sublime, who established it and rendered it usable, and to Him shall be its return, designating His servants as vicegerents to build upon the earth. He rendered them responsible for what is in their possession by way of property, and not to squander it or use it harmfully. God the Sublime says: "spend out of that in which he has made you vicegerents." [Qur'an 57:7] ... This is a delegation to the Guardian of Affairs to regulate in a manner that realizes the purposes [*maqāṣid*] of the sharia envisaged. These are purposes that prevent the management and administration of the property wastefully, frivolously, aggressively, or taking measures that conflict with public interest, or impose on those rights of others which are regarded as superior.

The clear import is that the state may—indeed, must—regulate property ownership so that the owners of property, who are no more than God's vicegerents, use it in a responsible fashion that corresponds to the public interest. However, as God has entrusted individuals who possess property to make use of it in the first instance, the state may not confiscate it, either directly or indirectly, through a form of regulatory taking that renders it impossible for the owner of the land to make productive use of it. Decision 6/JY9, Supreme Constitutional Court of Egypt, decided March 18, 1995.

The reasoning is not unsound. After all, one of the five primary purposes of the sharia is the protection of property, and Egypt's rent control system confirms the transfer of such broad tenancy rights at such artificially low rents that it seems to limit the property owner's ability to make productive use of the property. Certainly, the Court is not the first to observe this. Nevertheless, it is hard to see how Islamic law as it is traditionally understood is going to offer much by way of guidance to a court intending to adjudicate the line between legitimate regulation of private property on the one hand, and, on the other, a regulatory scheme that becomes so unduly burdensome that it constitutes a confiscation of property. This is simply not a question with which jurists have traditionally had to grapple. As such, given this lack of guidance, one wonders whether repugnancy is at all useful as a means to protect property, or whether common constitutional provisions that prohibit takings without compensation are sufficient. The references to Islamic law seem to add little to the analysis.

A third problem as concerns the implementation of repugnancy clauses is one of political interference. This is a problem that plagues courts across the Islamic world generally, where authoritarianism is more the rule than the exception, but it is particularly acute in the work of constitutional courts, whose work carries broader political implications.

Pakistan offers a useful example. The Federal Shariat Court, responsible for reviewing legislation under Pakistan's repugnancy clause, heard the case of *Hazoor Bakhsh v. Federation of Pakistan* (1981 PLD FSC 145) in 1981. The case involved the application of the stoning punishment to the Scriptural Crime of fornication. As explained in Chapter Six, the stoning punishment, applied under Sunni rules to those who are or have been married in the past, is curious, in that it does not seem to comport with Qur'an 24:2, which reads as follows:

> The woman or man found guilty of sexual intercourse—lash each one of them with a hundred lashes, and do not be taken by pity for them in the religion of Allah, if you should believe in Allah and the Last Day. And let a group of the believers witness their punishment.

Classical jurists came to the consensus conclusion that the Qur'anic verse only applied to those never married. (Indeed, common Qu'ran translations endorse this approach by placing the word "unmarried" in brackets in the text above, just before the words "man" and "woman." As that qualification does not appear in the Arabic, I do not include it here.) The basis for this conclusion was Sunna that revealed the Prophet applying the stoning punishment to adulterers.

In a series of opinions delivered by different judges on the Court, the court ultimately decided in a 4–1 vote that in fact the proper punishment for fornication, for the married and unmarried alike, was that specified in the Qur'an; namely, one hundred lashes, and that existing legislation that called for the punishment of stoning was invalid because repugnant to the Qur'an.

Unlike the Egyptian and Iraqi constitutional courts, the Pakistani Federal Shariat Court appeared to know juristic rules and methods quite well, and it was quite willing to engage Islamic jurisprudence in order to justify its conclusions. The judges raised a variety of arguments to explain their reasoning, and specifically to cast doubt on the Sunna that seemed to establish stoning as the punishment for adulterers. Among them were familiar reformist and modernist moves—for example, that a given statement of the Prophet was in fact more suspect in its authenticity than classical jurists acknowledged. They made other arguments as concerned the Sunna and stoning as well. One of the Prophetic traditions, for example, involved the application of the stoning punishment to Jewish fornicators and the argument ran that the Prophet was applying Jewish law rather than Islamic law, as a matter of deference and comity. Another argument among the judges on the Court concerned the temporal order of the Sunna and Qur'an 24:2. If, as some judges argued, the Prophetic Sunna favoring stoning *preceded* the revelation of Qur'an 24:2, then the relevant Sunna would be abrogated by Qur'anic verse, rather than Qur'anic verse being limited by the Sunna. Finally, the judges expounded at some length on the possibility of the punishment of stoning as being a discretionary one applied by the Prophet in a particular instance, rather than one that was mandatory in connection with the commission of a Scriptural Crime.

Overall, the various opinions struck a cautious note. They emphasized that the absolutely and unambiguously clear Qur'anic text ipso facto cast some doubt on the validity of the Sunna. When that doubt was combined with other, separate questions respecting the validity and authenticity of the relevant Sunna, as described above, the only conclusion was that the Scriptural Crime necessitated one hundred lashes rather than stoning. The contrary conclusion would be that, to quote Justice Hyder, "a commandment of such vital importance, with such serious consequences, [was] revealed [by God, in the Qur'an] only in half, and that too in an ambiguous way." That, to the court, seemed deeply improbable.

The judges involved in the case were quite aware that they were engaged in the process of *ijtihād,* in that they were by definition reviewing original sources to come to conclusions that were at odds with those of classical jurists. Moreover, the reasoning of the various judges of the court revealed a maturity and sophistication in approaching Islamic law. Such an approach could potentially have served as a harbinger for the emergence over time of a well-considered methodology to evaluate legislation on repugnancy grounds.

Unfortunately, however, this was not to be. Under pressure from traditional clerics, Pakistan's authoritarian leader, General Zia ul-Haq, reconstituted the court entirely following the case. The remade Court, which now included three traditionalist clerics, promptly overruled the *Hazoor Bakhsh* decision. While the overruling was not itself poorly reasoned, the overt political interference in the affairs of the courts rendered the decision highly suspect, and the development of a coherent method of Islamic constitutionalism all the more challenging. This process repeated itself in Pakistan yet again in the early 2000's, with General Musharraf replacing the Shariat Appellate Bench in order to induce a ruling more to his liking on the concept of *ribā*. It is hard to believe that a coherent form of jurisprudence could possibly emerge from courts that are so transparently politically compromised.

The fact that courts have such frail legitimacy—partly because of political interference and partly because of general distrust among large parts of the Muslim laity toward state institutions of any kind—leads to a fourth and final impediment to the creation of a coherent method to implement repugnancy. This is that courts are uncomfortable departing from long established medieval Islamic rules. Even where the judges are not then replaced, as they were in Pakistan in *Hazoor Bakhsh,* they are perceived as having somehow interfered with a more authentic version of Islamic law. This poses a particularly severe problem when the medieval rules, at least as they are commonly understood, impose limitations that are at odds with core realities of modernity. The most obvious of these is in the ban on money interest on a loan. A cautious constitutional court concerned about its legitimacy is neither willing to reinterpret Islamic rules to limit or eliminate such a prohibition, nor can it exactly declare interest unlawful without causing severe financial distress. This leaves it in a quandary.

Egypt's Supreme Constitutional Court responded to this problem with a form of jurisprudential incoherence. In a 1985 case involving the imposition of money interest on a debt owed by the premier Sunni Islamic center of learning, the Azhar, the Court summarily and without much analysis agreed with the Azhar that the taking of interest was clearly and unambiguously banned by Islamic law. It was quite uninterested in examining the word *ribā* as it appeared in the Qur'an to determine whether it actually applied to money interest, or to reinterpret Sunna on which the interest ban is based, despite the fact that such an approach is quite plausible, as discussed in Chapter Four.

Yet, aware that it could not exactly overrule the provisions of the Civil Code, which permitted this taking of interest without causing significant economic disruption, the Court ruled against the

Azhar on a different basis. It maintained that legislation enacted prior to the date that the constitution was amended to incorporate the concept of repugnancy was immune from judicial challenge on the grounds of repugnancy. It was left to the legislature to amend this sort of law to render it compatible with Islamic law, rather than for the court to strike it down because incompatible. Decision 20/JY 1, Supreme Constitutional Court of Egypt, decided May 4, 1985. The theory is unusual, almost bizarre, akin to suggesting that U.S. slavery laws in existence prior to the abolition of slavery in the Constitution's Thirteenth Amendment were immune from judicial challenge and therefore enforceable, even as the Thirteenth Amendment prevented new slavery laws from being enacted.

The impression that emerges from this is less of a Court actually seeking to implement some sort of comprehensible test to determine what is or is not repugnant to Islamic law, and one instead navigating a narrow course, however incoherently, between incompatible political and economic forces, on the one hand, and demands for consistency with classical law, on the other.

In the end, in light of these challenges, courts have had difficulty establishing a clear mechanism by which to determine whether or not law is Islamic, even as states have had difficulty establishing a means by which to demonstrate they are Islamic. The classical rules do not provide sufficient guidance, and constitutional practice is not sufficiently mature in most Islamic states as to have led to a method that could be regarded as effective, or even coherent. Islamic constitutionalism, in this sense, very much remains a work in progress.

CHAPTER 8
ISLAMIC INTERNATIONAL LAW AND RELATIONS

Islamic international law and relations, the final subject of this Nutshell, are somewhat distinct from the other areas of law we have examined. On the one hand, like family law and inheritance law, and unlike Islamic constitutionalism, classical jurists had a great deal to say on the core subject matter at issue. On the other hand, like Islamic finance, modernity has so shifted expectations and understandings of the subject that any coherent modernist theory on the subject must be considered more of a reinvention of what Islamic law means than it is a reinvigoration of Islamic law principles.

There is another unique dimension to add to this, however. Unlike the other mature areas of law we have examined in this Nutshell, which remained reasonably stable throughout much of the classical era, Islamic international law found itself in a near constant state of flux. This should be of little surprise. If there was any feature of the classical era Islamic state that was unstable and ever changing, it was the geopolitical realities in which it found itself. Islamic theories of international law, which include as a central plank the well-known and frequently misunderstood doctrine of jihad, needed to evolve to meet those realities, and continue to need to do so.

That rather obvious point leads to an important consequence that requires constant emphasis—any state or transnational organization that purports to operate in conformity with what it describes as Islamic principles of international law is necessarily operating with a tremendous amount of license when making the claim. In the process of reinvention, it is choosing from one of many options that have existed within the tradition over the course of existence millennium and a half rather than following some immutable, monolithic set of principles. In other words, in the absence of a stable classical corpus, virtually any claim of fidelity to some stable historical conception of Islamic law is a highly opportunistic one.

The first part of this Chapter lays out the origins of Islamic international law doctrine, which presume eternal hostility as between the Muslim state and non-Muslim states that surround it. The second part describes how some of the assumptions underlying the early doctrine, chief among them that Muslim armies do not lose many battles, began to fray during the classical era itself, with the onset of the Crusades and, centuries later, the sacking of Baghdad by the Mongols. The third part then moves to the late classical and then modern world, which are characterized by the rise of more established and sustained relationships between states. This Part shows how some of the underlying normative principles undergirding the modern systems, among them principles relating to mutual recognition and nonaggression, have now been internalized not only by Muslim states, but even by nationalist and Islamist "resistance" movements that claim fidelity to Islamic law. The final part then brings the focus to modern, transnational jihadist movements such as

Al Qaeda and ISIS. This section seeks to demonstrate how such movements are no more faithful to the classical tradition than modern states are. Instead, they are best understood as offering a different and highly tendentious Islamic law response of sorts to their own perceptions of modern conditions, one that in many ways turns the traditional doctrine of jihad nearly completely on its head.

A. THE ORIGINS OF ISLAMIC INTERNATIONAL LAW

1. THE ERA OF THE PROPHET MUHAMMAD

As might be unsurprising given the significant shifts in doctrine, referred to above, that Islamic international law has undertaken over the course of centuries, the revelatory source material on which the field is based is largely ambiguous. This has given advocates for almost every conceivable approach to international law an opportunity to stake their claim to Islamicity on the basis of revelatory text, whether that be the Qur'an itself or the example of the Prophet Muhammad set forth in the Sunna.

For example, those who seek to emphasize within Islam a principle of mutual recognition and respect among peoples frequently point to certain features of a treaty of sorts struck by the Prophet Muhammad known as the Medina Charter. The agreement was between the Muslim community, polytheist Arab tribes, and various Jewish tribes in the city of Medina, where the Prophet Muhammad had sought refuge, as further explored in Chapter Two. The

Medina Charter plainly recognizes the rights and obligations of the different tribes and faiths on a level of parity, and in this sense embraces a conception of interfaith pluralism that is broad and inclusive. To be clear, it is anachronistic to suggest that the Medina Charter is the seventh century realization of both secular constitutional democracy as well as the principles of mutual tolerance and respect for all peoples irrespective of religion or ethnicity. For example, the Charter prohibits a believer from supporting a disbeliever against another believer, and the Quraysh of Mecca are singled out as a people to whom none are permitted to give sanctuary. That said, the document clearly provides the roots for mutual respect and tolerance, and does not seek to subjugate any one faith to any other, thereby giving rise to a core set of values out of which modern, secular, and inclusive models of governance could be developed.

In addition to the Medina Charter, those who seek to accommodate Islam to the norms of modernity point out that the Prophet Muhammad sent a number of his closest companions and relatives to Abyssinia to seek sanctuary from a Christian king against the depredations of the Meccan Quraysh. The humane treatment of these Muslim emigres earns the non-Muslim Abyssinians praise in the Qur'an. Other source material suggesting recognition of non-Muslim polities include multiple Qur'anic verses that inform the Prophet Muhammad that his duty is only the clear delivery of the Message, and that God will call people to account for failing to abide by it. To quote the Qur'an further, "there shall be no compulsion in religion: truth stands out clear from error" [2:256]. From all of this, it is certainly plausible to establish a series of principles of international relations whereby the Muslim polity is to live alongside others according to a principle of mutual recognition and nonaggression.

On the other hand, it is fair to say that other source material from the Prophet Muhammad's era could be used to derive a very different set of principles in the area of international law and relations. These include, most saliently, the Prophet's military campaign from Medina back to his home city of Mecca, which he placed under Islamic control, clearing the Holy Shrine—the Ka`ba—of idols in the process. Similarly, the Prophet is reported to have written letters to the emperors of Persia and Byzantium, as well as the king of Abyssinia, urging them to accept Islam and thereby earn immunity from attack. Such material is supported by Qur'anic verse extolling the believers "to kill the [disbelievers] wherever you overtake them, and expel them from wherever they have expelled you, for tumult and oppression are worse than killing" [2:191].

The question ultimately left for Muslim jurists to decide was which source material to privilege, and which to narrow to specific places and times, in order to develop an overarching theory of international relations. Was the Medina Charter a concession to a certain reality of Muslim weakness in Islam's early years, rendered unnecessary and thereby abrogated by the Prophet himself once the polity was large enough to be in a position to spread itself through conquest? Or was the example of the Prophet's conquest of Mecca to be understood as *sui generis,* relating to the clearing of idols from the House of Abraham and not the manner in which non-Muslim houses of worship were to be treated generally? Could it be, in the same vein, that Qur'an 2:191, quoted above and urging believers to kill nonbelievers rather than accept oppression, is to be understood to refer solely to those engaged in aggression against the Muslim community itself, thereby explaining the next verse "and if they cease, then indeed, God is Forgiving and Merciful"? Alternatively, is the reference to the disbelievers "ceasing" the fighting intended to mean they have surrendered, and that thus the believers are under obligation to kill non-Muslims until they have accepted Islamic rule, at which point they can be forgiven for their previous aggression?

The answers to these questions are complex and a matter of continuous contestation within the Islamic tradition. Much depends on the ideological commitments of the juristic communities developing the rules as well as the social and political context in which they were writing. The next part describes the positions of the earliest jurists who attempted to systematize the source material into a coherent body of international law and international relations and further contextualizes the era in which such jurists were writing.

2. EARLY JURISTIC THEORY: SHAYBĀNĪ'S *SĪYĀR*

The first real attempts to systematize Islamic international law into a form of doctrine took place around the start of the eighth century C.E., approximately a century after the death of the Prophet Muhammad. By far the most important of these was a work entitled *Kitāb al-Sīyār* (literally, the "Book of Movements"), penned by one of the disciples of Abu Hanifa, the eponym of the Hanafi school, whose name was Muhammad al-Shaybāni. Shaybānī has been justifiably described as the Hugo Grotius of Islamic law, in that, like Grotius in the context of modern international law, Shaybānī's work establishes a framing of Islamic international relations that was then adopted by jurists for centuries after him. Indeed, Shaybānī's conceptions continue to capture the imagination of modern Muslim scholars today. It is quite hard to imagine any modernist, no matter how reformist or progressive, who would presume to propound a theory of Islamic international law that did not contend with Shaybānī's work, written almost a millennium and a half ago.

Yet, as with Grotius in the context of modern international law, there is a difference between suggesting that Shaybānī established the *framework* out of which Islamic international law developed, and that Shaybānī set forth an entire set of complete and determinative rules that were left undisturbed by later jurists. The former proposition is largely true, and the latter is certainly not. The fact is that over the course of Islamic history, jurists continued to develop and refine rules of Islamic international relations from within the Shaybānī framework, in a manner that in some cases severely strained it, but never entirely broke it. This process of reimagining rules within an existing framework continued until the cataclysmic disruptions of modernity, and the incursion of Grotian ideas into Islamdom.

Shaybānī's work, and those of the jurists after him, is built upon an implicit factual premise—highly contestable in our times, but obvious in his—that the relationship as between the Islamic world and the non-Muslim world is characterized by perduring enmity and hostility. There is thus no possibility of permanent peaceful relations, nor could such a relationship be rationally contemplated. Instead, in Shaybānī's framing, there is a "House of Islam" and a "House of War", and the goal of each is to exterminate the other. Shaybānī's concern lay exclusively with how the House of Islam should conduct itself in light of these underlying predicates.

The primary mechanism for Islamic expansion, in the Shaybānī vision, is the jihad. In essence, God has obligated the Muslim community to spread the House of Islam at the expense of the House of War and thereby bring about domination of the globe under the banner of Islam, God's True Faith, in accordance with God's Will. The jihad is a perfectly permissible means to fulfill that community obligation through military means. The imperative to spread Islam, in other words, overwhelms any hesitations or reticence respecting the use of force.

These conclusions, obvious from even a cursory reading of Shaybānī's work, must be tempered by two major qualifications. First, there was never a suggestion among early jurists, including Shaybānī, that the jihad was the preferred, much less the only, means by which Islam might spread. Hence, for example, there was an obligation prior to engaging in hostilities for the Muslim forces to "call" their enemies to Islam, and thereby avoid the hostilities altogether. It is a mistake of category to focus on the evident absurdity of two armies meeting on an open battlefield, and all fighting avoided through the decision from one side to accept the call of the enemy forces to embrace their faith. The point is not that the conversion of the non-Muslim forces is likely upon the making of such a call. The point, instead, is to underscore the preference to avoid bloodshed wherever possible, and to use jihad when no other means of propagating the faith are apparent. Hence, there is even debate among early jurists as to the extent to which the call to Islam needed to be repeated once hostilities had begun. Such debate reveals amply the concern of these jurists on how best to balance the ethical desire to hold to an ideal of avoiding violence wherever possible on the one hand with the practical realities of warfare on the other.

Second, and equally importantly, Shaybānī described the jihad as a communal obligation rather than an individual one. Thus, it is absolutely not the case that each individual believer has an obligation to fight unbelievers wherever they might be found, even if some Qur'anic verse quoted above might be read to suggest this. Rather, the *community* was expected to spread the faith through war, and so long as a sufficient number of believers did that, the obligation was deemed satisfied. Hence, there was an understanding that a significant number of believers would not be participating in the jihad. Jurists in fact created a series of limiting rules relating to who was even permitted participate. Some rules, such as that the participants be male and able bodied, are rather obvious in context. Others, however, include fighters who do not have the permission of their parents, or, among some jurists, debtors who do not have the permission of their creditors. The recently married could participate, though there was some expectation that they probably would not, and rules respecting distribution of war booty were adjusted to take account of this. As the Muslim empire expanded and the numbers of Muslims in the world consequently multiplied, the numbers of those not participating in the jihad exceeded those participating in it by a significant margin. There may have been some romanticism associated with the earliest period of Islamic history, when the Muslim community was a tiny one divided between the city states of Mecca and Medina, beset by enemies on all sides, and nearly every able bodied believer was called into battle with some frequency to defend the community from extinction. However, Islamic society did not have to evolve very much or for very long for jurists to recognize that not every able bodied male made an ideal soldier, and that society had interests well beyond those associated with making war. Thus, the jihad was an imperative, but not an all-consuming imperative. It was instead one of the many obligations upon the community, and not necessarily the central one around which Muslim society was organized.

Once it is established that the jihad is a communal obligation, the natural question that follows is *who* is supposed to organize and manage the jihad on the part of the community. In this, both Sunni and Shi'i scholars proved remarkably conservative, in that they designed the rules in order to ensure the preservation of institutions and hierarchies of power within the Islamic state. Specifically, among the early Sunni jurists, it was made amply clear that only the leader of the House of Islam himself—the caliph, in other words—could call the jihad. The caliph would determine how many fighters he needed, where to deploy them, and for how long any given military campaign would continue. Once the caliph had determined he had sufficient numbers of fighters to conduct a battle, the community had fulfilled its obligation. There was no need for anyone else to continue military operations. In fact, such military operations were specifically prohibited. Quite plainly, the aim was to privilege a caliph, even a tyrannical one, over any and all forces that might threaten to challenge him. The result would be a placid internal order where authority was never challenged and intra-Muslim civil strife rendered an impossibility. That this was more the reflection of an idealized (Sunni) juristic imagination than it was a description of the actual conduct of intra-Muslim politics was obvious virtually from the moment of the Prophet Muhammad's death.

Of course, Sunni jurists recognized to some limited extent that internal strife was inevitable. Hence, for example, Shaybānī and later jurists gave the subject of rebellion ample treatment. They accepted that the caliph could undertake military campaigns against Muslims who had rebelled against him. However, once subdued, the general juristic preference was to permit them to return to the fold with their properties and their weapons and free of any demands for compensation for harm done or lives lost. This conclusion is on the basis of the treatment received by those who had rebelled against the Fourth Caliph Ali, among whose ranks was the Prophet's wife A'isha.

Later Sunni jurists, most notable among them the chief Shafi'i judge of Baghdad Abu al-Hasan al-Mawārdi, would attempt to address intra Muslim disputes within the House of Islam differently. Mawārdi imagined concepts such as caliphal appointments of governorships that were procured through usurpation on the part of the governor. Under such an approach, competing Islamic polities are little more than various "governorships" (many taken by force) where true authority is technically held on behalf a caliph who theoretically rules over the entire House of Islam. Fictions of this sort proved useful, though they could only go so far, in particular as caliphal authority began to atrophy over the course of the Abbasid empire. It is fair to say in the end that Sunni jurists never managed to entirely accommodate their theories of international law and international relations in a manner that took sufficient cognizance of the very clear political divisions within the entire House of Islam. This problem generally became worse over time, as these divisions grew ever deeper.

For their part, early Shi'i jurists established the principle that only the Infallible Imam could call the jihad. Given that the final Imam went into hiding toward the end of the 9th century C.E., less than a century after Shaybānī had produced *Kitāb al-Siyār,* and given that he will only return to usher in the end times, the effect of such a limitation has been to render the jihad in traditional Shi'i accounts to be more a feature of eschatology than law. This has not prevented classical Shi'i jurists propounding the extensive rules of jihad at length, only to indicate, in the midst of them, that "to fight alongside someone other than the Imam ... is forbidden, like the consumption of carrion, blood, or the flesh of swine." [*Jawāhir al-Kalām* 21:11]. The ultimate result is broadly consonant with Shi'ism's longstanding Quietist tradition, which does not seek to challenge Muslim temporal authority so much as delegitimize it, thereby regarding the caliphate as an epiphenomenon from which the believer is ideally alienated until the return of the Hidden Imam.

Just as the caliph (or Imam, as the case may be) could call the jihad, so the caliph could call for a respite from warfare. There was not an expectation, that is, of incessant warfare on all fronts. There could very well be strategic advantage to sue for a truce for a time, before initiating fighting once again. As with all contracts, upholding the truce was considered a religious duty, to the extent of course that the counterparties to the truce uphold it was well. The term for the truce—*hudna*, which is the term used in modern Arabic to denote a cease fire—demonstrates its purpose amply, as well as its inherently temporary nature. Early jurists regarded ten years as the maximum permissible length of a truce, on the theory that the Prophet Muhammad's longest truce, the Pact of Hudaybiyya, with the Quraysh of Mecca, lasted that length of time.

Early jurists also contemplated the possibility of a temporary non-Muslim presence in Muslim lands, not only for the obvious purpose of diplomacy, but also for trade. Similarly, the jurists expected that Muslims might travel to the House of War, temporarily, for similar reasons. These sorts of sojourns were accommodated through the device of the *'amān* or guarantee of safe passage. Any Muslim could theoretically grant an *'amān* to a non-Muslim, and the holder of the *'amān* would then be able to travel safely within the House of Islam for its duration. The same was true in reverse, meaning that Muslims were permitted to travel through the House of War at least temporarily in order to engage in commerce or diplomacy. The *'amān* was deemed a form of a contract, and therefore upholding its terms was a religious duty, on the part of the Muslim holding an *'amān* in the House of War, and on the part of the Muslim community vis a vis a non-Muslim holding an *'amān* in the House of Islam. A Muslim who is travelling in the House of War under a guarantee of safe passage, in other words, is not permitted to engage in acts of violence against the state wherein he is located under a theory of jihad because he would be violating the *'amān* to do this. Rather, if the Muslim wished to participate in a jihad called by the caliph in fulfillment of the duty, the Muslim would be obligated to return to the House of Islam, thereby terminating the *'amān,* and then volunteer for the jihad from there.

Beyond non-Muslims guaranteed temporary safe passage, the other group of Muslims that Shaybānī and his contemporaries imagined as residing in the House of Islam were those known as the *dhimmīs*. Early jurists interpreted Prophetic traditions and related Qur'anic passages as obligating the Muslim polity to offer some limited level of respect to the followers of other Abrahamic faiths who preceded them. Such peoples are referred to in the Qur'an as "People of the Book," meaning adherents to a Divine Book. The terms set forth by the jurists under which the *dhimmīs* were permitted to continue to remain within the House of Islam were unenviable, at least by modern standards. Based largely on what is known as the Pact of 'Umar, concluded between the second caliph and the Christians of Syria, *dhimmīs* were clearly branded as a subjugated and conquered people within the House of Islam. Thus, they were required to pay a special tax, known as the *jizya,* and were supposed to be humiliated when doing so by whomever was collecting the tax. They were also denied the right to rebuild places of worship, forced to wear distinctive dress that would identify them as non-Muslims, not permitted to ring church bells, and expected to give up their seats at a gathering if Muslims wished to sit. These rules all arise on the basis of interpretations of the Qur'an and the

Prophet's example that are, to say the least, contestable.

One final point bears mentioning as concerns international relations and warfare within the conception of the early jurists. This relates to what in modern legal parlance would be referred to as *jus in bello,* meaning the law pertaining to how to conduct war, as opposed to the laws relating to when war may be entered into. This particular field of law, from its earliest stages, is far more amenable to the demands of modern conditions. There is a certain humanitarian ethos that permeates the early juristic literature. Derived largely from the instructions the first caliph directed to the Muslim armies initiating the Syria campaign, the war is to be directed against combatants, and the targeting of noncombatants is to be shunned. The believers are not permitted to cut down the trees or gardens belonging to the enemy. They may not slaughter the animals of the enemies, except for food, and they may not destroy their homes. Again, it would be anachronistic and absurd to suggest that these rules anticipate in their entirety the post World War II Geneva Conventions. The taking of war booty, for example, is very much part of the juristic tradition, based on a chapter of the Qur'an entitled "The Spoils of War." That said, the ethical framework called into being in the early juristic accounts is broadly consonant with modern developments and expectations concerning the conduct of war. The same is obviously not true of the manner in which Shaybānī envisages Muslim and non-Muslim relations more broadly, as demonstrated above.

B. INTERNATIONAL LAW AFTER THE EARLY YEARS

1. IBN TAYMIYYA AND THE DEFENSIVE JIHAD

The previous section described a key assumption under which Shaybānī operated, which was that the House of Islam and the House of War were engaged in a perduring conflict. A second assumption, key to the early juristic understanding of international relations, was that in military conflict, God was on the side of the believers. They might not win every battle—indeed, even in the Prophet's time there were military setbacks referenced in the Qur'an—but over time, the inexorable trend would be an expansion of the House of Islam until God's rule encompassed the earth. Accordingly, early Muslim jurists did not develop with any degree of depth or sophistication a set of principles to govern war to defend the House of Islam, as opposed to expand it. The most that appears on this subject are brief disquisitions on dispensing with the need to obtain the caliph's permission to conduct the jihad under circumstances where the House of Islam is suddenly attacked. These are exceptional rules arising out of expediency more than they are the establishment of a comprehensive doctrine.

Shaybānī's position respecting inevitable Islamic triumph was both theologically grounded, and, in his context, entirely consonant with objective realities. The speed with which the believers had expanded the House of Islam from two tiny desert city states on the

Arabian Gulf so insignificant Rome never thought to conquer them to an empire stretching from the west coast of Africa to the virtual gates of Byzantium and across to India was astonishing. There was absolutely no reason for the empire to think that somehow this trend would stop. Indeed, a Christian soldier in an army fighting to stop the Muslim advance through the Pyrenees and into France might be forgiven for questioning on whose side God was truly on.

Circumstances changed, of course, over time, with the first major collective psychological shock to Muslim self-assurance being the Crusades. The idea that European powers—referred to collectively by jurists of the era as the *faranj*, or Franks—would be able to wrest a city of such importance as Jerusalem from Muslim hands, and that they would be control it for significant periods of time, caused significant consternation within Islamdom. Out of that experience and the later Mongol conquests, which ultimately led to the ignominious sacking of Baghdad and the end of the Abbasid empire, later jurists added important dimensions to Shaybānī's doctrine.

There were a number of jurists over the course of centuries who worked to develop the idea of the defensive jihad, but among the most important and influential, certainly among modern jihadist movements, was Ibn Taymiyya, writing in the specific time of the Mongol conquests. Deploying *ijtihād* to reason from Prophetic example, Ibn Taymiyya based his ideas on the Prophet's famed Battle of the Ditch. Ibn Taymiyya noted that in digging a ditch to protect Medina from attack from the Quraysh of Mecca, the Prophet required the participation of every able bodied male. However, once the immediate threat had passed, and the armies of Medina gave chase to the Meccans, not every believer needed to, or did, participate. Thus, Ibn Taymiyya reasoned, there is a distinction to be drawn as between a defensive jihad and an aggressive one. Shaybānī's rules apply only as to the aggressive jihad. The defensive jihad, by contrast, is an individual duty. When the House of Islam is under attack, each individual believer must participate until the threat has been repelled. From this seed ultimately grew many theories of modern international terrorism, as the final subsection will show.

2. THE OTTOMANS AND PERMANENT INTERNATIONAL RELATIONS

Other changes to Shaybānī's early doctrines came later, in particular in the context of the Ottoman Empire. Based as they were on Europe's doorstep, the Ottomans enjoyed a relationship with non-Muslim Europe that was by its nature more sustained than previous Islamic empires. This became truer over time, as the Ottomans weakened and grew more dependent on stronger European states. Shaybānī's notions of permanent hostility seemed, in this context, rather quaint.

One manner to accommodate these changes was through expansion of the idea of the *hudna,* or truce, described above. Specifically, the mere fact that the

Prophet Muhammad had not executed a truce longer than ten years no longer seemed to be a sufficient justification to require all treaties to be no longer than this. Accordingly, Ottoman sultans extended the period of truces to as long as the lifetime of the sultan, it being doctrinally harder to justify extending a peace in a manner that would prevent the next sultan from reinstituting the jihad if strategically advantageous to do so.

The other change was through extensions of the principle of the 'amān. Over time, European powers extracted powerful concessions from the Ottomans that granted all of their citizens the right to travel and do business throughout the Empire. Every citizen of particular states, in other words, now possessed an 'amān and could enter the House of Islam. The roots of Islamic law justifications for both permanent relations with non-Muslim states on the principle of mutual recognition as well as the permanent presence of non-Muslims in Muslim states, and Muslims in non-Muslim states, were beginning to deepen.

C. MODERN INTERNATIONAL LAW AND RELATIONS

1. CONVENTIONAL DEVELOPMENTS

Though this Nutshell concerns modern Islamic law, this more extended account of classical doctrine is necessary in order to better understand the panoply of different understandings of Islamic international law and relations as they have emerged in the modern world. This is because there is significant contestation of the classical tradition in modernity, leading to wildly diverging understandings of what Islam requires in the areas of international law, international relations, and the jihad. This section begins with what might be fairly termed the "mainstream" approach, meaning the approach adopted by the Muslim states across the globe, and that broad set of scholars and advocates of Islamic law who support it.

This "mainstream" approach domesticates Islamic law largely within a Grotian framing, meaning that it basically accepts the division of the world into separate sovereign entities, under principles of mutual recognition and nonaggression. The justification for this sort of arrangement with non-Muslim states relies on extending the principles embodied in the traditional truce and the *'amān* in the same way that the Ottomans did, but to a greater extent. The United Nations Charter thus serves as a form of a truce, just a longer one than that which existed in earlier times. Muslim residence in non-Muslim lands, even on a permanent basis, are a form of *'amān*. These extensions, and the types of political relationships and loyalties they inevitably engender across religious boundaries, constitute of course a significant departure from what Shaybānī might have envisioned. However, they may be justified as merely a continuation of the doctrinal evolution that has been taking place since his death more than a millennium ago.

Ironically, despite the intense focus in the contemporary world among media and academic commentators alike on whether Islam has the tools necessary to support coexistence with non-Muslim polities, the more difficult doctrinal questions are internal to the House of Islam itself. The modern international system presupposes the division of the House of Islam into separate political entities. Particularly problematic is the idea that the relationship of these states to one another is governed by the same U.N. Charter as those that govern the relationship of Muslim states to non-Muslim states. After all, if the U.N. Charter is a permanent truce that leads to permanent recognition of non-Muslim states, the problem is that "truce" is not the means by which classical jurists would define the relations of disparate Muslim polities to one another. There are solutions, though most focus less on juristic texts and more on earlier Prophet example—deploying *ijtihād,* as it were, to reimagine intra Muslim relations as well as Muslim non-Muslim relations.

Equally difficult is the principle of equality of citizenship across religion within any given Muslim majority state, given the history of subjugated status historically afforded to non-Muslims within the House of Islam. In this area, Islamic law reformists and progressives from Hashim Kemali to Abdulaziz Sachedina have defended a variety of different theories of coexistence in the Islamic tradition, largely on the basis of *ijtihad*. It is fair to say that in doing so, they are forced in some important ways to depart from the classical tradition and engage in more creative exercises of interpretation.

For the most part, such disquisitions relate far more to Islamic law theory than they do to Islamic law practice. The fact is that very few Muslims in modern conventional states view themselves as somehow part of a global political unit known as an Islamic state, and fewer still have shown any inclination to institute formal discrimination against non-Muslim citizens by instituting a special tax against them. This is more likely to be a charge leveled by secular candidates against Islamist ones than it is to be one that the Islamists themselves are likely to openly embrace. That said, the fact that Islamist groups across the Muslim world seek to deflect charges of this sort by describing them as not part of their party's agenda rather than as an affront to Islamic law itself is an indication of the continued strength of elements of Shaybānī's framework even in contemporary times.

2. JIHAD AND THE MODERN WORLD

To state that modern Muslim states have accommodated themselves to a Grotian framing of international relations, as described in the previous section, is different from stating that there is no broad dissatisfaction with current geopolitical arrangements, or that Islam has not supplied some distinctive elements to modern international discourse. To be sure, as is the case with much of the developing world, there is a broad sense of unfairness that permeates Muslim understandings of the contemporary international system, where larger powers are able to ignore legal rules that smaller states are not, and where states are held to differing standards depending on their level of influence. Yet, importantly, even when seeking to frame objections in Islamic terms, Muslim actors end up adopting the ethical presuppositions and commitments of modern international law rather than classical Islam. Nowhere is this clearer than in discourse that surrounds the jihad.

In the first place, the point is often made in modern Muslim discussions on jihad that lexically, the word refers to "struggle" and does not necessarily implicate violence, let alone war. The struggle may be personal and spiritual in nature, or it may be societal and not involve violence, such as a "social jihad" to open hospitals and other nonprofit social service organizations. It might even be political, and relate to the establishment of a political party seeking a greater role for Islam in public life, but committed to the use of democratic politics to achieve it. Many mainstream Muslim leaders and organizations argue that such forms of personal and social struggle are the more important forms of jihad. This is on the basis of a statement from the Prophet Muhammad returning from a military campaign that he had completed the lesser jihad and was now coming back to engage in the greater one. Such treatment of jihad is unquestionably plausible, but it is a form of *ijtihād,* in that it involves reasoning from primary sources in a fashion that departs sharply from the established classical legal tradition. Specialists in Sunna historically regarded the Prophetic statement reflected above as being of questionable authenticity, and classical manuals of Islamic law certainly paid no attention to it at all—discussing jihad exclusively in the context of war.

Where jihad is contemplated among mainstream organizations in connection with violence and war, it is infused with modern terminology that creates almost unmanageable tension with the classical doctrine. The best example of this might be provided by the Organization of Islamic Cooperation ("OIC"), comprised of all of the Muslim majority nations in the world. While not specifically using the term jihad, the OIC has indicated on various occasions that the true teachings of Islam prohibit the killing of innocent people. Yet the OIC also endorses as Islamic "resistance to foreign aggression and the struggle of peoples under colonial or alien domination and foreign occupation for national liberation and self-determination," which it rather controversially exempts from any definition of terrorism.

Importantly, the idea of jihad as having something to do with resistance to occupation and foreign aggression is not exclusive to more mainstream organizations such as the OIC. The broad (and often quite popular) Islamist movements that claim the right to violence almost always use the term jihad alongside the word "resistance", in rhetoric that sounds as much in national liberation theory as it does in Islam. The Islamist Palestinian movement Hamas is an acronym in Arabic for the "Islamic Resistance Movement." Hizbollah likewise refers to its own military activities against Israel as "resistance". The insurrection against the United States that took place in Iraq shortly after 2003 among Islamist groups frequently described itself as a "resistance" to American occupation.

Such violent, postcolonial resistance is not directed solely at putatively non-Muslim regimes or occupiers within the militant framework. The highly popular work *The Neglected Duty,* published by militants shortly after the assassination of Anwar Sadat in Egypt, indicated that it was a duty of Muslims to overthrow virtually all regimes throughout the Muslim world because they refuse to uphold Islamic law, and because they cooperate with Western regimes in a colonialist fashion to subvert a just Islamic order.

The appeal of an Islamic call to resistance against oppression and injustice, whether directed at external, non-Muslim targets, or internal, indigenous, "colonialist" leaders, has proven quite alluring in significant parts of the Muslim world and quickly supplanted other forms of violent radicalism in much of it. The sharia, in modern times, has become deeply imbued with the language of national resistance to existing centers of power, and the jihad serves as its primary justificatory vehicle.

The extent to which each of these calls to violence is in fact "defensive" and designed to resist oppression and injustice is, obviously, contestable. The important point to note, however, is how deeply rooted in modern conceptions of legitimacy this reinvigoration of the jihad happens to be. To a jurist like Shaybānī, the idea of an "occupation" being somehow illegitimate and an object to which "resistance" is warranted is positively incoherent. The expectation was that the House of Islam and the House of War were at war with one another, with each seeking to exterminate the other, and that this state of affairs would continue so long as both continued to exist on the earth. While the expansion of the House of War at the expense of the House of Islam would then be of course rather disappointing, it was not illegitimate or a demonstration of non-Muslim perfidy—the House of Islam would do the same, after all, if and when it had the opportunity. By contrast, a conception of jihad as resistance to occupation presupposes a right of peoples to self determination and freedom from imperialist and colonialist meddling that did not exist within the classical framework. The evolutions, among Islamist and mainstream alike, are remarkable.

Moreover, it might be noted, the division of the House of Islam into independent nation states is not at all questioned in this version of jihad. Few of the violent liberation movements claiming to be engaged in jihad are truly international in nature. Hizbollah is Lebanese, Hamas is Palestinian, and the Gama`a Islamiyya is Egyptian. While there were, and still may be, limited forms of cooperation between them, none have showed any desire or inclination to unite as a single movement. The goal of each of these movements is to establish *an* Islamic state, but not *the* Islamic state. Each, that is, effectively accepts the modern division of the House of Islam into separate states, even when the boundaries of those states was largely set by the very imperialist and colonialist powers they purport to be resisting.

Finally, this section has focused almost exclusively on Sunnism in modernity. However, it is important to address evolutions that have transpired in Shi'i doctrine as well. As noted at the start of the Chapter, the longstanding Shi'i view was that only the Hidden Imam could call the jihad, which more or less relegated the doctrine to irrelevance for most of Islamic history. Interestingly, however, as the notion of jihad began in modernity to take on a more defensive character, and came to be understood as an instrument of anticolonialism and resistance to occupation, Shi'i movements proved as amenable to it as Sunni movements did. While formally Shi'i jurists continued to favor passivity to state authority through the middle of the twentieth century, prominent jurists were involving themselves in movements designed to resist colonial occupation. This began as early as the start of the twentieth century, in particular in the 1920 uprising in Iraq against the British. Decades later, Ayatollah Khomeini and his contemporaries and successors added some level of theory to these practices. They maintained that while aggressive jihad to spread the House of Islam was suspended pending the return of the Imam, defensive jihad to resist injustice and oppression, which included the overthrow of tyrannical regimes throughout the Muslim world, was not only permissible, but vitally necessary. Khomeini used as his model the Third Imam, Husayn bin Ali. As further described in Chapter Two, the Imam Husayn is primarily known for having taken up arms against the tyrannical leader of his time, the caliph Yazid, and died a martyr on the plains of Karbala, where the faithful lament his death to this day.

Despite the hold of the Karbala tragedy on the Shi'i imagination, Khomeini's idea that it could be used as a basis upon which to resist oppression and engage in jihad was a significant departure from traditional Shi'i doctrine, which counselled patience and forbearance pending the return of the Hidden Imam. Yet the position proved quite alluring among the Shi'a devout. It opened the door for various violent revivalist movements in a Shi'i mold, from Hizbollah in Lebanon to the Party of the Islamic Call in Iraq, to claim to be engaged in forms of defensive jihad against oppression and injustice that resembled those led by their Sunni counterparts. Given the broad popularity of this transmogrified conception of jihad, it is perhaps unsurprising that even Najaf's high jurist of our times, Ali Sistani—a traditionally more Quietist jurist hardly associated with political radicalism—came to embrace the concept. Quite ironically, he did so not to replace a supposedly "colonialist" regime under American occupation, but rather to *preserve and defend* the current Iraqi state from the depredations of the Islamic State, which was calling for its own jihad *against* the Iraqi state. This brings us to the matter of the Islamic State and its more significant challenge to contemporary international frameworks, discussed in the final section of this Chapter below.

3. THE CHALLENGE OF THE TRANSNATIONAL MOVEMENTS: AL QAEDA AND THE ISLAMIC STATE

A summary account of jihad in the contemporary world published at the end of the twentieth century would probably end the story with the last subsection. The conclusion would then describe the near total absorption of the Islamic world into the Grotian framework, including the division of the House of Islam into separate nation states, the equality of citizens within each nation state irrespective of religion, and the principle of mutual recognition of nation states for the territorial integrity of one another. It could then be pointed out that even Islamist movements of the most violent and radical sort tend to internalize this vision, describing their entire enterprise as a means to "resist" colonialism, imperialism, injustice, and oppression in terms and framings that are unmistakably modern. A commentator might be forgiven for looking past the one rather perplexing contrary example that did not then quite manage to fit within this framework. This was the Afghan jihad against the Soviet invasion of 1979, at least as envisioned by the tens of thousands of international fighters who came to Afghanistan from across the world to participate in it. They were fighting for the liberation of Muslim lands, far from their putative states of citizenship, thereby reflecting a more pristine sense of a House of Islam that permeated national boundaries.

From a purely military standpoint, these fighters were not well trained and did not prove particularly helpful. Far more crucial to the ultimate military outcome were the Afghan fighters and the equipment provided to them by both the United States and Saudi Arabia. The high significance of the fighters came to light afterwards, when the jihad was over. By then, the they were thoroughly radicalized and indoctrinated into the notion of a universalist struggle on behalf of oppressed Muslims against the enemies that oppressed them. Though few might have predicted it at the time, the result was the spread of an internationalist jihadist ideology throughout Muslim states. From these roots grew the respective organizations of Al Qaeda and the Islamic State.

What is most interesting about Al Qaeda, which came first, is that in its rejection of modern international law as it stands in the current day, it adopts some elements of classical law while still managing to turn the classical concept of jihad as nearly entirely on its head. There are three aspects to Bin Laden's conception of jihad that are particularly notable.

First, Bin Laden's 1996 declaration of jihad against the United States adopts very much the modern, conventional paradigm of Islamic radicalism, where jihad is primarily a response to occupation rather than an effort to expand the House of Islam. This is obvious from its title, which refers to a jihad against the "Americans Occupying the Land of the Two Holiest Sites." The sites in question are the holy cities of Mecca and Medina. Bin Laden's position—made clear in the Declaration—is that by permitting an American military presence in Saudi Arabia, and by putatively failing to uphold sharia in its entirety, the Saudi government has lost its legitimacy and is in fact merely an instrument of American occupation. The repeated reference to the United States either as "Crusader" or at the forefront of a "Jewish-Crusader alliance", and the litany of aggressions and massacres laid at the feet of that alliance, from places that are well known (Burma and Kashmir) to those that are so obscure as to be unrecognizable (Fattani and Ugadin), reflect a deep sense of victimization characteristic of Islamic radical movements generally.

Second, Bin Laden does not focus violent efforts within some sort of geographically defined territory such as a nation state. Rather he uses it as part on behalf of the House of Islam generally. Where other defensive jihads were therefore much more nationalist in character (and, indeed, remain so), Bin Laden's jihad is far more global and in this sense more attuned to the classical framing.

The problem is that, contrary to the situation that may have existed in the classical era, whether in Shaybānī's time or during the considerably more turbulent period when Ibn Taymiyya was writing, Bin Laden finds no legitimate authority on earth to whom to turn to reinstitute proper Islamic rule within the House of Islam. Even Ibn Taymiyya's robust articulation of defensive jihad presupposed *some* authority under whose leadership each individual believer was obligated to fight, in a more or less conventional military campaign.

This leads to the third notable plank in Bin Laden's conception of jihad, and the one that is by far the most radical and the most astonishing. This was to turn the long established duty to fight under a rightful leader into an individualized obligation that is dislocated from authority entirely. The analogy—Bin Laden's own—is to performance of ritual daily prayers. One may perform them alone, or with a few others, even as one may in this view properly conduct jihad through an individual lone wolf attempt to explode a car in Times Square, or in coordination with eighteen fellow believers in the hijacking of various aircraft to fly them into skyscrapers. All of this disassociated violence comes together within a rubric of jihad that serves almost as the precise opposite of that which Shaybānī envisioned. Shaybānī, it is important to reemphasize, imagined the doctrine of jihad as fundamentally *conservative*. It preserved the authorities and systems of power as they existed within the House of Islam, and permitted their gradual expansion at the expense of the House of War, at the strategic and tactical discretion of the caliph. Bin Laden's violence is deliberately disruptive, and intended to upend existing Muslim hierarchies and power structures, out of whose ashes a caliphate might be reestablished. The jihad in this conception is no longer a theory of just war under a leader to whom all owe obedience. It is instead the instrument of the anarchist, designed to spread unrest, terror, and social and political dislocation. The departure from classical origins is vast indeed.

The other major disruptive jihadist movement, the so-called Islamic State evolved quite differently. Contrary to the general geographic dislocation of Al Qaeda, the Islamic State sought to establish control over a geographically defined area—ultimately self-described as a caliphate—from which it would expand outward. In its obvious contempt for existing national boundaries, its suggestion that it served as the true Islamic state to which all Muslims owed obedience, and its reference to its leader as caliph, the Islamic state clearly sought to invoke the glories of the Abbasid empire at its height.

Moreover, it is important to note, the Islamic State caused some embarrassment to modern Muslims in its reinvigoration of some of Islamic law's more sordid elements, which many had hoped had long been confined to history's dustbin. These include the permissibility of taking female slaves in a jihad and using them for sexual enjoyment and imposing special taxes on Christians living within their territories. That such reinvocations were contestable, but in many cases at least plausible understandings of classical juristic opinion, demonstrated amply the limitations of the classical law in establishing norms pursuant to which modern Muslims seek to live.

At the same time, it is important not to overestimate the extent of the fidelity of the Islamic State to traditionalist teachings. Their treatment of war prisoners, which include beheadings and burning some prisoners alive, seems grossly inconsistent with the classical texts, and at best an opportunistic and highly selective reading of some very small number of them. Their participation in both the illicit antiquities trade and the kidnapping market to fund themselves is so transparently contrary to Islamic law that the Islamic State denied these activities rather than attempt to legitimize them through tendentious interpretations of classical law. And, finally, it is an odd caliphate that finds itself in perpetual, internal conflict with other Muslim polities rather than non-Muslim ones. This in the end may have been the Islamic State's most radical departure from Islam's rich, pluralistic and internally inclusive tradition. The movement refused to even try to come to terms with alternative approaches to Islamic law—to engage, that is, with the Muslim mainstream or indeed any Islamic approaches other than its own—and turned to military campaigns instead, against other Muslims, all in the name of jihad on behalf of a caliphate it had created only months earlier.

In any event, the Islamic State's vision of reimagined caliphate was not long for this world. To the extent that the group could be said to continue to exist now that it has lost all of its territory, it relies primarily on the same forms of dislocated, disorganized, and atomized acts of violence that long characterized Al Qaeda, and that bear no resemblance to the classical jihad as it evolved over the ages. This is hardly a surprise. The modern world is simply not politically organized as the world of the Abbasids was. Even as classical jurists adapted their own rules to fit the times as they evolved, modern Islamic scholars have found it necessary to do no less. To insist instead on the rules of the Abbasid era is no more possible for the Islamic State to do than reversing time is.

INDEX

References are to Pages

ADOPTION
Generally, 156
Classical Islamic law, 156
Inheritance law and, 158, 193
Kafāla (sponsorship) as alterative, 158
Modern Islamic law, 158
Orphans, protection of, 158

AL QAEDA, 398

'AMĀN (PROTECTION)
Muslim residents in non-Muslim lands, 22, 389

CHILD CUSTODY
Generally, 144 et seq.
Abandonment of marital home, 146
Adoption, this index
Age of discernment, 153
Best interests standard
    Gulf states rules, 154
    Modern Islamic law, 151
Classical Islamic law
    Generally, 145
    Wilāya (guardianship), 152
Convention on the Rights of the Child, 145, 151
Ḥaḍana (rearing)
    Generally, 153
    Age of discernment, 153
    Classical Islamic law, 147
    Maternal presumption, 147, 153
    Reforms, 155
    Wilāya distinguished, 146
International expectations and treaties, tension with Islamic law, 145, 151

Maternal presumption, Ḥaḍana, 147, 153
Modern Islamic law
    Generally, 150 et seq.
  Best interests standard, 151, 155
  Child custody, international expectations and treaties
    tensions, 145, 151
  Reforms, 155
Modifications in favor of mothers, 149
Patriarchal rules, 149
Reforms, 150, 155
Sunni-Shi'a split, 148
Visitation, 149
Wilāya (guardianship)
    Generally, 152
  Age of discernment, 153
  Classical Islamic law, 152
  Ḥaḍana distinguished, 146

CLASSICAL ISLAMIC LAW

  Generally, 1 et seq.
Abrogated verses, Sunnism development, 10
Adoption, 156
Analogy as source, 12
Authority of
    Generally, 1
  Interpretation in the Sunni paradigm, 13
Caliph selections, 14
Chains of trustworthy narrators developing, 8
Child custody, 145
Consensus as source, 12
Contract law, 5
Criminal law punishments, 10
Evolution of, 1
Finance law development
    Generally, 8, 20
  Workarounds, 274
Fixed punishments, Qur'anic text vs modern practices, 200
Geopolitical realities impacting, 369
Ḥaḍana, rearing of children, 147
Holy Qur'an and Prophet Muhammad, 2

Idol worship era, 4
'Ijtihād reasoning as source
    Closing the doors of 'ijtihād, 19
    Compensated divorce laws in modern states, 128
Inheritance Law, this index
International law and relations, 369
Jurists, this index
Marriage laws development, 35
Medinan verses, 5
Modern Islamic law compared, 2
Monotheism, 5
Nation-state era's impacts, 36
Occultation, Shi'ism in era of, 32
Political states vs schools of jurists as sources, 15
Polygamy, 66
Prophet Muhammad and the Holy Qur'an, 2
Qur'an, Sunna as equivalent source of law to, 9
Schools of Islamic jurisprudence, 16
Social justice, Muhammad's message of, 4
Sources of law
    Generally, 2
  Analogy as, 12
  Consensus as, 12
  'Ijtihād reasoning from
    Generally, 18
  Qur'an as, 3
  Sunnism, development, 7, 11
Sunna as, 6
Sunni paradigm, authority to interpret in, 13
Sunni-Shi'a Split, this index
Taqlīd (imitation)
    Generally, 18
  Sunni-Shi'a split, 34
Waqfs, 214 et seq.
Wilāya (guardianship), 152

CONSTITUTIONALISM
    Generally, 337 et seq.
Classical era principles, translation of, 338
Criminal law, legality principle internalization, 319

Edicts of rulers
    Generally, 340
    Repugnancy determinations, 352
International "Islamic" commitments, 342
Islamicity of legislation
    Determining, 353
    Repugnancy, above
Jurists pronouncements, edicts of rulers distinguished, 340
Legality principle internalization, 319
Mechanism for determination of repugnancy, 350
Medieval rules, implementations of repugnancy, 365
Political interference with implementations of repugnancy, 362
Purposes, 338, 351
Religious Freedom, this index
Repugnancy
    Generally, 342, 352 et seq.
    Ambiguities confounding, 359
    Dower valuation law example, 357
    Edicts of rulers, 352
    'Ijtihād role, 353
    Interest provisions, 366
    Leasing law example, 359
    Mechanism for determination, 350
    Medieval rules, 365
    Origin of term, 349
    Political interference, 362
    Purposes measure of repugnancy, 351
    Scriptural Crimes punishments, 362
Roots of Islamic constitutionalism, 339
Rulers' edicts
    Generally, 340
    Repugnancy determinations, 352
Scriptural Crimes punishments, repugnancy determinations, 362
Siyāsa shar'īyya, 339
State law, Islamic law as a source of, 342, 345
Validity of state laws
    Islamic law precepts as measure, 348
    Repugnancy of state laws inconsistent with Islamic law, above
Women's Rights Concerns, this index

CONTRACT LAW, 5

CRIMINAL LAW
Generally, 289 et seq.
Adultery, 326
Alcohol drinking, 298
Apostasy
    Generally, 298, 311
  Blasphemy distinguished, 329
Banditry, 297
Blasphemy, 328
Cursing of the Prophet, 299
Desecration of religion, 333
Domestic violence, reforms and state court practices, 95
Embezzlement, 318
European legal system impacting, 289
False weights or measures use, 301
Fornication
    Generally, 292
  Female vs male proof standards in Maliki school, 304
  Modern criminal law, 323
Ḥudūd (Scriptural Crimes)
    Generally, 291 et seq.
  Blasphemy, 328
  Fornication, 292
  Modern codifications, 303
  Political dissidents, persecution of, 316
  Punishments
    Generally, 317
    Qur'anic text vs modern practices, 200
    Repugnancy determinations, 362
  Religious minorities persecution, 308
  Repressive effect of, 304
  Retraction of confessions to, 305
  Ta`zīrāt distinguished in modern era, 300
  Women, persecution of, 304
Immodest behavior, 326
Khulwa, seclusion, 324
Legality principle, internalization in modern criminal law, 319

Modern criminal law
- Generally, 303 et seq.
- Blasphemy, 328
- Discretionary sexual crimes, 323
- Fornication, 323
- Legality principle internalization, 319
- Secular procedural rules adoption, 316

Muḥṣan persons, disparate punishments applicable to, 294

Punishments
- Classical Islamic law, 10
- Ḥudūd (Scriptural Crimes), 200, 317, 362
- Muḥṣan persons, disparate punishments applicable to, 294
- Ta`zīrāt (Discretionary Crimes), 302

Qadhf (defamation or slander), 296

Qur'an burning, 329

Reforms, domestic violence, 95

Religious freedom restraints through blasphemy laws, 332

Retaliation, 334

Same-sex relations, 295

Sexual crimes, discretionary, 323

Speech restraints through blasphemy laws, 330

Ta`zīrāt (Discretionary Crimes)
- Generally, 300
- Blasphemy, 328
- Ḥudūd distinguished, 300
- Judicial discretion as to, 302
- Punishments, 302
- Reinvention of, 319
- Sexual crimes, discretionary, 323

Theft, 297

CRUSADES, 370

DIVORCE
Capricious ṭalāq, 115
Conditional or delegated ṭalāq, 121
Dower issues, 115
Effects of ṭalāq, 105
Faskh (annulment) on wife's petition, 130

Khul` (compensated divorce)
      Generally, 126
  Shiqāq compared, 142
  Talāq relationship, 127
No fault divorce reforms, 130
Notification of talāq, 110
Other marital dissolutions, 121 et seq.
Patriarchy in Islamic societies, 117
Post marital support
      Generally, 115
  India (Shah Bano case), 118
Registration of talāq, 110, 114
Shiqāq (irreconcilable differences)
      Generally, 139
  Khul` compared, 142
State divorce laws, talāq tensions, 104
Sunni-Shi'a split
      Generally, 102
  Conditional talāq, 122, 125
  Triple talāq, 107
Talāq
      Generally, 101 et seq.
  Capricious, 115
  Delayed dower, 142
  Effects, 105
  Invalid talāq, 112
  Khul`, relationship to, 127
  Limitations on wife's declaration of, 121
  Notification, 110
  Patching together rules from different schools, 132
  Reforms and state court practices, 108
  Registration, 110, 114
  State divorce laws, talāq tensions with, 104
  State marriage contracts limiting, 124
  Sunni-Shi'a distinctions, 102
  Triple talāq, below
  Wife's declaration of talāq, below
Triple talāq
      Generally, 106, 111
  Disapproval, 108

Marriage contracts limiting, 124
Reforms, 119
Tensions with divorce laws, 104
Wife's declaration of ṭalāq
    Generally, 103
Conditional declarations, 122
Faskh petitions, 130
Limitations, 121

DOWER
See also Marriage, this index
Delayed dower, 75, 204
Divorce dower issues
    Generally, 115
Capricious Ṭalāq, 115
Shiqāq, irreconcilable differences dissolution, 139

FAMILY LAW
Generally, 41 et seq.
Adoption, this index
Children
    Age of discernment, 153
    Child Custody, this index
    Marriage of, 48
Divorce, this index
Inheritance law relationship, 161
Marriage, this index
Non-Muslim states, governing law for Muslim populations, IX
Patriarchy in Islamic societies, 117

FINANCE
Generally, 241 et seq.
Capital markets, 280
Classical Islamic law, development within
    Generally, 8, 20
Workarounds, 274
Derivative markets, 286
Dow Jones fatwa, 281
Forbidden businesses, investments in, 283
Gharar, excessive speculation, 269
Insurance, speculation prohibition, 277

Lease contracts, 268 et seq.
Profit sharing ideal, 246
Ribā interest prohibition
    Generally, 243
    Artifices and their risks, 247, 256 et seq.
Risk gharar and, 271
Speculation prohibition, 277
Ṣukūk bonds, 284
Sunni-Shi'a differences, 29

GUARDIANSHIP
Wilāya (Guardianship), this index

'IJTIHĀD
Closing the doors of 'ijtihād, 18
Constitutional repugnancy determinations, 'ijtihād role, 353
Jihad doctrine, 'ijtihād development, 392

INHERITANCE LAW
    Generally, 161 et seq.
Adopted children
    Generally, 193
    Kafāla (sponsorship) as alternative to adoption, 158
Agnatic system
    Generally, 168
    Reforms, 170, 197
Bequests
    Classical Islamic law, 194
    Constitutionality of bequests to heirs, 211
    Modern state practices, 210
    Obligatory bequest fictions, 208
Classical Islamic law
    Development, 10
    Modern Islamic law compared, 161
    Wills and bequests, 194
Dower, delayed, 204
Family law relationship, 161
Females, apparent discrimination against in the verses
    Generally, 165
    Modern reforms, 198
Heir, bequest to, 211

Interfaith inheritance, 193
Kafāla (sponsorship) as alternative to adoption, 158
Modern state practices
    Generally, 195 et seq.
  Agnatic system reforms, 197
  Daughters and sisters inheritance, 202
  Marital status disputes, 195
  Nephews, orphaned, 207
  Obligatory bequest fictions, 208
  Orphaned grandchildren, 207
  Property ownership assignments, 206
  Qur'anic text, practical limitations, 198
  Talfiq, patching together rules from different schools, 202
  Valuation disputes, 195
  Wife's portion, 204
  Wills, 210
Non-Muslim states, governing law for Muslim populations, IX
Nonmarital children, 193
Obligatory bequest fictions, 208
Orphaned grandchildren, 207
Parental support obligations, 206
Priority classes, Shi'a, 187
Property ownership assignments, 206
Qur'anic heirs, 169
Qur'anic text, practical limitations, 198
Qur'anic verses as source, importance of, 162 et seq.
Slayer rule, 193
Sunni-Shi'a law distinctions
    Generally, 28, 162
  Sunni system, 168, 184
Uterine Heirs, 176
Waqf principles contrasted
    Generally, 214
  Waqf use to avoid inheritance rules, 223
Wife's portion, modern state practices, 204
Wills
  Classic Islamic law, 194
  Modern state practices, 210

INTERNATIONAL LAW AND RELATIONS

Generally, 369
Al Qaeda and ISIS, 398
Classical Islamic law, 369
Coexistence issues in non-Muslim states in modern era, 390
Crusades era, 370
Defensive jihad, 394
Defensive vs aggressive jihad, 387
Division of House of Islam into independent nation states, 395
Geopolitical realities impacting classical Islamic law, 369
House of War conception
    Generally, 376
  Jihad doctrine and, 39, 376
Ibn Taymiyya and the defensive jihad, 385
Independent nation states, division of House of Islam into, 395
Islamic State as concept, persistence of in modern era, 391
Jihad doctrine
  Al Qaeda and ISIS perversions of, 398
  Defensive jihad, 394
  Defensive vs aggressive jihad, 387
  House of War conception and, 39, 376
  Ibn Taymiyya and the defensive jihad, 385
  'Ijtihād development, 392
  Leaders of jihad, 379
  Misunderstandings, 369, 377
  Modern era, 391
  Muslim nation-states. doctrine in era of, 392
  Participants in jihad, 378
  Resistance interpretation, 393
  Social jihad, 392
  Spiritual struggle vs actual war, 392
  Taqlīd (imitation) development, 20
Kitāb al-Sīyār (Book of Movements), 375
Laws of war edicts, 384
Leaders of jihad, 379
Mainstream approach in modern era, 389
Medina Charter, 371
Modern era
    Generally, 388 et seq.
  Al Qaeda and ISIS, 398

'Amān, or covenant of protection, 22, 389
Coexistence issues in non-Muslim states, 390
Islamic State as concept, persistence of, 391
Jihad doctrine in, 391
Mainstream approach, 389
Organization of Islamic Cooperation, 393
Sunni-Shi'a split, 396
U.N. Charter, role of, 390
Non-Muslim persons in Muslim states
Generally, 390
Non-Muslim states
Coexistence issues, 390
Presumptive hostility
Generally, 370
Kitāb al-Sīyār (Book of Movements), 376
Organization of Islamic Cooperation, 393
Origins, 371
Ottoman Empire era, 387
Participants in jihad, 378
Prophet Muhammad era, 371
Resistance interpretation of jihad, 393
Safe passage, non-Muslims guarantees of, 383
Shaybānī framework, 375
Social jihad, 392
Sunni-Shi'a split in modern era, 396
U.N. Charter, role of in modern era, 390

ISIS/ISIL, 89, 314, 398

JIHAD DOCTRINE
International Law and Relations, this index

JURISTS
Classical Islamic law, interpretive roles, 15
Declining roles in modern Muslim state law, 37
'Ijtihād, right to pronounce Islamic law as exclusive province of, 355
Judges distinguished, 15
Modern Islamic law, declining roles of, 37
Political states vs schools of jurists as classical Islamic law sources, 15

Pronouncements of, rulers' edicts distinguished, 340
Reforms, jurists' roles, 17, 36
Repugnancy, role of jurists to determine
> Generally, 349
> See also Constitutionalism, this index

Rulers' edicts distinguished from pronouncements of, 340
Schools and seminaries, jurists' classical roles within, 15
Sharia, as distinguished from fiqh, 16
Waqfs
> Generally, 223
> Difficulties in modern era, 234

MARRIAGE
> Generally, 43 et seq.

Abstention, 85
Capacity to marry, 49
Child Custody, this index
Child marriage, 48
Classical Islamic law development, 35
Competency restraints, 75
Consanguinity rules, 79
Consent to marriage, 51
Contractual vs sacramental nature of relationship, 44
Dower
> Classical and modern views, 55 et seq.
> Consent issues, 62
> Delayed dower, 75, 142
> Enforceability in American courts, 60
> Prenuptial agreements distinguished, 60
> Purposes, 58
> Sale of wife's reproductive organs analogy, 45
> Temporary marriage and, 97

Formalities, 46
Forming the marriage contract, 48 et seq.
Guardian authorization of child marriage, 49
Hajr (abstention), 86
Inheritance law, marital status disputes, 195
Interfaith, 80
'Ihtibas (confinement) of wives, 86, 89
Maintenance obligations, 81

Obedience obligations
    Classical rules, 86
    Modern rules, 89
    Sexual obedience, 95
Patriarchy in Islamic societies, 117
Procreation relationship, 47
Social class competency restraints, 75
Sunni-Shi'a split
    Competency, 77
    Interfaith, 80
    Relationship, 45
Ṭalāq, state marriage contracts limiting, 124
Temporary marriage, 97

MEDINA CHARTER, 371

MONOTHEISM, 5

MUSLIM STATES' LAWS

Adoption, 158
Child Custody, this index
Child marriage, 54
Classical Islamic law
    Impacts in nation-state era, 36
    Influences, 2
    Politicians vs jurists as sources, 15
    Tensions, 40
Codifications of family law, 41
Constitutionalism, this index
Criminal law, legality principle internalization, 319
Development, 'ijtihād development contrasted, 14
Divorce, this index
Domestic violence, 95
Family law codifications, 41
Ḥudūd, Scriptural Crimes, modern codifications, 303
Inheritance Law, this index
Interfaith marriage, 80
Islamic law authorities, search for, 39
Islamic State as concept, persistence of in modern era, 391
Islamic values, struggle of states to reflect within, 40
Jurists, declining roles, 37

Legality principle, internalization in modern criminal law, 319
Maintenance standards
    Divorce, 128
    Marriage, 83
Marital obedience obligations, 89
Nation-state era, classical Islamic law impacts, 36
No fault divorce, 130, 132
Non-Muslims in Muslim states
    Constitutionalism protections for religious minorities, 309
    Conversions to Islam, 308
    Ḥudūd, Scriptural Crimes, religious minorities persecution, 308
    International law modern era, 390
Ottoman Empire era development, 340
Personal status codes, 161
Polygamy, 69
Reforms, jurists' roles, 17, 36
Religious freedom, court practices conflicts, 64
Search for Islamic law authorities, 39
Shi'i communities compliance with, 38
Struggle of states to reflect Islamic values within, 40
Sunni-Shi'a split and modern Islamic law, 37
Talfiq, patching together rules from different schools
      Generally, 202
    Divorce, 132
Triple ṭalāq reforms, 119
Waqfs, this index

NATION-STATE ERA
Classical Islamic law impacts, 36
Colonial powers' drawing of, 36
Division of House of Islam into independent nation states, 395
Muslim nation-states, reconciliation of with principles of jihad, 398
Muslim States' Laws, this index
Non-Muslim States' Laws, this index

NON-MUSLIM STATES' LAWS
'Amān (covenant of protection), 22, 389
Anti-sharia legislation, 65
Coexistence issues in modern era, 390

Divorce formalities, 111
Dower enforceability in American courts, 60
Governing law for Muslim populations, IX
Jihad resistance calls, 394, 398
Muslim residence in non-Muslim lands, 22, 389
Nation-state era and classical Islamic law, 36

ORGANIZATION OF ISLAMIC COOPERATION, 393

ORPHANED GRANDCHILDREN, 207

ORTHODOXY
Religious Freedom, this index

OTTOMAN EMPIRE ERA
   Generally, 36
International law and relations, 387
Muslim state law development, 340

PARENTAL SUPPORT OBLIGATIONS, 206

PATRIARCHY IN ISLAMIC SOCIETIES, 117

PERSONAL STATUS CODES, 161

POLYGAMY, 66 et seq.

REFORMS
   Generally, 13, 16
Child custody, best interests standard, 155
Conditional ṭalāq, female empowerment through, 122
Domestic violence, 95
Islamic progressivism, 155
Jurists' roles, 17, 36
Marriage contracts limiting ṭalāq, 124
Non-Muslims in Muslim states, 390
Polygamy, 66
Ṭalāq, marriage contracts limiting, 124
Triple ṭalāq reforms, 108, 119
Women's Rights Concerns, this index

RELIGIOUS FREEDOM
Apostasy. See Criminal law, this index
Constitutionalism, religious minorities protections, 309

Desecration of religion, 333
Ḥudūd (Scriptural Crimes), religious minorities persecution, 308
Muslim states' laws
 Constitutionalism protections for religious minorities, 309
 Court practices tensions, 64
Orthodoxy, blasphemy laws enforcing, 332

REPUGNANCY
Colonial origin of term, 349
Jurists selected by state to determine
 Generally, 349
 See also Constitutionalism, this index

SCHOOLS AND SEMINARIES
 Generally, 15, 16
 See also Jurists, this index
Modern Islamic law, declining roles of seminaries, 37

SEX DISCRIMINATION
Women's Rights Concerns, this index

SOCIAL JUSTICE
Muhammad's message of, 4

STATE LAWS
Muslim States' Laws, this index
Non-Muslim States' Laws, this index

SUNNI-SHI'A SPLIT
 Generally, 23 et seq.
Child custody, 148
Divorce, this index
Finance law differences, 29
Historical sources of tension, 24
Inheritance Law, this index
International law and relations, 396
Jurists, authority of, 33
Marriage, this index
Political dimensions, 25
Taqlīd imitation of past rulings, 34

TRUSTS
Waqfs, this index

WAQFs
Generally, 213 et seq.
Administration, 213, 219
Beneficiary designations, 220
Cash waqfs, 218
Classical Islamic law, 214 et seq.
Corrupt use, reforms challenging, 225
Decline of importance of, 223
Exchanges of waqf property, 217
Family waqfs
    Generally, 221
  State restrictions, 227
Impermanent waqfs, 218
Inheritance law principles contrasted
    Generally, 214
  Waqf use to avoid inheritance rules, 223
Irrevocability of, 215
Jurist vs state control
    Generally, 223
  Difficulties in modern era, 234
Leasing the property under waqf, 216
Maintenance, classical vs modern Islamic law, 37
Modern era relevance
    Generally, 232
  Sunni-Shi'a split, 233
Moveable property, 217
Neglected waqfs, 228
Perpetual nature of relationship, 215
Reformist challenges to classical waqf doctrine, 224
Reinvention in modern states, 238
Revenue from the waqf, 215
State vs jurist control
    Generally, 223
  Difficulties in modern era, 234
Supervisory functions, 220
Trusts distinguished, 215

WILĀYA (GUARDIANSHIP)
Child Custody, this index
Child marriage authorizations, 49

Ḥaḍanā distinguished, 146
Kafāla (sponsorship) as alternative to adoption, 158
Property rights, 146

WOMEN'S RIGHTS CONCERNS
Child custody
   Age of discernment, 153
   Maternal presumption, 147, 153, 154
   Modifications in favor of mothers, 149
   Reforms, 155
Empowerment of women through conditional ṭalāq, 122
Fornication, female vs male proof standards in Maliki School, 304
Ḥudūd (Scriptural Crimes) as modern instrument of repression
   against women, 304
Inheritance law discrimination
     Generally, 165
   Modern reforms, 198
'Iḥtibas (confinement) of wives, 86, 89
Marital obedience obligations
     Generally, 89
   Sexual obedience, 95
Patriarchy in Islamic societies, 117
Ṭalāq, wife's declaration of
     Generally, 103
   See also Divorce, this index